Tom Lochray

COAST TO COAST

Senior Authors

Roger C. Farr

Dorothy S. Strickland

Authors

Richard F. Abrahamson ♦ Alma Flor Ada ♦ Barbara Bowen Coulter
Bernice E. Cullinan ♦ Margaret A. Gallego
W. Dorsey Hammond
Nancy Roser ♦ Junko Yokota ♦ Hallie Kay Yopp

Senior Consultant

Asa G. Hilliard III

Consultants

V. Kanani Choy ♦ Lee Bennett Hopkins ♦ Stephen Krashen ♦ Rosalia Salinas

Harcourt Brace & Company

Orlando Atlanta Austin Boston San Francisco Chicago Dallas New York Toronto London

Printed in the United States of America

ISBN 0-15-309116-9

2 3 4 5 6 7 8 9 10   048   99 98 97

Dear Reader,

The land that we call the United States is an enormous place, bordered by two oceans. In this book, you will read about the people of this land, adventurous people who came here from every direction—Native Americans from the north; Spanish explorers from the south; Asians from the west; Africans and Europeans from the east.

They are now all part of one great people, and their stories are as different and as fascinating as their backgrounds. So join us now to read about a great land and its adventurous people—from the fictional to the historical; from the past to the present; from coast to coast.

Sincerely,

The Authors

The Authors

Our Fifty States

SIDEWAYS STORIES FROM WAYSIDE SCHOOL
LOUIS SACHAR

Whose Side Are You On?
Emily Moore

SHILOH Phyllis Reynolds Naylor

BEVERLY CLEARY
Dear Mr. Henshaw
ILLUSTRATED BY PAUL O. ZELINSKY

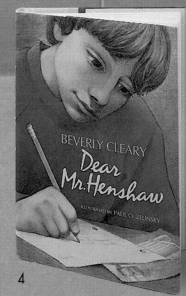

IN AND OUT OF SCHOOL

CONTENTS

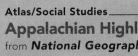

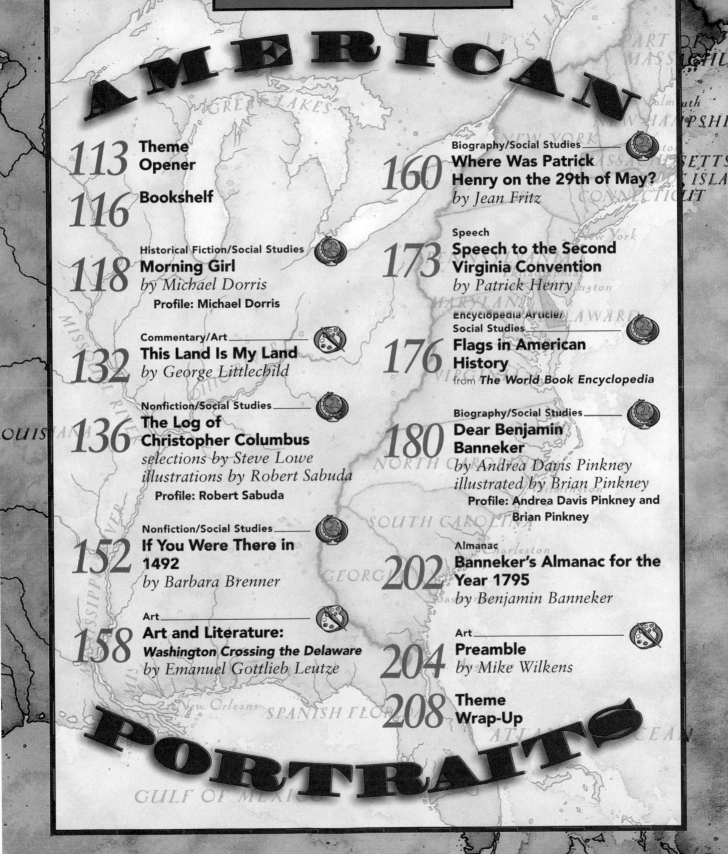

★ CONTENTS ★

AMERICAN

PORTRAITS

·CONTENTS·

Personal Journeys

BEETHOVEN
LIVES
UPSTAIRS

RADIO
FIFTH GRADE
Gordon Korman

Lensey Namioka

Yang the Youngest
and
His Terrible Ear

Illustrated by Kees de Kiefte

A Very Young
Musician

by Jill
Krementz

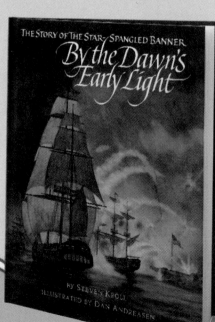

THE STORY OF THE STAR-SPANGLED BANNER
By the Dawn's
Early Light

BY STEVEN KROLL
ILLUSTRATED BY DAN ANDREASEN

Listen to This!

CONTENTS

THE PEOPLE WHO HUGGED THE TREES

THE THIRD PLANET
EXPLORING THE EARTH FROM SPACE

STILL MORE STORIES TO SOLVE
FOURTEEN FOLKTALES FROM AROUND THE WORLD
Edited by GEORGE SHANNON
Illustrated by PETER SÍS

Amish Home
RAYMOND BIAL

The American Family Farm
A Photo Essay by GEORGE ANCONA   Text by JOAN ANDERSON

PLANET OF LIFE

CONTENTS

A PIONEER SAMPLER

Hector
LIVES IN
THE UNITED STATES NOW

The Story of a Mexican-American Child
By Joan Hewett · Photographs by Richard Hewett

Children of the
Wild West

RUSSELL FREEDMAN

THE ORPHAN TRAIN ADVENTURES
A FAMILY
APART
Joan Lowery Nixon

ROADS TO THE WEST

CONTENTS

IN AND OUT OF SCHOOL

We communicate with different people in different ways. In the following selections, you'll read about a boy who learns to express himself through writing, a girl who struggles to communicate with her mother and her teacher, and a boy whose special relationship with a dog needs no words at all.

17

IN AND OUT OF SCHOOL

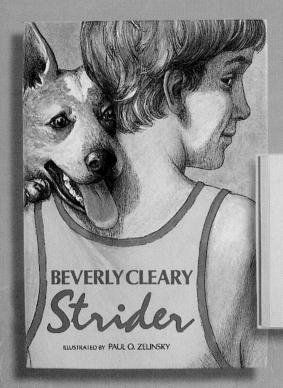

Strider
by Beverly Cleary

Four years later, *Dear Mr. Henshaw*'s
Leigh Botts continues to tell his story.
Signatures Library

BOOKSHELF

Just My Luck
by Emily Moore

A pair of kid detectives discover something
they weren't looking for—the truth.
Signatures Library

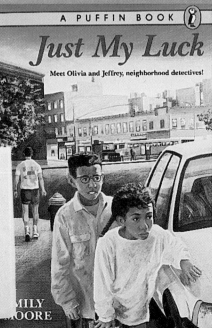

After Fifth Grade, the World!
by Claudia Mills

Heidi—determined, confident, and headstrong—has a plan to solve every problem. But when it comes to Mrs. Richardson, the meanest teacher in school, Heidi may have met her match.

The Facts and Fictions of Minna Pratt
by Patricia MacLachlan

As she plays her many roles in life—daughter, sister, friend, musician—Minna Pratt struggles to sort out the facts from the fictions.

ALA Notable Book

Mariah Keeps Cool
by Mildred Pitts Walter

Mariah spends her summer swimming for glory and getting to know Denise, a half sister she has just met.

DEAR MR. HENSHAW

WRITTEN BY BEVERLY CLEARY

LEIGH BOTTS has been keeping a diary and writing to his favorite author since second grade. Now, as a sixth grader, Leigh has new problems: His mother and his father, a truck driver, are divorced. His father's girlfriend has a son his age that Leigh calls the pizza boy. Someone at school is stealing the best part of Leigh's lunch every day. His story for the Young Writers' Yearbook is not going well.

Can Leigh find solutions to any of these problems?

ILLUSTRATIONS BY ANDREW POWELL

FROM THE DIARY OF LEIGH BOTTS/VOLUME 2

I AM GETTING BEHIND in this diary for several reasons, including working on my story and writing to Mr. Henshaw (really, not just pretend). I also had to buy a new notebook because I had filled up the first one.

The same day, I bought a beat-up black lunchbox in the thrift shop down the street and started carrying my lunch in it. The kids were surprised, but nobody made fun of me, because a black lunchbox isn't the same as one of those square boxes covered with cartoon characters that first and second graders carry. A couple of boys asked if it was my Dad's. I just grinned and said, "Where do you think I got it?" The next day my little slices of salami rolled around cream cheese were gone, but I expected that. But I'll get that thief yet. I'll make him really sorry he ate all the best things out of my lunch.

Next I went to the library for books on batteries. I took out a couple of easy books on electricity, really easy, because I have never given much thought to batteries. About all I know is that when you want to use a flashlight, the battery is usually dead.

I finally gave up on my story about the ten-foot wax man, which was really pretty dumb. I thought I would write a poem about butterflies for Young

Writers because a poem can be short, but it is hard to think about butterflies and burglar alarms at the same time, so I studied electricity books instead. The books didn't have directions for an alarm in a lunchbox, but I learned enough about batteries and switches and insulated wires, so I think I can figure it out myself.

FRIDAY, MARCH 2

BACK TO THE POEM TONIGHT. The only rhyme I can think of for "butterfly" is "flutter by." I can think up rhymes like "trees" and "breeze" which are pretty boring, and then I think of "wheeze" and "sneeze." A poem about butterflies wheezing and sneezing seems silly, and anyway a couple of girls are already writing poems about monarch butterflies that flutter by.

Sometimes I start a letter to Dad thanking him for the twenty dollars, but I can't finish that either. I don't know why.

SATURDAY, MARCH 3

TODAY I TOOK MY LUNCHBOX and Dad's twenty dollars to the hardware store and looked around. I found an ordinary light switch, a little battery and a cheap doorbell. While I was looking around for the right kind of insulated wire, a man who had been watching me (boys my age always get watched when they go into stores) asked if he could help me. He was a

nice old gentleman who said, "What are you planning to make, son?" *Son*. He called me son, and my Dad calls me kid. I didn't want to tell the man, but when he looked at the things I was holding, he grinned and said, "Having trouble with your lunch, aren't you?" I nodded and said, "I'm trying to make a burglar alarm."

He said, "That's what I guessed. I've had workmen in here with the same problem."

It turned out that I needed a 6-volt lantern battery instead of the battery I had picked out. He gave me a couple of tips and, after I paid for the things, a little slap on the back and said, "Good luck, son."

I tore home with all the things I bought. First I made a sign for my door that said

KEEP OUT MOM
THAT MEANS YOU

Then I went to work fastening one wire from the battery to the switch and from the other side of the switch to the doorbell. Then I fastened a second wire from the battery to the doorbell. It took me a while to get it right. Then I taped the battery in one corner of the lunchbox and the doorbell in another. I stood the switch up at the back of the box and taped that in place, too.

Here I ran into a problem. I thought I could take the wire clamp meant to hold a thermos bottle inside the lunchbox lid and hook it under the

"LEIGH, WHAT ON EARTH IS GOING ON IN THERE?" SHE SHOUTED ABOVE THE ALARM.

switch if I reached in carefully as I closed the box. The clamp wasn't quite long enough. After some thinking and experimenting, I twisted a wire loop onto it. Then I closed the box just enough so I could get my hand inside and push the wire loop over the button on the switch before I took my hand out and closed the box.

Then I opened the box. My burglar alarm worked! That bell inside the box went off with a terrible racket that brought Mom to my door. "Leigh, what on earth is going on in there?" she shouted above the alarm.

I let her in and gave her a demonstration of my burglar alarm. She laughed and said it was a great invention. One thing was bothering me. Would my sandwich muffle the bell? Mom must have been wondering the same thing, because she suggested taping a piece of cardboard into the lid that would make a shelf for my sandwich. I did, and that worked, too.

I can't wait until Monday.

MONDAY, MARCH 5

TODAY MOM PACKED my lunch carefully, and we tried the alarm to see if it still worked. It did, good and loud. When I got to school, Mr. Fridley said, "Nice to see you smiling, Leigh. You should try it more often."

I parked my lunchbox behind the partition and waited. I waited all morning for the alarm to go off. Miss Martinez asked if I had my mind on my work. I pretended I did, but all the time I was really waiting for my alarm to go off so I could dash behind the partition and tackle the thief. When nothing happened, I began to worry. Maybe the loop had somehow slipped off the switch on the way to school.

Lunchtime came. The alarm still hadn't gone off. We all picked up our lunches and went off to the cafeteria. When I set my box on the table in front of me, I realized I had a problem, a big problem. If the loop hadn't slipped off the switch, my alarm was still triggered. I just sat there, staring at my lunchbox, not knowing what to do.

"How come you're not eating?" Barry asked with his mouth full. Barry's sandwiches are never cut in half, and he always takes a big bite out of one side to start.

Everybody at the table was looking at me. I thought about saying I wasn't hungry, but I was. I thought about taking my lunchbox out into the hall to open, but if the alarm was still triggered, there was no way I could open it quietly. Finally I thought, Here goes. I unsnapped the two fasteners on the box and held my breath as I opened the lid.

Wow! My alarm went off! The noise was so loud it startled everybody at the table including me and made everyone in the cafeteria look around. I looked up and saw Mr. Fridley grinning at me over by the garbage can. Then I turned off the alarm.

Suddenly everybody seemed to be noticing me. The principal, who always prowls around keeping an eye on things at lunchtime, came over to examine my lunchbox. He said, "That's quite an invention you have there."

"Thanks," I said, pleased that the principal seemed to like my alarm.

Some of the teachers came out of their lunchroom to see what the noise was all about. I had to give a demonstration. It seems I wasn't the only one who had things stolen from my lunch, and all the kids said they wanted lunchboxes with alarms, too, even those whose lunches were never good enough to have anything stolen. Barry said he would like an alarm like that on the door of his room at home. I began to feel like some sort of hero. Maybe I'm not so medium after all.

One thing bothers me, though. I still don't know who's been robbing my lunch.

TUESDAY, MARCH 6

TODAY BARRY ASKED ME to come home with him to see if I could help him rig up a burglar alarm for his room because he has a bunch of little sisters and stepsisters who get into his stuff. I thought I could, because I had seen an alarm like that in one of the electricity books from the library.

Barry lives in a big old house that is sort of cheerful and messy, with little girls all over the place. As it turned out, Barry didn't have the right kind of battery so we just fooled around looking at his models. Barry never uses directions when he puts models together, because the directions are too hard and spoil the fun. He throws them away and figures out how the pieces fit by himself.

I still don't know what to write for Young Writers, but I was feeling so good I finally wrote to Dad to thank him for the twenty dollars because I had found a good use for it even if I couldn't save it all toward a typewriter. I didn't say much.

I wonder if Dad will marry the pizza boy and his mother. I worry about that a lot.

THURSDAY, MARCH 15

THIS WEEK SEVERAL KIDS turned up with lunchboxes with burglar alarms. You know that song about the hills ringing with the sound of music? Well, you might say our cafeteria rang with the sound of burglar alarms. The fad didn't last very long, and after a while I didn't even bother to set my alarm. Nobody has robbed my lunchbox since I set it off that day.

I never did find out who the thief was, and now that I stop to think about it, I am glad. If he had set off the alarm when my lunchbox was in the classroom, he would have been in trouble, big trouble. Maybe he was just somebody whose mother packed bad lunches—jelly sandwiches on that white bread that tastes like Kleenex. Or maybe he had to pack his own lunches and there was never anything good in the house to put in them. I have seen people look into their lunches, take out the cookies and throw the rest in the garbage. Mr. Fridley always looks worried when they do this.

I'm not saying robbing lunchboxes is right. I am saying I'm glad I don't know who the thief was, because I have to go to school with him.

FRIDAY, MARCH 16

TONIGHT I WAS STARING at a piece of paper trying to think of something to write for Young Writers when the phone rang. Mom told me to answer because she was washing her hair.

It was Dad. My stomach felt as if it was dropping to the floor, the way it always does when I hear his voice. "How're you doing, kid?" he asked.

"Fine," I said, thinking of the success of my burglar alarm. "Great."

"I got your letter," he said.

"That's good," I said. His call took me so by surprise that I could feel my heart pounding, and I couldn't think of anything to say until I asked, "Have you found another dog to take Bandit's place?" I think what I really meant was, Have you found another boy to take my place?

"No, but I ask about him on my CB," Dad told me. "He may turn up yet."

"I hope so." This conversation was going no place. I really didn't know what to say to my father. It was embarrassing.

Then Dad surprised me. He asked, "Do you ever miss your old Dad?"

I had to think a minute. I missed him all right, but I couldn't seem to get the words out. My silence must have bothered him because he asked, "Are you still there?"

"Sure, Dad, I miss you," I told him. It was true, but not as true as it had been a couple of months ago. I still wanted him to pull up in front of the house in his big rig, but now I knew I couldn't count on it.

"Sorry I don't get over your way more often," he said. "I hear the sugar refinery in Spreckels is closing down."

"I read about it in the paper," I said.

"Is your mother handy?" he asked.

"I'll see," I said even though by then she was standing by the phone with her hair wrapped in a towel. She shook her head. She didn't want to talk to Dad.

"She's washing her hair," I said.

"Tell her I'll manage to send your support check sometime next week," he said. "So long, kid. Keep your nose clean."

"So long, Dad," I answered. "Drive carefully." I guess he'll never learn that my name is Leigh and that my nose is clean. Maybe he thinks I'll never learn that he drives carefully. He doesn't really. He's a good driver, but he speeds to make time whenever he can avoid the highway patrol. All truckers do.

After that I couldn't get back to thinking about Young Writers, so I picked up *Ways to Amuse a Dog* and read it for the thousandth time. I read harder books now, but I still feel good when I read that book. I wonder where Mr. Henshaw is.

SATURDAY, MARCH 17

TODAY IS SATURDAY, so this morning I walked to the butterfly trees again. The grove was quiet and peaceful, and because the sun was shining, I stood there a long time, looking at the orange butterflies floating through the gray and green leaves and listening to the sound of the ocean on the rocks. There aren't as many butterflies now. Maybe they are starting to go north for the summer. I thought I might write about them in prose instead of poetry, but on the way home I got to thinking about Dad and one time when he took me along when he was hauling grapes to a winery and what a great day it had been.

TUESDAY, MARCH 20

YESTERDAY MISS NEELY, the librarian, asked if I had written anything for the Young Writers' Yearbook, because all writing had to be turned in by tomorrow. When I told her I hadn't, she said I still had twenty-four hours and why didn't I get busy? So I did, because I really would like to meet a Famous Author. My story about the ten-foot wax man went into the wastebasket. Next I tried to start a story called *The Great Lunchbox Mystery*, but I couldn't seem to turn my lunchbox experience into a story because I don't know who the thief (thieves) was (were), and I don't want to know.

Finally I dashed off a description of the time I rode with my father when he was trucking the load of grapes down Highway 152 through Pacheco Pass to a winery. I put in things like the signs that said STEEP GRADE, TRUCKS USE LOW GEAR and how Dad down-shifted and how skillful he was handling a long, heavy load on the curves. I put in about the hawks on the telephone wires and about that high peak where Black Bart's lookout used to watch for travelers coming through the pass so he could signal to Black Bart to rob

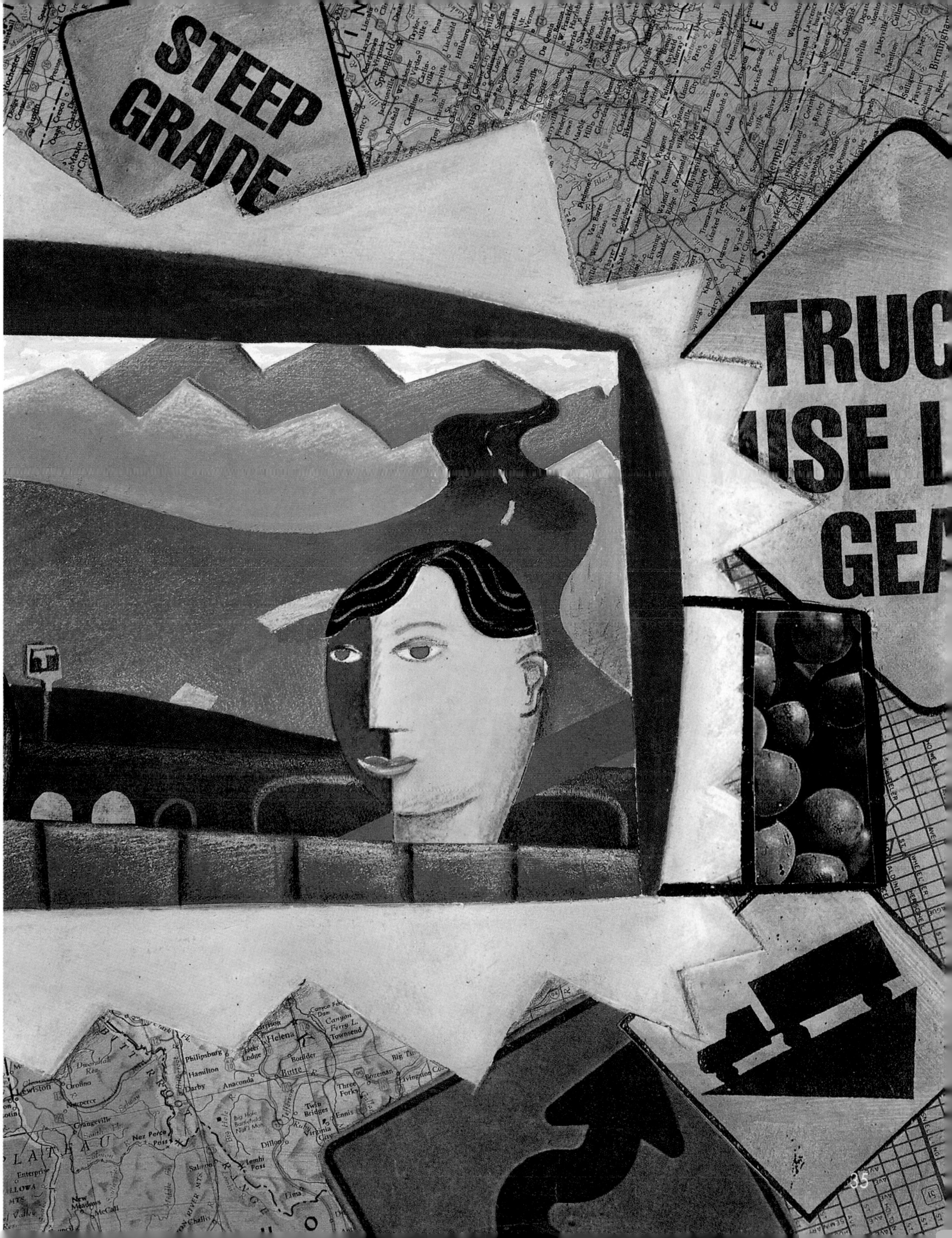
STEEP GRADE

them, and how the leaves on the trees along the stream at the bottom of the pass were turning yellow and how good tons of grapes smelled in the sun. I left out the part about the waitresses and the video games. Then I copied the whole thing over in case neatness counts and gave it to Miss Neely.

SATURDAY, MARCH 24

MOM SAID I HAD TO invite Barry over to our house for supper because I have been going to his house after school so often. We had been working on a burglar alarm for his room which we finally got to work with some help from a library book.

I wasn't sure Barry would like to come to our house which is so small compared to his, but he accepted when I invited him.

Mom cooked a casserole full of good things like ground beef, chilies, tortillas, tomatoes and cheese. Barry said he really liked eating at our house because he got tired of eating with a bunch of little sisters waving spoons and drumsticks. That made me happy. It helps to have a friend.

Barry says his burglar alarm still works. The trouble is, his little sisters think it's fun to open his door to set it off. Then they giggle and hide. This was driving his mother crazy, so he finally had to disconnect it. We all laughed about this. Barry and I felt good about

making something that worked even if he can't use it.

Barry saw the sign on my door that said KEEP OUT MOM THAT MEANS YOU. He asked if my Mom really stays out of my room. I said, "Sure, if I keep things picked up." Mom is not a snoop.

Barry said he wished he could have a room nobody ever went into. I was glad Barry didn't ask to use the bathroom. Maybe I'll start scrubbing off the mildew after all.

SUNDAY, MARCH 25

I KEEP THINKING about Dad and how lonely he sounded and wondering what happened to the pizza boy. I don't like to think about Dad being lonesome, but I don't like to think about the pizza boy cheering him up either.

Tonight at supper (beans and franks) I got up my courage to ask Mom if she thought Dad would get married again. She thought awhile and then said, "I don't see how he could afford to. He has big payments to make on the truck, and the price of diesel oil goes up all the time, and when people can't afford to build houses or buy cars, he won't be hauling lumber or cars."

I thought this over. I know that a license for a truck like his costs over a thousand dollars a year. "But he always sends my support payments," I said, "even if he is late sometimes."

TONIGHT AT SUPPER (BEANS AND FRANKS) I GOT UP MY COURAGE TO ASK MOM IF SHE THOUGHT DAD WOULD GET MARRIED AGAIN.

"Yes, he does that," agreed my mother. "Your father isn't a bad man by any means."

Suddenly I was mad and disgusted with the whole thing. "Then why don't you two get married again?" I guess I wasn't very nice about the way I said it.

Mom looked me straight in the eye. "Because your father will never grow up," she said. I knew that was all she would ever say about it.

Tomorrow they give out the Young Writers' Yearbook! Maybe I will be lucky and get to go have lunch with the Famous Author.

MONDAY, MARCH 26

TODAY WASN'T THE greatest day of my life. When our class went to the library, I saw a stack of Yearbooks and could hardly wait for Miss Neely to hand them out. When I finally got mine and opened it to the first page, there was a monster story, and I saw I hadn't won first prize. I kept turning. I didn't win second prize which went to a poem, and I didn't win third or fourth prize, either. Then I turned another page and saw Honorable Mention and under it:

A Day on Dad's Rig
by Leigh M. Botts

There was my title with my name under it in print, even if it was mimeographed print. I can't say I wasn't disappointed because I hadn't won a prize, I was. I was really disappointed about not getting to meet the mysterious Famous Author, but I liked seeing my name in print.

Some kids were mad because they didn't win or even get something printed. They said they wouldn't ever try to write again which I think is pretty dumb. I have heard that real authors sometimes have their books turned down. I figure you win some, you lose some.

Then Miss Neely announced that the Famous Author the winners would get to have lunch with was Angela Badger. The girls were more excited than the boys because Angela Badger writes mostly about girls with problems like big feet or pimples or something. I would still like to meet her because she is, as they say, a real live author, and I've never met a real live author. I am glad Mr. Henshaw isn't the author because then I would *really* be disappointed that I didn't get to meet him.

TODAY TURNED OUT to be exciting. In the middle of second period Miss Neely called me out of class and asked if I would like to go have lunch with Angela Badger. I said, "Sure, how come?"

Miss Neely explained that the teachers discovered that the winning poem had been copied out of a book and wasn't original so the girl who submitted it would not be allowed to go and would I like to go in her place? Would I!

Miss Neely telephoned Mom at work for permission and I gave my lunch to Barry because my lunches are better than his. The other winners were all dressed up, but I didn't care. I have noticed that authors like Mr. Henshaw usually wear old plaid shirts in the pictures on the back of their books. My shirt is just as old as his, so I knew it was OK.

Miss Neely drove us in her own car to the Holiday Inn, where some other librarians and their winners were waiting in the lobby. Then Angela Badger arrived with Mr. Badger, and we were all led into the dining room which was pretty crowded. One of the librarians who was a sort of Super Librarian told the winners to sit at a long table with a sign that said Reserved. Angela Badger sat in the middle and some of the girls pushed to sit beside her. I sat across from her. Super Librarian explained that we could choose our lunch from the salad bar. Then all the librarians went off and sat at a table with Mr. Badger.

There I was face to face with a real live author who seemed like a nice lady, plump with wild hair, and I couldn't think of a thing to say because I hadn't read her books. Some girls told her how much they loved her books, but some of the boys and girls were too shy to say anything. Nothing seemed to happen until Mrs. Badger said, "Why don't we all go help ourselves to lunch at the salad bar?"

What a mess! Some people didn't understand about salad bars, but Mrs. Badger led the way and we helped ourselves to lettuce and bean salad and potato salad and all the usual stuff they lay out on salad bars. A few of the younger kids were too short to reach anything but the bowls on the first rows. They weren't doing too well until Mrs. Badger helped them out. Getting lunch took a long time, longer than in a school cafeteria, and when we carried our plates back to our table, people at other tables ducked and dodged as if they expected us to dump our lunches on their heads. All one boy had on his plate was a piece of lettuce and a slice of tomato because he thought he was going to get to go back for roast beef and fried chicken. We had to straighten him out and explain that all we got was salad. He turned red and went back for more salad.

I was still trying to think of something interesting to say to Mrs. Badger while I chased garbanzo beans around my plate with a fork. A couple of girls did all the talking, telling Mrs. Badger how they wanted to write books exactly like hers. The other librarians

were busy talking and laughing with Mr. Badger who seemed to be a lot of fun.

Mrs. Badger tried to get some of the shy people to say something without much luck, and I still couldn't think of anything to say to a lady who wrote books about girls with big feet or pimples. Finally Mrs. Badger looked straight at me and asked, "What did you write for the Yearbook?"

I felt myself turn red and answered, "Just something about a ride on a truck."

"Oh!" said Mrs. Badger. "So you're the author of *A Day on Dad's Rig*!"

Everyone was quiet. None of us had known the real live author would have read what we had written, but she had and she remembered my title.

"I just got honorable mention," I said, but I was thinking, She called me an author. *A real live author called me an author.*

"What difference does that make?" asked Mrs. Badger. "Judges never agree. I happened to like *A Day on Dad's Rig* because it was written by a boy who wrote honestly about something he knew and had strong feelings about. You made me feel what it was like to ride down a steep grade with tons of grapes behind me."

"But I couldn't make it into a story," I said, feeling a whole lot braver.

"Who cares?" said Mrs. Badger with a

A REAL LIVE AUTHOR HAD CALLED ME AN AUTHOR. A REAL LIVE AUTHOR HAD TOLD ME TO KEEP IT UP.

wave of her hand. She's the kind of person who wears rings on her forefingers. "What do you expect? The ability to write stories comes later, when you have lived longer and have more understanding. *A Day on Dad's Rig* was splendid work for a boy your age. You wrote like *you,* and you did not try to imitate someone else. This is one mark of a good writer. Keep it up."

I noticed a couple of girls who had been saying they wanted to write books exactly like Angela Badger exchange embarrassed looks.

"Gee, thanks," was all I could say. The waitress began to plunk down dishes of ice cream. Everyone got over being shy and began to ask Mrs. Badger if she wrote in pencil or on the typewriter and did she ever have books rejected and were her characters real people and did she ever have pimples when she was a girl like the girl in her book and what did it feel like to be a famous author?

I didn't think answers to those questions were very important, but I did have one question I wanted to ask which I finally managed to get in at the last minute when Mrs. Badger was autographing some books people had brought.

"Mrs. Badger," I said, "did you ever meet Boyd Henshaw?"

"Why, yes," she said, scribbling away in someone's book. "I once met him at a meeting of librarians where we were on the same program."

"What's he like?" I asked over the head of a girl crowding up with her book.

"He's a very nice young man with a wicked twinkle in his eye," she answered. I think I have known that since the time he answered my questions when Miss Martinez made us write to an author.

On the ride home everybody was chattering about Mrs. Badger this, and Mrs. Badger that. I didn't want to talk. I just wanted to think. A real live author had called *me* an author. A real live author had told me to keep it up. Mom was proud of me when I told her.

The gas station stopped pinging a long time ago, but I wanted to write all this down while I remembered. I'm glad tomorrow is Saturday. If I had to go to school I would yawn. I wish Dad was here so I could tell him all about today.

MEET BEVERLY CLEARY

How did you happen to write Leigh's story?

I had been writing about a girl, Ramona, for a while, when several boys suggested I write a story about a boy whose parents were divorced.

Did you know that you were going to write it in journal style when you began?

I prefer to write in the third person, but I know that first-person books are popular with children, so I decided that presenting this book in the form of a diary and letters might be an interesting change of pace for me.

Like Mr. Henshaw, as a popular author you must get many letters.

Yes, more than I can possibly answer and still have time for writing. I do the best I can. It rather surprises me that children want to write to an author. When I was young I was only interested in the book itself, not in the person who had written it. I remember there was an author who lived in my town and after I saw him, I thought, well, I certainly wouldn't want to read any books *he's* written.

There is a scene in *Dear Mr. Henshaw* when a well-known author goes to lunch with several writing students. Did anything like this ever happen to you?

Yes. Even though I usually don't write

so specifically from life, this incident did happen. I was asked to lunch with a group of about 20 children who had won a reading contest. We were only allowed to eat from the salad bar. There was one boy who did not understand this, and he took just one piece of lettuce and tomato because he thought he was going back for roast beef and fried chicken. We had to set him straight, and the children had a good laugh.

You must like dogs because you've written about them since way back in your Ribsy series.

Yes, but I write about cats and hamsters and mice, too! When I was growing up, everyone had a dog like Ribsy that roamed around the neighborhood. In *Strider,* the sequel to *Dear Mr. Henshaw,* there is a dog, a Queensland Heeler. My son has a dog of this breed, so we sent pictures of him to the artist who illustrated the book.

What is your next project?

I'm working on the second volume of my autobiography, *Girl from Yamhill.* I received many letters after that book asking what happened next. So this book recalls how I went to college during the Depression and worked as a children's librarian and an Army librarian. It ends with the acceptance of my first book.

Fifth Grade

From today on, I'm in fifth grade! My chest felt tight as I took the road to school. It felt like I was taking that road for the first time. Fourth grade seemed like a dream to me. When I got to school everything was quiet and when I came to the classroom suddenly everyone was looking at me. I felt like a transfer student. I was all shy. But I steeled my shoulders and entered the classroom. In my heart I was shouting, "I *am* a part of this class!" Everybody seemed much taller. I thought I had gotten smaller. I was a little embarrassed. But at that moment a fifth grade wind began to blow.

Endō Mina, fifth grade

44

I Love the Look of Words

by Maya Angelou
illustrated by Tom Feelings

Popcorn leaps, popping from the floor
of a hot black skillet
and into my mouth.
Black words leap,
snapping from the white
page. Rushing into my eyes. Sliding
into my brain which gobbles them
the way my tongue and teeth
chomp the buttered popcorn.

When I have stopped reading,
ideas from the words stay stuck
in my mind, like the sweet
smell of butter perfuming my
fingers long after the popcorn
is finished.

I love the book and the look of words
the weight of ideas that popped into my mind
I love the tracks
of new thinking in my mind.

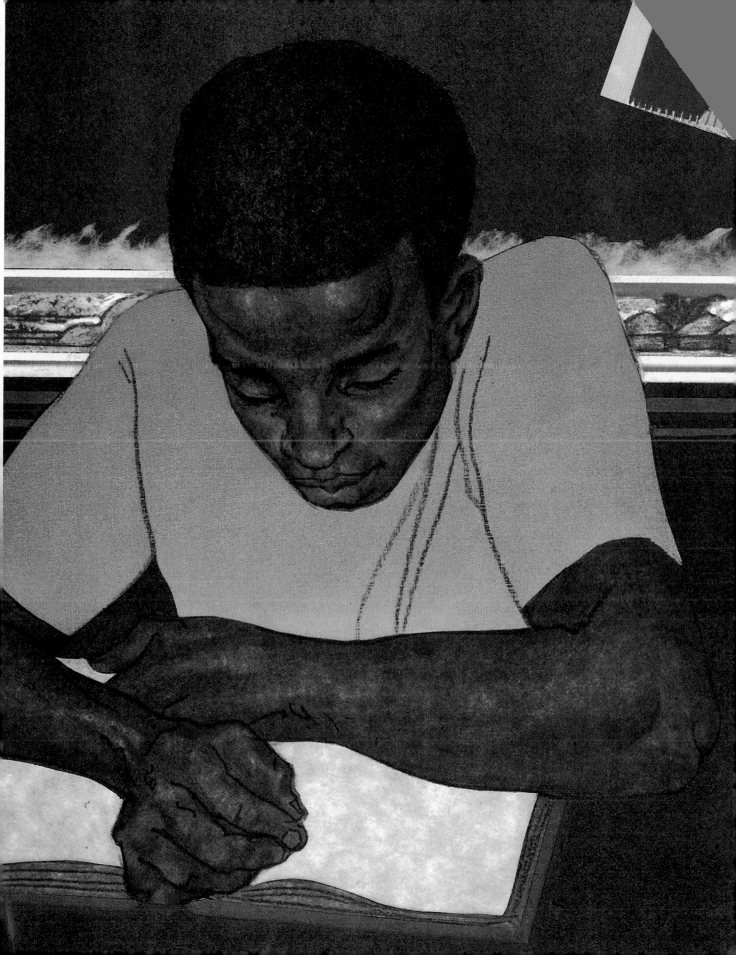

RESPONSE

CLEVER CONTRAPTION

Work with a partner to design an alarm that will trap Leigh's lunchbox thief. Draw your trap on poster paper, labeling all the parts. Then explain the trap to your classmates. If you wish, make the trap and display it in the classroom.

EXPERIENCE THIS

Remember Mrs. Badger's encouraging words about writing honestly about something you know. Write a personal narrative about an interesting experience you have had in fifth grade.

CORNER

THE RIGHT DIET

How could you make better food choices at lunchtime? Design a colorful menu for a healthful lunch you could bring from home or buy in the school cafeteria. Tell why each choice would be good for you.

WHAT DO YOU THINK?

• What does Leigh learn about himself by outsmarting the lunchbox thief and by writing his story for the Young Writers' Yearbook?

• How did you feel about Leigh by the end of the story? Explain why.

• Who do you think Leigh is more like—the narrator of "Fifth Grade" or the narrator of "I Love the Look of Words"?

by Sarah Jane Brian
from *3-2-1 CONTACT*

INVEN

Every year, thousands of kids come up with ideas for futuristic inventions. They enter a science competition called the ExploraVision Awards.

These inventions don't exist—yet. But the kids used real scientific research to show how their designs could become real someday.

50

TiONS

Yakity-Yak ... Watches Talk Back

"The Amazing Calculator" is designed to look like a watch. But it's a talking computer!

The calculator has no keys, so you could use it even if your hands were busy. It would also store information, like a computer.

The calculator would listen to questions, and might even ask you some! "Say you were painting a room, and you wanted to know how much paint to buy," says inventor Malissa Andring. "The calculator would ask, 'How thick do you want the paint to be?'"

INVENTORS: *Malissa Andring, Ben Howie, Bradley Wilson*

Shake and Wake

The smoke detector of the future would do more than just broadcast a siren. It might also give loud, spoken instructions with escape routes. Plus, the detector could be wired to every bed in the house. In case of a fire, the beds would shake to wake up anyone who's sleeping!

INVENTORS:
Corey Beasley, James Davis, Giles Sydnor, Graham Whitley

Looking to the Future

Here's an invention that could be a sight for sore eyes: "The Superglasses!"

The glasses would be so soft and flexible that you could even sleep with them on. Change the color of the frames by turning a screw. A built-in camera would let you take a picture of anything you see. Plus, the glasses would have a built-in heater to defrost the lenses if they fog up!

INVENTORS: *Nana Furukubo, Ann Garlid, Katherine Saviskas, Madeline Shapiro*

Thumbs Up

A lock can keep your bicycle safe from theft. But what if you forget the combination, or lose the key? This solution locked up an ExploraVision award last year: a computerized bike lock. It would lock and unlock by reading your thumbprint!

INVENTORS: *Elizabeth Hartz, Jessica Pederson, Katherine Layman*

Code Green

How will we take care of the environment in the future? This new bar-coding system could help.

The system would tell how "green" a product is before you buy it. Shoppers would use a hand-held scanner to "read" the codes on products in a store. The code would say how much energy it took to make the item, how much waste was produced and what natural resources were used. You'd also find out if the product is recyclable.

INVENTORS: *Jennifer Kalansky, Alpa Patel, Rupa Patel, Heather Fisch*

The Write Stuff

We've got to hand it to the kids who invented the Infrared Tipper glove. If you had one, you'd never need to sharpen a pencil. Just let your fingers do the writing!

The glove would reflect infrared radiation made by your hand's heat. This would let you write with your fingertip on special infrared-sensitive paper. All write!

INVENTORS!
Diana Crowe, Kyra Deutsch, Daniel Guido, Ryoichi Yamamoto

Wacky Patents

Ben Franklin sez: *These inventions may seem weird. But they are real! Each one was recently patented by the U.S. Patent Office. We wouldn't invent a story like this. Honest!*

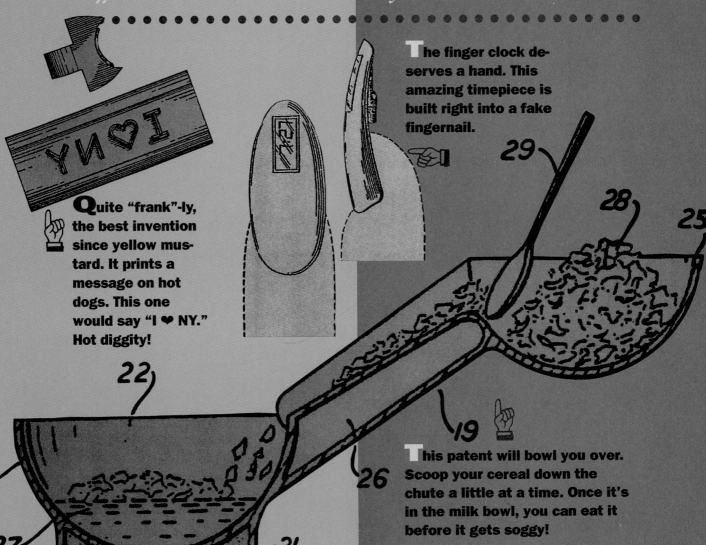

Quite "frank"-ly, the best invention since yellow mustard. It prints a message on hot dogs. This one would say "I ♥ NY." Hot diggity!

The finger clock deserves a hand. This amazing timepiece is built right into a fake fingernail.

This patent will bowl you over. Scoop your cereal down the chute a little at a time. Once it's in the milk bowl, you can eat it before it gets soggy!

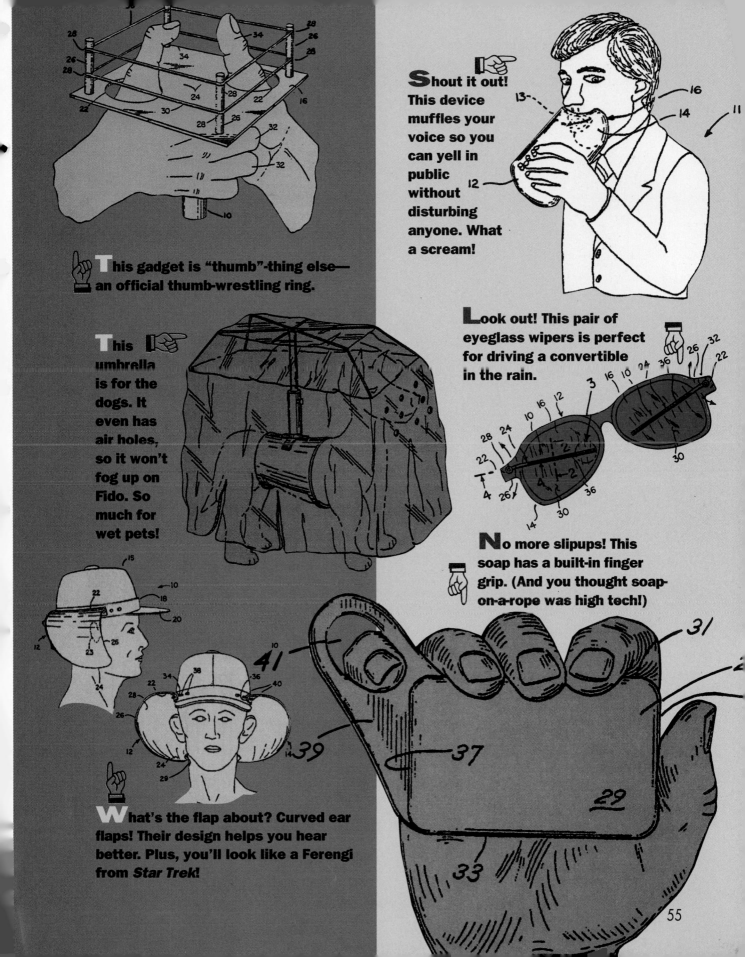

This gadget is "thumb"-thing else—an official thumb-wrestling ring.

Shout it out! This device muffles your voice so you can yell in public without disturbing anyone. What a scream!

This umbrella is for the dogs. It even has air holes, so it won't fog up on Fido. So much for wet pets!

Look out! This pair of eyeglass wipers is perfect for driving a convertible in the rain.

No more slipups! This soap has a built-in finger grip. (And you thought soap-on-a-rope was high tech!)

What's the flap about? Curved ear flaps! Their design helps you hear better. Plus, you'll look like a Ferengi from *Star Trek*!

Whose Side

by Emily Moore
illustrated by Tyrone Geter

Are You On?

REPORT-CARD DAY

THE CLOCK ON THE TEACHER'S DESK TICKED AWAY.

Just fifteen minutes to go, I thought, as I shifted nervously in my seat.

If only it had snowed hard enough for school to be closed, I could be

anywhere else but here, sitting at my desk, waiting for my report card. I

dreaded getting it because my grades for the first marking period had

been lousy compared to last year. It wasn't my fault, though. Everything

was so much harder in sixth grade, especially my teacher, Mrs. Stone.

The sound of jangling bracelets brought me back to the chalky smell

of the classroom and to the sight of Mrs. Stone standing over my desk.

"Barbra," she said in her metallic voice, "if you're ready to join us,

I'll now distribute report cards."

I gulped so loud that the kids around me heard and started giggling. Mrs. Stone shook her head and walked to the front of the room, undoing the rubber band binding the packet of report cards. She began to give them out. I sat on my hands, anxiously waiting for her to get to me. Mrs. Stone had promised that in the second marking period she was going to be even tougher than before. I didn't see how. She was hard enough on me the first time.

Several kids whooped and hollered when they opened their cards. Mrs. Stone smiled at my best friend, Claudia. She patted my other friend, Patricia, on the shoulder and said, "Nice work."

Finally it was my turn. From across the room, Claudia made an A-okay sign at me. I drew in my breath and opened the card.

Tears came to my eyes when I saw my grades. I never dreamed it would be this bad! Not one *Excellent*. In my favorite subject, reading, Mrs. Hernandez only gave me a *Satisfactory*. But that wasn't the worst of it. In math, Mrs. Stone gave me a *U. Unsatisfactory* is the nice word for *failed*. I couldn't believe that Mrs. Stone had actually flunked me! I felt a thump on my back and jerked around.

Nosy Kim was grinning at me. Kids called her Gumdrop because she ate a lot of candy and was fat. "Show me your report card; I'll show you mine." She stuck her report card in my face.

I pushed her hand away.

"What did you get?" she whined.

"Leave me alone, Gumdrop," I snapped.

I stuffed my report card into my schoolbag before anyone else asked to see it, and as soon as Mrs. Stone dismissed us, I took off down the block.

"Barbra, wait up!" Claudia called, walking with Patricia.

"Got to go," I called back, as if I had to get someplace fast.

Since we all lived in the River View Co-ops, I went in the opposite direction. As I ran up the snow-slicked street, my unzipped boots flapped against my legs. I didn't stop to zip them or to swipe at my tear-stained eyes. I kept running until I passed Harlem Hospital.

Out of breath, I stopped and opened the report card again. There it was—a fat, red *U*—the first one of my life. It made me feel like a real failure. Nobody in my family had ever failed at anything before. I couldn't bring this report card home. What was I going to do?

Then I saw the solution to my problem: a trash can on the corner. The sign tacked on it said *Throw It Here*. So I did. A feeling of lightness came over me. I twirled around, holding my mouth open to catch snowflakes. The next moment, a snowball splattered against my back, making me stumble forward.

"Hey!" I said out loud, and looked around to see who threw it.

The street was empty except for a woman in a fur coat hurrying along and two old men talking in the doorway of Patricia's father's barbershop on 138th Street. I was sure it couldn't have been any of them. Then I saw the real culprit peer up from behind a car and duck down again. I should have known.

"What's the big idea, T.J.?" I yelled, marching over to him.

T.J. was tall, with gleaming black eyes and deep, round dimples. Even though he was twelve, a year older than me, he was in Mrs. Stone's class, too. A long time ago, he told me that the reason he got left back in first grade was that his teacher said he wasn't mature enough to be promoted to second grade. She was probably right.

He opened his mouth wide, pretending to be astonished.

"Don't play innocent," I said. "You hit me."

"You're hallucinating."

"Then why were you trying to hide?"

"I dropped some money." He poked around in the snow. I could tell it was all a big act by the way he kept looking up, grinning that sneaky, crooked grin of his.

"Why weren't you in school today?" I asked.

"Playing hookey," he said sarcastically.

"Seriously."

He took an Oreo cookie from his pocket, waved it in my face, then popped it into his mouth whole. I walked away, disgusted.

"If you must know," he said, tagging after me, "I was getting Pop's asthma medicine and the newspaper." Pop was his grandfather, whom he lived with.

"All day?" Not that I was complaining. In school I sat next to him. It was a relief that he was absent and could not pester me, for a change.

He hitched his old green knapsack on his shoulders, ignoring my question. "Weren't we supposed to get report cards?" he asked.

"What of it?"

"How did you do?"

"Why does everybody care how I did?"

He made tsk-tsking noises. "That bad, huh?"

"Good as yours, I bet."

He stuck out his pinky and thumb. I knew better than to bet with T.J. He'd always done well in school. He never failed math or anything else. He may have been immature, but he certainly was smart.

Turning up my nose at him, I glanced away and saw a garbage truck stop in front of the trash can. A second later, I realized the terrible thing that was about to happen. I had to get that report card back before it got dumped in the trash for real.

"Stop!" I shouted.

"I'm not doing anything," T.J. said.

I waved him off and ran back to the trash can. "Wait! Stop," I called again, but the sanitation man paid no attention. He picked up the can and shook the contents into the garbage chute in the back of the truck. He climbed inside the cab. The driver put the truck into gear. The truck rumbled away and disappeared around the corner. My report card was on its way to the city dump.

What had I been thinking? My mother was going to be mad

enough about my grades, let alone a thrown-away report card. I stamped my foot and kicked over the can. Without a word, T.J. righted it and gave me a strange look.

"Well, I know you're dying to ask me what's wrong," I said.

"Here," he said, offering me a cookie from his pocket.

"No, thanks." I loved Oreos, but I didn't trust T.J. The last time he offered me ice cream, it was a Dixie cup filled with mushed-up peas and mashed potatoes. Besides, I was in no mood to eat now. I sniffed and crossed the street.

He kept walking with me toward my building on Harlem River Drive. The River View Co-ops took up the entire square block from 139th to 140th Streets and from Fifth Avenue to the Drive. The buildings were red and beige brick and were built around an inner courtyard. I lived in building number 4, which faced the Drive and the East River. From halfway down the block, I heard the swishing sound of traffic on the Drive.

"Come on, take it," he said gently. "It will make you feel better."

"Nothing could make me feel better." But the thought of the bittersweet chocolate and sweet, creamy center made my mouth water. "Okay," I finally said. "I'll take one, thanks."

I bit into the cookie and almost broke my tooth. It wasn't a cookie at all, but a wooden disk made to look like one. T.J. bent over, laughing.

I threw the fake cookie at him and pushed through the doors of my building's lobby. "I hate you, Anthony Jordan Brodie!" I'd never fall for one of his tricks again.

"Can't you take a joke?" he called after me.

I turned around, sticking my tongue between my teeth, and gave him a loud, sloppy raspberry.

WISHFUL THINKING

I dumped my books on the kitchen counter and poured myself a glass of ice-cold chocolate milk, hoping it would make the burning in my stomach go away. It only gave me the chills. I stomped upstairs to where our bedrooms were. All the second-floor apartments in our co-op were duplexes.

The door to my brother Billy's room was slightly opened. His baseball and swimming trophies were lined up on his dresser, along with his comb, brush, and cologne bottle in the shape of a steam engine. He loved trains. The Tyco train set he'd received for Christmas took up much of the floor space in his room. Pushing the door open a bit more, I could see the brown report-card envelope leaning up against his mirror like another trophy on display.

"Hey," he said, glancing up from his homework. "What took you so long to get home?"

"I bumped into you-know-who. The pain." I told him about T.J.'s trick and finished by saying, "I felt like smashing his face in the snow."

But Billy only laughed. "He likes you. That's what grownups always say about kids teasing each other."

"They sure don't know anything about me and T.J."

"If you say so," he said and reached into the old, battered briefcase that had belonged to Daddy when he was a reporter. Daddy died in a plane crash when we were four years old. Billy's named after him.

Billy pulled his protractor out of the briefcase. He carefully measured angles and made calculations. While I was still struggling with division and word problems, he was doing geometry. It was hard to believe we were twins. I was ten minutes older; he was ten times smarter—which is why I was in a regular sixth-grade class and he was in the IGC, the class for "intellectually gifted children."

I pushed aside his blue plaid curtains. The snow continued to fall thick and steady. How I hoped school would be closed tomorrow. Hmmph! Fat chance! I let the curtain fall back in place and went to my own room. After changing into old jeans, I got out my schoolbooks and worked on my homework until it was almost dinnertime.

Passing Billy's room on my way downstairs, I heard his trains chugging around the track. He'd be in for it when Ma saw he hadn't set the table. But as I entered the kitchen, I was surprised to see the yellow dishes on top of the daisy-patterned place mats. Billy had even made a tossed salad. Everything was ready for when Ma came home in a few minutes. Now I would be the only one she'd scold.

When I heard her at the door, I figured it was best to try to be extra nice. I kissed her hello and helped her off with her coat. "Let me take that," I said, putting her briefcase on the lacquered parson's table next to the coat closet.

"My, what did I do to get such treatment?" She pulled off her hat and ran her fingers through her short, curly hair.

"You work hard, and I'm sure you're tired."

She sank down on the sofa. "It's worth it." I put her boots in the bathroom to dry.

She sat with her eyes closed for a while, then got up and stretched. "After I change, I'll warm up the leftover turkey and gravy for sandwiches."

However, instead of going up to her room, she went into Billy's. I tried to hear what they were saying, but the sound of the trains drowned out their voices. All I could do was hope for two things— that Ma did not notice the brown envelope on Billy's dresser and that Billy didn't start blabbing.

In any case, report cards would have to come up during supper, the time when important family discussions took place. Usually, the first thing Ma did once we sat down to eat was to ask us about school. But tonight she started telling us about what happened to her at Citibank, where she is a manager.

"I got a promotion," she said. "It's now official. I'm a vice president."

"Wow!" Billy said. "That's just one step from president."

"It's many steps away, but it's exactly what I've been working toward. It will mean longer hours," she said and then gave us some other details about her new job.

"More money, too?" Billy asked.

She nodded. "Most definitely."

"Oh, Ma, that reminds me," said Billy.

I knew he was going to tell her about his report card. In the excitement of Ma's news, I had almost forgotten about it. My heart began to beat faster.

"Ma," Billy said, "I'm going to need a new baseball uniform. My old one is too small."

"No problem," Ma said, then faced me. "Are you all right? You're awfully quiet."

"I'm okay."

"You sure?" Ma ate a forkful of salad.

"Uh-huh." I pushed my plate to one side. All this suspense took away my appetite.

"Is something wrong with your food?" Ma asked.

"Big lunch," I said, getting up from the table.

"It's almost eight hours since lunch."

"I ate a big snack, too."

Ma told me to sit back down. "You know the rules. We eat as a family."

Rules, rules. Rules made me sick. I propped my elbows on the table, but one look from Ma and I began to eat slowly. Billy was cutting his sandwich into bite-size pieces. Whoever heard of eating a sandwich with a knife and fork, even if it was a sloppy kind of sandwich? Everything about him was so proper and right. He would never even *think* of throwing away his report card, let alone do it.

"Can I go upstairs now?" I asked after forcing down the last of my turkey sandwich.

Ma put her hand to my forehead. "What's the matter?"

"Nothing."

"You call T.J. nothing?" asked Billy, with a silly grin on his face.

"He's such a pain,"
I said, grateful to him for changing the subject.

"The way you and T.J. needle each other," Ma said, shaking her head. "It's . . ."

"It's his fault," I said, cutting her off. "Like when he put that caterpillar down my back."

"That was last summer at the Labor Day picnic," said Billy, as if a few months made a difference. "And the caterpillar was made from a pipe cleaner and yarn."

"It wiggled like it was real. I thought I was going to die."

"Oh, Barbra," Ma said. "You're exaggerating."

"He's always bugging me, Ma."

"You know what they say." Billy was hinting again about T.J. liking me. I kicked at him under the table.

Ma ate some more salad. "Anyway, I've invited his grandfather and him to dinner Friday night," Ma said.

I nearly jumped out of my seat. "Oh, no. You didn't!"

"Since T.J.'s mom is still away, it's probably lonely for him."

"So what," I blurted out.

She gave me a look and I knew I had said the wrong thing. So I quickly said, "I don't feel well. May I be excused?"

Ma drew in a long sigh. "Go on."

I ran up the stairs to my room, shut the door, and got ready for bed, even though it was way before my bedtime. Going to sleep was the only way out of my mess. Why, oh, why did I ever do such a stupid thing?

I hugged Brown Bear close until he was all squished up. Ever since I was a little girl, hugging him always comforted me. Just as I was falling asleep, I heard the click of my door.

Ma came into the room. She stood over me a long time before sitting down on the edge of my bed. When she turned on the lamp, my eyelids fluttered, but I kept my eyes squeezed shut.

Brushing down my bangs, she said, "Whatever is bothering you, you can tell me. I'll understand."

I looked up at her. This is silly, I thought. Sooner or later she's going to find out. I should just get it over with. I sat up and finally told her about how Mrs. Stone failed me in math.

"No wonder you're upset. But, honey, I'll see that you get help. And I suspect it's not as bad as you make out."

"It's worse."

"Let me see." She held out her hand.

I looked down. "You can't." Twisting the blanket around, I said, "See, there was this trash can, and a sign. Then T.J. hit me with a snowball and I forgot all about it. Then a garbage truck came . . ."

"Talk plainly, Barbra."

"I threw my report card in a trash can."

She didn't say anything.

"I tried to get it back," I rushed on to explain, "but I was too late. The garbage man wouldn't listen."

She sat there, not saying a word. The change in her expression was like what happened to that Dr. Jekyll in the movie. One minute he looked like a regular person and then the next he looked real mean and evil.

"How could you do such a thing?" she said in such a quiet voice I got goose pimples.

"It was an accident. I never meant to throw it away. Not really. But that T.J. . . ."

"Don't blame him," she said.

While my voice was high and shrieky, Ma stayed quietly angry.

"In a way, it's kind of funny. Don't you think?" I looked at her hopefully, but she was not amused.

"It wasn't on purpose!" I said.

"Wasn't it?" she asked. "You never think. And now look what's happened."

"I was so upset. I never got a *U* before, and I was scared of what you would say."

"I'm disappointed in you." She got up and left. I threw Brown Bear across the room. He could stay in that corner forever.

After a while, Ma came back into the room with a long, white envelope in her hand. She laid it on the dresser. "Give this to Mrs. Stone. She'll write you another report card, and I'll talk to her tomorrow at the parent-teacher's conference." She saw Brown Bear in the corner, picked him up, and put him on my chair. "You're grounded. You won't have any special privileges."

"Forever?" I asked in a panic.

"Let me finish. No special privileges until your math grades improve."

That may as well be forever, I thought, as she closed the door behind her.

GOOD NEWS AND BAD

First thing the next morning, Mrs. Stone asked for the signed report cards. I pulled Ma's letter halfway out of my schoolbag, but I didn't have the nerve to give it to her in front of the whole class.

"Do I have them all?" Mrs. Stone asked, waving the packet in the air. I wondered if she could feel that one was missing. Sometime later, in private, I would give the letter to her. Until then, I would just act normally. I put my homework on my desk to be collected, then went to sharpen my pencils. On my way back to my seat, I noticed the envelope on the floor. It must have fallen from my schoolbag. Before I could get it, Kim picked it up.

"Give me that," I said, reaching for the envelope.

She hid it behind her back, all the while chomping on something—a gooey gumdrop, no doubt. "Mrs. Stone's name is written on it."

"It's mine."

Kim bit her lip as if thinking it over. Meanwhile, Mrs. Stone noticed. "Kim, bring that up here."

If Mrs. Stone read that letter aloud, I'd be the laughingstock of the whole, entire sixth grade. And all because of Gumdrop. I'd fix her but good. I stuck my foot out into the aisle, but she stepped over it without tripping.

"Thank you, Kim." Mrs. Stone opened the envelope. "And empty your mouth," she added, not even looking at Kim as she spat a wad of gum into the trash can.

Over the rim of her glasses, Mrs. Stone glanced at me as she read the letter. After she finished, she called me to her desk.

"Why do you need
another report card?" Mrs. Stone asked in
a low voice.

"The letter explains it."

She showed me the letter. Ma requested another report card
without any explanation. How could she have done this to me?

"Well, Barbra," Mrs. Stone said. Her head bobbed, showing her
impatience.

"I lost it." I swallowed and went on. "I, um, reached into my
schoolbag to give it to my mother, you know, um, to sign. And it
wasn't there."

She gave me a long, hard look to see if I was really telling the
truth. "Why wasn't it in your schoolbag?"

"It was, but . . ." I shifted uneasily, then asked, "Will you give me
another one?"

The bell rang for first period and Mrs. Stone said, "Barbra will stay behind. The rest of you may go to your reading classes." She went into the hall to ask her reading group to wait outside.

On her way out with Patricia, Claudia whispered, "We'll wait by the water fountain."

The last person to leave was T.J. At the door, he brushed his two pointer fingers together and said, "Shame, shame."

I threw an ink eraser at him just as Mrs. Stone was coming back. She scolded me, then made me pick it up.

"Do you have a problem, Anthony?" Mrs. Stone asked T.J.

"No, ma'am," he said and hiked out of the room fast.

I knew what Mrs. Stone was going to say—I'd heard it before. "You have to try harder. Don't say you can't." And that's just what she said, adding, "Until you change your attitude, you will continue to do poorly. Losing your report card is an example of your carelessness." With that, she slipped Ma's letter into her roll book and told me to go to reading.

By now, only a few kids were straggling through the hall, but as they promised, Claudia and Patricia were waiting by the water fountain. I hurried to meet them.

Ever since this past summer when Patricia moved into River View, she, Claudia, and I were together every chance we got. Claudia was the lucky one, because she and Patricia both lived in building number 6 and went to the same ballet school. Ma refused to pay for lessons for me on account of what happened last year. She had signed me up and after three lessons I begged her to let me stop. Even though I promised not to drop out this time, she wouldn't let me take them.

"What did Mrs. Stone say?" asked Patricia.

"Gave me a lecture. I lost my report card," I said, trying to sound nonchalant.

"Anybody can lose a report card," said Claudia.

"True," I said and crossed my fingers, hoping they would never find out about the dumb thing I had done.

Emily Moore

I was born in Harlem, the next to the youngest of seven children. I wasn't very much like Barbra in *Whose Side Are You On?* I was more like her brother, Billy—the kind of student who always got good grades. I certainly never had to throw my report card in the trash! When I grew up, I became a teacher. I've taught all different grades all over the New York area.

When I was writing this book, I kept thinking about things like friendship, loyalty, and caring about other people. It's interesting to me that although times change, kids worry about the same things. There's a lot of talk today about drugs and violence and homelessness. But kids still worry about who will be their best friend, whether a certain boy or girl likes them, and what they're going to do tomorrow. And that's the way it should be.

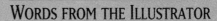

WORDS FROM THE ILLUSTRATOR

Tyrone Geter

American artist Tyrone Geter (JEE ter) spent seven years living and working in West Africa. This experience inspired the name of his studio/gallery in Akron, Ohio, Hikima Creations. Mr. Geter explains, "The name *Hikima* comes from an Arabic-Hausa-Swahili word meaning 'the creativity and wisdom of the elders.' Many of the models you see in my paintings – including the ones for *Whose Side Are You On?* – are local kids, right out of this studio."

Under the Back Porch

by Virginia Hamilton • illustrated by Pat Cummings

Our house is two stories high
shaped like a white box.
There is a yard stretched around it
and in back
a wooden porch.

Under the back porch is my place.
I rest there.
I go there when I have to be alone.
It is always shaded and damp.
Sunlight only slants through the slats
in long strips of light,
and the smell of the damp
is moist green,
like the moss that grows here.

My sisters and brothers
can stand on the back porch
and never know
I am here
underneath.
It is my place.
All mine.

RESPONSE

MAKE A LIST

Rules of the Roost

Barbra's family had dinner-time rules. What rules does your family like to follow? Make a list of those rules and illustrate some of them. Post the list on the refrigerator as a colorful reminder.

ROLE-PLAY A CONVERSATION

Critical Choices

When the truth comes out about the missing report card, whose side are you on—Barbra's or her mother's? Role-play with a partner the conversation that follows the discovery.

CORNER

Hidden Feelings

Barbra probably felt as though she wanted to hide under the back porch rather than face her mother. Have you ever felt that way? Share with a small group your thoughts about whether it is better to face something unpleasant right away or later.

What Do You Think?

· How does Barbra feel about what she did? What does this tell you about her?

· Would you like to read more about Barbra? Explain why or why not.

· How are Barbra and the narrator of "Under the Back Porch" alike? Explain your answer.

75

ART AND LITERATURE

The stories in this theme are about getting along with people in and out of school. How does the painting *School's Out* fit in with this theme? The painting shows an after-school scene on a day in 1936. How is the scene like one you might see today? How is it different?

School's Out
by Allan Rohan Crite

Allan Rohan Crite was born in New Jersey in 1910 and moved to Boston when he was still a baby. He received his first drawing lessons from his mother. Later, he became the first African American to attend the School of the Boston Museum of Fine Arts. School's Out *is one of Crite's many paintings showing Boston street life.*

Oil on canvas 1936,
National Museum of American Art, Washington, DC

SIDEWAYS STORIES FROM WAYSIDE SCHOOL

by Louis Sachar
illustrated by Michael Sours

It began with a simple mistake. Wayside School was supposed to be built with thirty classrooms side by side. Instead, the builder put them one on top of the other, making Wayside School only one classroom wide, but thirty classrooms high! No wonder so many strange things happen there, especially in Mrs. Jewls's class—all the way up on the thirtieth floor.

Todd

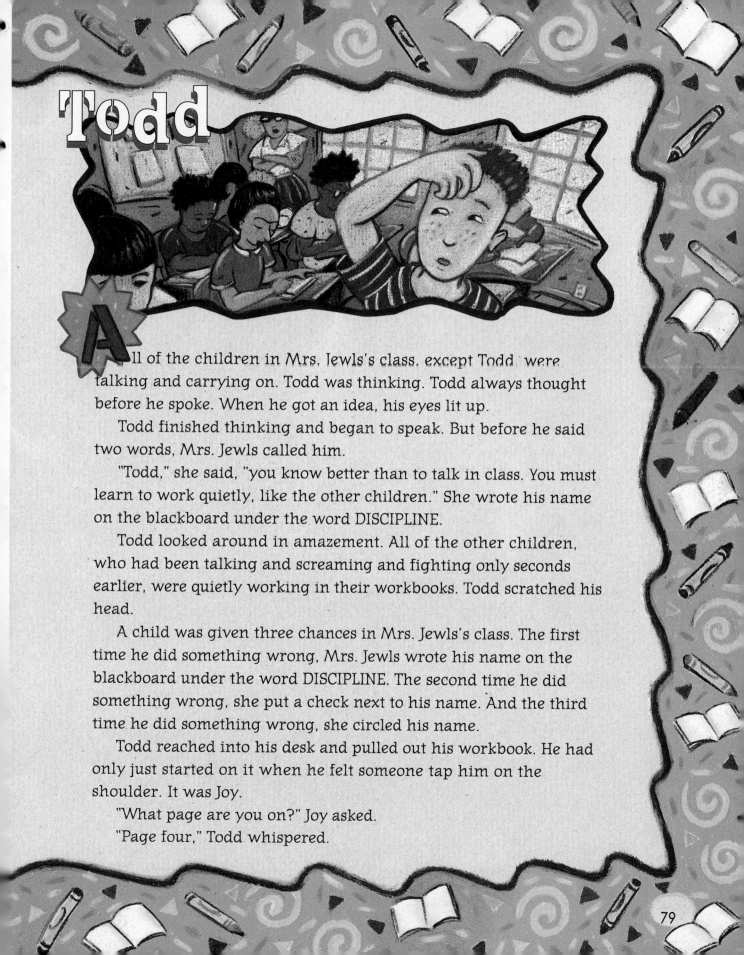

All of the children in Mrs. Jewls's class, except Todd, were talking and carrying on. Todd was thinking. Todd always thought before he spoke. When he got an idea, his eyes lit up.

Todd finished thinking and began to speak. But before he said two words, Mrs. Jewls called him.

"Todd," she said, "you know better than to talk in class. You must learn to work quietly, like the other children." She wrote his name on the blackboard under the word DISCIPLINE.

Todd looked around in amazement. All of the other children, who had been talking and screaming and fighting only seconds earlier, were quietly working in their workbooks. Todd scratched his head.

A child was given three chances in Mrs. Jewls's class. The first time he did something wrong, Mrs. Jewls wrote his name on the blackboard under the word DISCIPLINE. The second time he did something wrong, she put a check next to his name. And the third time he did something wrong, she circled his name.

Todd reached into his desk and pulled out his workbook. He had only just started on it when he felt someone tap him on the shoulder. It was Joy.

"What page are you on?" Joy asked.

"Page four," Todd whispered.

"I'm on page eleven," said Joy.

Todd didn't say anything. He didn't want to get into trouble. He just went back to work.

Five minutes later, Joy tapped him again. Todd ignored her. So Joy poked him in the back with her pencil. Todd pretended he didn't notice. Joy got up from her seat and sharpened her pencil. She came back and poked it in Todd's back. "What page are you on?" she asked.

"Page five," Todd answered.

"Boy, are you dumb," said Joy, "I'm on page twenty-nine."

"It isn't a race," Todd whispered.

Five minutes later Joy pulled Todd's hair and didn't let go until he turned around. "What page are you on?" she demanded.

"Page six," Todd answered as quietly as he could.

"I'M ON PAGE TWO HUNDRED!" Joy shouted.

Todd was very angry. "Will you please let me do my work and stop bothering me!"

Mrs. Jewls heard him. "Todd, what did I say about talking in class?"

Todd scratched his head.

Mrs. Jewls put a check next to Todd's name on the blackboard under the word DISCIPLINE.

Todd really tried to be good. He knew that if he talked one more time, Mrs. Jewls would circle his name. Then he'd have to go home early, at twelve o'clock, on the kindergarten bus, just as he had the day before and the day before that. In fact, there hadn't been a day since Mrs. Jewls took over the class that she didn't send Todd home early. She said she did it for his own good. The other children went home at two o'clock.

Todd wasn't really bad. He just always got caught. He really wanted to stay past twelve o'clock. He wanted to find out what the class did from twelve to two. But it didn't look as though this was going to be his day. It was only ten-thirty, and he already had two strikes against him. He sealed his lips and went back to work.

There was a knock on the door. Mrs. Jewls opened it. Two men stepped in wearing masks and holding guns. "Give us all your money!" they demanded.

"All I have is a nickel," said Mrs. Jewls.

"I have a dime," said Maurecia.

"I have thirteen cents," said Leslie.

"I have four cents," said Dameon.

"What kind of bank is this?" asked one of the robbers.

"It's not a bank, it's a school," said Todd. "Can't you read?"

"No," said the robbers.

"Neither can I," said Todd.

"Do you mean we walked all the way up thirty flights of stairs for nothing?" asked the robber. "Don't you have anything valuable?"

Todd's eyes lit up. "We sure do," he said. "We have knowledge." He grabbed Joy's workbook and gave it to the robbers. "Knowledge is much more valuable than money."

"Thanks, kid," said one of the robbers.

"Maybe I'll give up being a criminal and become a scientist," said the other.

They left the room without hurting anybody.

"Now I don't have a workbook," complained Joy.

Mrs. Jewls gave her a new one. Joy had to start all the way back at the beginning.

"Hey, Joy, what page are you on?" asked Todd.

"Page one," Joy sighed.

"I'm on page eight," laughed Todd triumphantly.

Mrs. Jewls heard him. She circled his name. Todd had three strikes against him. At twelve o'clock he left the room to go home early on the kindergarten bus.

But this time when he left, he was like a star baseball player leaving the field. All the children stood up, clapped their hands, and whistled.

Todd scratched his head.

Bebe

Bebe was a girl with short brown hair, a little beebee nose, totally tiny toes, and big brown eyes. Her full name was Bebe Gunn. She was the fastest draw in Mrs. Jewls's class.

She could draw a cat in less than forty-five seconds, a dog in less than thirty, and a flower in less than eight seconds.

But, of course, Bebe never drew just one dog, or one cat, or one flower. Art was from twelve-thirty to one-thirty. Why, in that time, she could draw fifty cats, a hundred flowers, twenty dogs, and several eggs or watermelons. It took her the same amount of time to draw a watermelon as an egg.

Calvin sat next to Bebe. He didn't think he was very good at art. Why, it took him the whole period just to draw one airplane. So instead, he just helped Bebe. He was Bebe's assistant. As soon as Bebe would finish one masterpiece, Calvin would take it from her and set down a clean sheet of paper. Whenever her crayon ran low, Calvin was ready with a new crayon. That way Bebe didn't have to waste any time. And in return, Bebe would draw five or six airplanes for Calvin.

It was twelve-thirty, time for art. Bebe was ready. On her desk was a sheet of yellow construction paper. In her hand was a green crayon.

Calvin was ready. He held a stack of paper and a box of crayons.

"Ready, Bebe," said Calvin.

"Ready, Calvin," said Bebe.

"Okay," said Mrs. Jewls, "time for art."

She had hardly finished her sentence when Bebe had already drawn a picture of a leaf.

Calvin took it from her and put another piece of paper down.

"Red," called Bebe.

Calvin handed Bebe a red crayon.

"Blue," called Bebe.

He gave her a blue crayon.

They were quite a pair. Their teamwork was remarkable. Bebe drew pictures as fast as Calvin could pick up the old paper and set down the new—a fish, an apple, three cherries, bing, bing, bing.

At one-thirty Mrs. Jewls announced, "Okay, class, art is over."

Bebe dropped her crayon and fell over on her desk. Calvin sighed and leaned back in his chair. He could hardly move. They had broken their old record. Bebe had drawn three hundred and seventy-eight pictures. They lay in a pile on Calvin's desk.

Mrs. Jewls walked by. "Calvin, did you draw all these pictures?"

Calvin laughed. "No, I can't draw. Bebe drew them all."

"Well, then, what did you draw?" asked Mrs. Jewls.

"I didn't draw anything," said Calvin.

"Why not? Don't you like art?" asked Mrs. Jewls.

"I love art," said Calvin. "That's why I didn't draw anything."

Mrs. Jewls did not understand.

"It would have taken me the whole period just to draw one picture," said Calvin. "And Bebe would only have been able to draw a hundred pictures. But with the two of us working together, she was able to draw three hundred and seventy-eight pictures! That's a lot more art."

Bebe and Calvin shook hands.

"No," said Mrs. Jewls. "That isn't how you measure art. It isn't how many pictures you have, but how good the pictures are. Why, a person could spend his whole life just drawing one picture of a cat. In that time I'm sure Bebe could draw a million cats."

"Two million," said Bebe.

Mrs. Jewls continued. "But if that one picture is better than each of Bebe's two million, then that person has produced more art than Bebe."

Bebe looked as if she was going to cry. She picked up all the pictures from Calvin's desk and threw them in the garbage. Then she ran from the room.

"I thought her pictures were good," said Calvin. He reached into the garbage pail and took out a crumpled-up picture of an airplane.

Bebe walked outside into the playground.

Louis, the yard teacher, spotted her. "Where are you going?" he asked.

"I'm going home to draw a picture of a cat," said Bebe.

"Will you bring it to school and show it to me tomorrow?" Louis asked.

"Tomorrow!" laughed Bebe. "By tomorrow I doubt if I'll even be finished with one whisker."

Calvin

Calvin had a big, round face.

"Calvin," said Mrs. Jewls, "I want you to take this note to Miss Zarves for me."

"Miss Zarves?" asked Calvin.

"Yes, Miss Zarves," said Mrs. Jewls. "You know where she is, don't you?"

"Yes," said Calvin. "She's on the nineteenth story."

"That's right, Calvin," said Mrs. Jewls. "Take it to her."

Calvin didn't move.

"Well, what are you waiting for?" asked Mrs. Jewls.

"She's on the nineteenth story," said Calvin.

"Yes, we have already established that fact," said Mrs. Jewls.

"The nineteenth story," Calvin repeated.

"Yes, Calvin, the nineteenth story," said Mrs. Jewls. "Now take it to her before I lose my patience."

"But, Mrs. Jewls," said Calvin.

"Now, Calvin!" said Mrs. Jewls. "Unless you would rather go home on the kindergarten bus."

"Yes, ma'am," said Calvin. Slowly he walked out the door.

"Ha, ha, ha," laughed Terrence, "take it to the nineteenth story."

"Give it to Miss Zarves," hooted Myron.

"Have fun on the nineteenth story," called Jason.

Calvin stood outside the door to the classroom. He didn't know where to go.

As you know, when the builder built Wayside School, he accidentally built it sideways. But he also forgot to build the nineteenth story. He built the eighteenth and the twentieth, but no nineteenth. He said he was very sorry.

There was also no Miss Zarves. Miss Zarves taught the class on the nineteenth story. Since there was no nineteenth story, there was no Miss Zarves.

And besides that, as if Calvin didn't have enough problems, there was no note. Mrs. Jewls had never given Calvin the note.

"Boy, this is just great," thought Calvin. "Just great! I'm supposed to take a note that I don't have to a teacher who doesn't exist, and who teaches on a story that was never built."

He didn't know what to do. He walked down to the eighteenth story, then back up to the twentieth, then back down to the eighteenth, and back up again to the twentieth. There was no nineteenth story. There never was a nineteenth story. And there never will be a nineteenth story.

Calvin walked down to the administration office. He decided to put the note in Miss Zarves's mailbox. But there wasn't one of those, either. That didn't bother Calvin too much, however, since he didn't have a note.

He looked out the window and saw Louis, the yard teacher, shooting baskets. "Louis will know what to do," he thought. Calvin went outside.

"Hey, Louis," Calvin called.

"Hi, Calvin," said Louis. He tossed him the basketball. Calvin dribbled up and took a shot. He missed. Louis tipped it in.

"Do you want to play a game?" Louis asked.

"I don't have time," said Calvin. "I have to deliver a note to Miss Zarves up on the nineteenth story."

"Then what are you doing all the way down here?" Louis asked.

"There is no nineteenth story," said Calvin.

"Then where is Miss Zarves?" asked Louis.

"There is no Miss Zarves," said Calvin.

"What are you going to do with the note?" asked Louis.

"There is no note," said Calvin.

"I understand," said Louis.

"That's good," said Calvin, "because I sure don't."

"It's very simple," said Louis. "You are not supposed to take no notes to no teachers. You already haven't done it."

Calvin still didn't understand. "I'll just have to tell Mrs. Jewls that I couldn't deliver the note," he said.

"That's good," said Louis. "The truth is always best. Besides, I don't think I understand what I said, either."

Calvin walked back up the thirty flights of stairs to Mrs. Jewls's class.

"Thank you very much, Calvin," said Mrs. Jewls.

Calvin said, "But I—"

Mrs. Jewls interrupted him. "That was a very important note, and I'm glad I was able to count on you."

"Yes, but you see—" said Calvin.

"You delivered the note to Miss Zarves on the nineteenth story?" asked Jason. "How did you do it?"

"What do you mean, how did he do it?" asked Mrs. Jewls. "He gave Miss Zarves the note. Some people, Jason, are responsible."

"But you see, Mrs. Jewls—" said Calvin.

"The note was very important," said Mrs. Jewls. "I told Miss Zarves not to meet me for lunch."

"Don't worry," said Calvin. "She won't."

"Good," said Mrs. Jewls. "I have a coffee can full of Tootsie Roll pops on my desk. You may help yourself to one, for being such a good messenger."

"Thanks," said Calvin, "but really, it was nothing."

SHILOH

by **Phyllis Reynolds Naylor**

illustrated by **Bob Dombrowski**

Newbery Medal

We live high up in the hills above Friendly, but hardly anybody knows where that is. Friendly's near Sistersville, which is halfway between Wheeling and Parkersburg. Used to be, my daddy told me, Sistersville was one of the best places you could live in the whole state. You ask *me* the best place to live, I'd say right where we are, a little four-room house with hills on three sides.

Afternoon is my second-best time to go up in the hills, though; morning's the best, especially in summer. Early, *early* morning. On one morning I saw three kinds of animals, not counting cats, dogs, frogs, cows, and horses. Saw a groundhog, saw a doe with two fawns, and saw a gray fox with a reddish head. Bet his daddy was a gray fox and his ma was a red one.

My favorite place to walk is just across this rattly bridge where the road curves by the old Shiloh schoolhouse and follows the river. River to one side, trees the other—sometimes a house or two.

And this particular afternoon, I'm about halfway up the road along the river when I see something out of the corner of my eye. Something moves. I look, and about fifteen yards off, there's this shorthaired dog—white with brown and black spots—not making any kind of noise, just slinking along with his head down, watching me, tail between his legs like he's hardly got the right to breathe. A beagle, maybe a year or two old.

I stop and the dog stops. Looks like he's been caught doing something awful, when I can tell all he really wants is to follow along beside me.

"Here, boy," I say, slapping my thigh.

Dog goes down on his stomach, groveling about in the grass. I laugh and start over toward him. He's got an old worn-out collar on, probably older than he is. Bet it belonged to another dog before him. "C'mon, boy," I say, putting out my hand.

The dog gets up and backs off. He don't even whimper, like he's lost his bark.

Something really hurts inside you when you see a dog cringe like that. You know somebody's been kicking at him. Beating on him, maybe.

"It's okay, boy," I say, coming a little closer, but still he backs off.

So I just take my gun and follow the river. Every so often I look over my shoulder and there he is, the beagle. I stop; he stops. I can see his ribs—not real bad—but he isn't plumped out or anything.

There's a broken branch hanging from a limb out over the water, and I'm wondering if I can bring it down with one shot. I raise my gun, and then I think how the sound might scare the dog off. I decide I don't want to shoot my gun much that day.

It's a slow river. You walk beside it, you figure it's not even moving. If you stop, though, you can see leaves and things going along. Now and then a fish jumps— big fish. Bass, I think. Dog's still trailing me, tail tucked in. Funny how he don't make a sound.

Finally I sit on a log, put my gun at my feet, and wait. Back down the road, the dog sits, too. Sits right in the middle of it, head on his paws.

"Here, boy!" I say again, and pat my knee.

He wiggles just a little, but he don't come.

Maybe it's a she-dog.

"Here, girl!" I say. Dog still don't come.

I decide to wait the dog out, but after three or four minutes on the log, it gets boring and I start off again. So does the beagle.

Don't know where you'd end up if you followed the river all the way. Heard some-body say it curves about, comes back on itself, but if it didn't and I got home after dark, I'd get a good whopping. So I always go as far as the ford, where the river spills across the path, and then I head back.

When
I turn around
and the dog
sees me coming,
he goes off into the
woods. I figure that's the last
I'll see of the beagle, and I get
halfway down the road again
before I look back. There he is. I
stop. He stops. I go. He goes.

And then, hardly thinking on it,
I whistle.

It's like pressing a magic button.
The beagle comes barreling toward
me, legs going lickety-split, long ears
flopping, tail sticking up like a
flagpole. This time, when I put out
my hand, he licks all my fingers and
jumps up against my leg, making
little yelps in his throat. He can't get
enough of me, like I'd been saying no
all along and now I'd said yes, he
could come. It's a he-dog, like I'd
thought.

"Hey, boy! You're really somethin'
now, ain't you?" I'm laughing as the
beagle makes circles around me. I
squat down and the dog licks my
face, my neck. Where'd he learn to
come if you whistled, to hang back if
you didn't?

I'm so busy watching the dog I don't even notice it's started to rain. Don't bother me. Don't bother the dog, neither. I'm looking for the place I first saw him. Does he live here? I wonder. Or the house on up the road? Each place we pass I figure he'll stop—somebody come out and whistle, maybe. But nobody comes out and the dog don't stop. Keeps coming even after we get to the old Shiloh schoolhouse. Even starts across the bridge, tail going like a propeller. He licks my hand every so often to make sure I'm still there—mouth open like he's smiling. He *is* smiling.

Once he follows me across the bridge, though, and on past the gristmill, I start to worry. Looks like he's fixing to follow me all the way to our house. I'm in trouble enough coming home with my clothes wet. My ma's mama died of pneumonia, and we don't ever get the chance to forget it. And now I got a dog with me, and we were never allowed to have pets.

If you can't afford to feed 'em and take 'em to the vet when they're sick, you've no right taking 'em in, Ma says, which is true enough.

I don't say a word to the beagle the rest of the way home, hoping he'll turn at some point and go back. The dog keeps coming.

I get to the front stoop and say, "Go home, boy." And then I feel my heart squeeze up the way he stops smiling, sticks his tail between his legs again, and slinks off. He goes as far as the sycamore tree, lies down in the wet grass, head on his paws.

"Whose dog is that?" Ma asks when I come in.

I shrug. "Just followed me, is all."

"Where'd it pick up with you?" Dad asks.

"Up in Shiloh, across the bridge," I say.

"On the road by the river? Bet that's Judd Travers's beagle," says Dad. "He got himself another hunting dog a few weeks back."

"Judd got him a hunting dog, how come he don't treat him right?" I ask.

"How you know he don't?"

"Way the dog acts. Scared to pee, almost," I say.

Ma gives me a look.

"Don't seem to me he's got any marks on him," Dad says, studying him from our window.

Don't have to mark a dog to hurt him, I'm thinking.

"Just don't pay him any attention and he'll go away," Dad says.

"And get out of those wet clothes," Ma tells me. "You want to follow your grandma Slater to the grave?"

I change clothes, then sit down and turn on the TV, which only has two channels. On Sunday afternoons, it's preaching and baseball. I watch baseball for an hour. Then I get up and sneak to the window. Ma knows what I'm about.

"That Shiloh dog still out there?" she asks.

I nod. He's looking at me. He sees me there at the window and his tail starts to thump. I name him Shiloh.

Sunday-night supper is whatever's left from noon. If nothing's left over, Ma takes cold cornmeal mush, fries up big slabs, and we eat it with Karo syrup. But this night there's still rabbit. I don't want any, but I know Shiloh does.

I wonder how long I can keep pushing that piece of rabbit around my plate. Not very long, I discover.

"You going to eat that meat, or you just playing with it?" Dad asks. "If you don't want it, I'll take it for lunch tomorrow."

"I'll eat it," I say.

"Don't you be giving it to that dog," says Ma.

I take a tiny bite.

"What's the doggy going to *eat,* then?" asks Becky. She's three, which is four years younger than Dara Lynn.

"Nothing here, that's what," says Ma.

Becky and Dara Lynn look at Dad. Now I had *them* feeling sorry for the beagle, too. Sometimes girl-children get what they want easier than I do. But not this time.

"Dog's going right back across the river when we get through eating," says Dad. "If that's Judd's new dog, he probably don't have sense enough yet to find his way home again. We'll put him in the Jeep and drive him over."

Don't know what else I figured Dad to say. Do I really think he's going to tell me to wait till morning, and if the beagle's still here, we can keep him? I try all kinds of ways to figure how I could get that rabbit meat off my plate and into my pocket, but Ma's watching every move I make.

So I excuse myself and go outside and over to the chicken coop. It's off toward the back where Ma can't see. We keep three hens, and I take one of the two eggs that was in a nest and carry it out behind the bushes.

I whistle softly. Shiloh comes loping toward me. I crack the egg and empty it out in my hands. Hold my hands down low and Shiloh eats the egg, licking my hands clean afterward, then curling his tongue down between my fingers to get every little bit.

"Good boy, Shiloh," I whisper, and stroke him all over.

I hear the back screen slam, and Dad comes out on the stoop. "Marty?"

"Yeah?" I go around, Shiloh at my heels.

"Let's take that dog home now."
Dad goes over and opens the door of
the Jeep. Shiloh puts his tail between
his legs and just stands there, so I go
around to the other side, get in, and
whistle. Shiloh leaps up onto my lap,
but he don't look too happy about it.

For the first time I have my arms
around him. He feels warm, and
when I stroke him, I can feel places
on his body where he has ticks.

"Dog has ticks," I tell my dad.

"Judd'll take 'em off," Dad says.

"What if he don't?"

"It's his concern, Marty, not yours.
It's not your dog. You keep to your
own business."

I press myself against the back of
the seat as we start down our bumpy
dirt driveway toward the road. "I
want to be a vet someday," I tell my dad.

"Hmm," he says.

"I want to be a traveling vet. The
kind that has his office in a van and
goes around to people's homes, don't
make folks come to him. Read about
it in a magazine at school."

"You know what you have to do to
be a vet?" Dad asks.

"Got to go to school, I know that."

"You've got to have college training.
Like a doctor, almost. Takes a lot of
money to go to veterinary school."

My dream sort of leaks out like water in a paper bag. "I could be a veterinarian's helper," I suggest, my second choice.

"You maybe could," says Dad, and points the Jeep up the road into the hills.

Dusk is settling in now. Still warm, though. A warm July night. Trees look dark against the red sky; lights coming on in a house here, another one there. I'm thinking how in any one of these houses there's probably somebody who would take better care of Shiloh than Judd Travers would. How come this dog had to be his?

The reason I don't like Judd Travers is a whole lot of reasons, not the least is that I was in the corner store once down in Friendly and saw Judd cheat Mr. Wallace at the cash register. Judd gives the man a ten and gets him to talking, then—when Mr. Wallace gives him change—says he give him a twenty.

I blink, like I can't believe Judd done that, and old Mr. Wallace is all confused. So I say, "No, I think he give you a ten."

Judd glares at me, whips out his wallet, and waves a twenty-dollar bill in front of my eye. "Whose picture's on this bill, boy?" he says.

"I don't know."

He gives me a look says, I thought so. "That's Andrew Jackson," he says. "I had two of 'em in my wallet when I walked in here, and now I only got one. This here man's got the other, and I want my change."

Mr. Wallace, he's so flustered he just digs in his money drawer and gives Judd change for a twenty, and afterward I thought what did Andrew Jackson have to do with it? Judd's so fast-talking he can get away with anything. Don't know anybody who likes him much, but around here folks keep to their own business, like Dad says. In Tyler County that's important. Way it's always been, anyhow.

Another reason I don't like Judd Travers is he spits tobacco out the corner of his mouth, and if he don't like you—and he sure don't like me—he sees just how close he can spit to where you're standing. Third reason I don't like him is because he was at the fairgrounds last year same day we were, and seemed like everyplace I was, he was in front of me, blocking my view. Standin' in

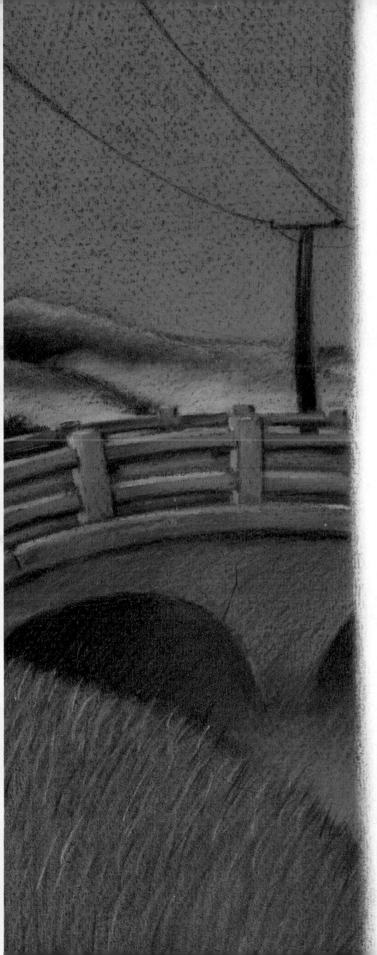

front of me at the mud bog, sittin' in front of me at the tractor pull, and risin' right up out of his seat at the Jorden Globe of Death Motorcycle Act so's I missed the best part.

Fourth reason I don't like him is because he kills deer out of season. He says he don't, but I seen him once just about dusk with a young buck strapped over the hood of his truck. He tells me the buck run in front of him on the road and he accidentally run over it, but I saw the bullet hole myself. If he got caught, he'd have to pay two hundred dollars, more than he's got in the bank, I'll bet.

We're in Shiloh now. Dad's crossing the bridge by the old abandoned gristmill, turning at the boarded-up school, and for the first time I can feel Shiloh's body begin to shake. He's trembling all over. I swallow. Try to say something to my dad and have to swallow again.

"How do you go about reporting someone who don't take care of his dog right?" I ask finally.

"Who you fixing to report, Marty?"

"Judd."

"If this dog's mistreated, he's only about one out of fifty thousand animals that is," Dad says. "Folks even bring 'em up here in the hills and let 'em out, figure they can live on rats and rabbits. Wouldn't be the first dog that wasn't treated right."

"But this one come to me to help him!" I insist. "*Knew* that's why he was following me. I got hooked on him, Dad, and I want to know he's treated right."

For the first time I can tell Dad's getting impatient with me. "Now you get that out of your head right now. If it's Travers's dog, it's no mind of ours *how* he treats it."

"What if it was a child?" I ask him, getting too smart for my own good. "If some kid was shaking like this dog is shaking, you wouldn't feel no pull for keeping an eye on him?"

"Marty," Dad says, and now his voice is just plumb tired. "This here's a dog, not a child, and it's not our dog. I want you to quit going on about it. Hear?"

I shut up then. Let my hands run over Shiloh's body like maybe everywhere I touch I can protect him somehow. We're getting closer to the trailer where Judd lives with his other dogs, and already they're barking up a storm, hearing Dad's Jeep come up the road.

Dad pulls over. "You want to let him out?" he says.

I shake my head hard. "I'm not lettin' him out here till I know for sure he belongs to Judd." I'm asking for a slap in the face, but Dad don't say anything, just gets out and goes up the boards Judd has laid out in place of a sidewalk.

Judd's at the door of his trailer already, in his undershirt, peering out.

"Looks like Ray Preston," he says, through the screen.

"How you doin', Judd?"

Judd comes out on the little porch he's built at the side of his trailer, and they stand there and talk awhile. Up here in the hills you hardly ever get down to business right off. First you say your howdys and then you talk about anything else but what you come for, and finally, when the mosquitoes start to bite, you say what's on your mind. But you always edge into it, not to offend.

I can hear little bits and pieces floating out over the yard. The rain . . . the truck . . . the tomatoes . . . the price of gasoline . . . and all the while Shiloh lays low in my lap, tail between his legs, shaking like a window blind in a breeze.

102

And then, the awful words: "Say, Judd, my boy was up here along the river this afternoon, and a beagle followed him home. Don't have any tags on his collar, but I'm remembering you got yourself another hunting dog, and wondered if he might be yours."

I'm thinking this is a bad mistake. Maybe it isn't Judd's at all, and he's such a liar he'd say it was, just to get himself still another animal to be mean to.

Judd hardly lets him finish; starts off across the muddy yard in his boots. "Sure bet it is," he says. "Can't keep that coon dog home to save my soul. Every time I take him hunting, he runs off before I'm through. I been out all day with the dogs, and they all come back but him."

I can hear Judd's heavy footsteps coming around the side of the Jeep, and I can smell his chewing tobacco, strong as coffee.

"Yep," he says, thrusting his face in the open window. "That's him, all right." He opens the door. "*Git* on down here!" he says, and before I can even give the dog one last pat, Shiloh leaps off my lap onto the ground and connects with Judd's right foot. He yelps and runs off behind the trailer,

tail tucked down, belly to the ground. All Judd's dogs chained out back bark like crazy.

I jump out of the Jeep, too. "Please don't kick him like that," I say. "Some dogs just like to run."

"He runs all over creation," Judd says. I can tell he's studying me in the dark, trying to figure what's it to me.

"I'll keep an eye out for him," I say. "Anytime I see him away from home, I'll bring him back. I promise. Just don't kick him."

Judd only growls. "He could be a fine huntin' dog, but he tries my patience. I'll leave him be tonight, but he wanders off again, I'll whup the daylights out of him. Guarantee you that."

I swallow and swallow, and all the way home I can't speak a word, trying to hold the tears back.

I don't sleep more than a couple hours that night. When I do, I dream of Shiloh. When I don't, I'm thinking about him out in the rain all afternoon, head on his paws, watching our door. Thinking how I'd disappointed him, whistling like I meant something that first time, gettin' him to come to me, then taking him on back to Judd Travers to be kicked all over again.

By five o'clock, when it's growing light, I know pretty much what I have to do: I have to buy that dog from Judd Travers.

I don't let my mind go any further; don't dwell on what Judd would want for Shiloh, or even whether he'd sell. Especially don't ask myself how I'm supposed to get the money. All I know is that I can think of only one way to get that dog away from Judd, and that's what I'm going to have to do.

Marty is determined to get Shiloh away from Judd. Phyllis Reynolds Naylor tells of the obstacles he must overcome in Shiloh.

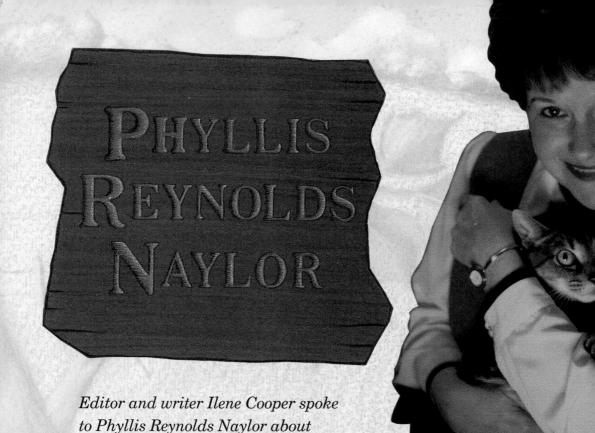

PHYLLIS REYNOLDS NAYLOR

Editor and writer Ilene Cooper spoke to Phyllis Reynolds Naylor about writing and about Shiloh.

Cooper: Shiloh was based on a real dog, wasn't he?

Naylor: Yes. I was visiting West Virginia once and saw a dog wandering around—the saddest-looking dog I'd ever seen. After I came home, I couldn't get that animal out of my mind, so I wrote a book about it.

Cooper: Does anything else in the book come from real life?

Naylor: Not really. My husband is from West Virginia, and my family is from the South, so that's where I picked up the dialect. I did have a dog when I was growing up, but it was a springer spaniel.

Cooper: When did you start writing?

Naylor: I had a real burst of writing when I was 10 or 11 years old. I wrote books on scrap paper, and my mother saved them all. I wrote books about Dutch children, fantasy stories, and a mystery series about a beautiful woman detective.

Cooper: So you knew pretty early that you were going to be a writer.

Naylor: Oh, no. I never dreamed writing would be something I could make a living at. I wrote because it was fun. My parents read aloud at night, so I enjoyed hearing stories. Also, we were very poor when I was growing up, and there wasn't any money for toys. But we did have paper and pencils, so writing stories was how I played.

Cooper: Then how did you decide to make writing a career?

Naylor: I was in my twenties, I had finished college, and I decided I wanted to write more than I wanted to be a psychologist. I began by writing stories for magazines.

Cooper: Did winning the Newbery award affect your writing at all? Did you feel as if you had a standard to live up to?

Naylor: No. I had written for many years before I won the Newbery and knew that you could fall just as easily as you could rise, so I just sat down and wrote my next book. It helps that my books are usually very different from one another.

Cooper: Does that mean you won't write another *Shiloh* book?

Naylor: It's interesting that you should ask that question. I had vowed that I would not write another book about Shiloh, but one day the whole idea for a sequel just swept into my mind. I fought it at first, but finally I decided to write it. It's called *Shiloh Season*.

Cooper: I understand there was a happy ending for the dog that was the model for *Shiloh*.

Naylor: Yes. Some friends in West Virginia found that dog that I had seen. They took her home and named her Clover. Whenever we're down there, we get to visit with her.

Appalachian

L ike giant ripples on the land, the Appalachian Mountains sweep along the eastern United States for some 2,000 miles (3,200 km) from central Alabama to Maine and on into Canada. Many mountain ranges make up the Appalachian system. Here the Blue Ridge Mountains form the range's eastern front. Behind them, other mountains roll westward to forested interior highlands bordered by rivers.

Kentucky

Rolling pastures surround a gabled barn at Calumet Farm near Lexington. The farm has owned eight Kentucky Derby winners, twice as many as any other stable.

Tennessee

Cumberland Gap, here a spillway for clouds beneath Pinnacle Overlook, also provided a route through the Appalachian Mountains for westward-bound settlers.

Highlands

from **National Geographic Picture Atlas of Our Fifty States**

Along the Blue Ridge, foothills called the Piedmont slope eastward, then step down onto the Atlantic Coastal Plain fringed with low wetlands and long, thin islands. The barrier islands of the Outer Banks, once sand ridges that were flooded when ocean levels rose after the Ice Age, act as a buffer between the mainland and the open ocean. Shallow sounds and lagoons between the islands and the shore also provide food and shelter for fish and wildlife.

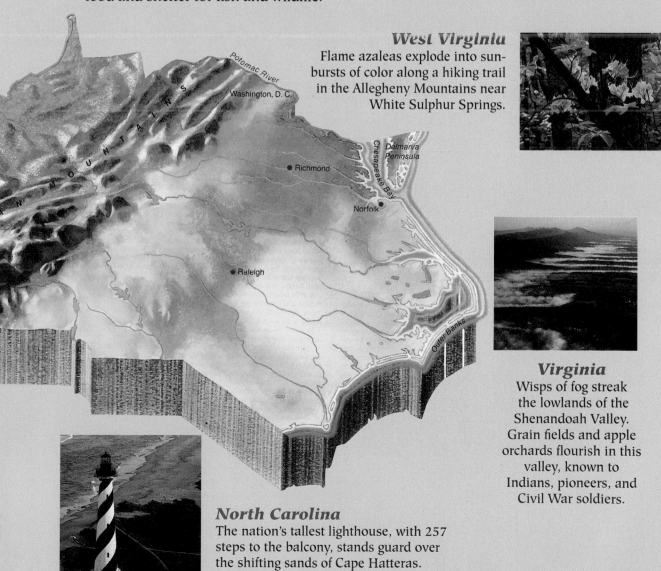

West Virginia
Flame azaleas explode into sunbursts of color along a hiking trail in the Allegheny Mountains near White Sulphur Springs.

Virginia
Wisps of fog streak the lowlands of the Shenandoah Valley. Grain fields and apple orchards flourish in this valley, known to Indians, pioneers, and Civil War soldiers.

North Carolina
The nation's tallest lighthouse, with 257 steps to the balcony, stands guard over the shifting sands of Cape Hatteras.

RESPONSE CORNER

WRITE A POEM

MY FAVORITE HOUR

Marty likes the early, early morning best. Write a poem about your favorite time of day. Describe what you do then and what makes that time special to you. Add your poem to a class bulletin board titled "The Times of Our Lives."

MAKE A LIST

MONEY MATH

Judd Travers informs Marty that Andrew Jackson's picture appears on a twenty-dollar bill. Make a list of the past Presidents and other patriots who appear on coins and bills. Then write math problems using the names of the people in place of the types of money. Exchange problems with classmates.

BEYOND THE BEAGLE

What kinds of dogs do you find interesting, beautiful, or cute? Research several kinds of dogs and create a poster about them. Display your poster as you describe your choices.

WHAT DO YOU THINK?

- Why does Marty want to keep the dog? Why can't he?

- How did you feel at the end of the selection? Why did you feel this way?

- How do the pictures in "Appalachian Highlands" compare to the picture you formed in your mind while reading "Shiloh"?

THEME WRAP-UP

You have met characters in this theme who live in the suburbs, the city, and the country. How are their lives different? How are they the same?

In your opinion, which of the characters has the most important problem? Why?

ACTIVITY CORNER

Use both sides of a poster to create a two-sided backdrop—one side representing "In School" and the other side "Out of School." Then work with a partner to develop a two-scene puppet play featuring any two characters from the theme.

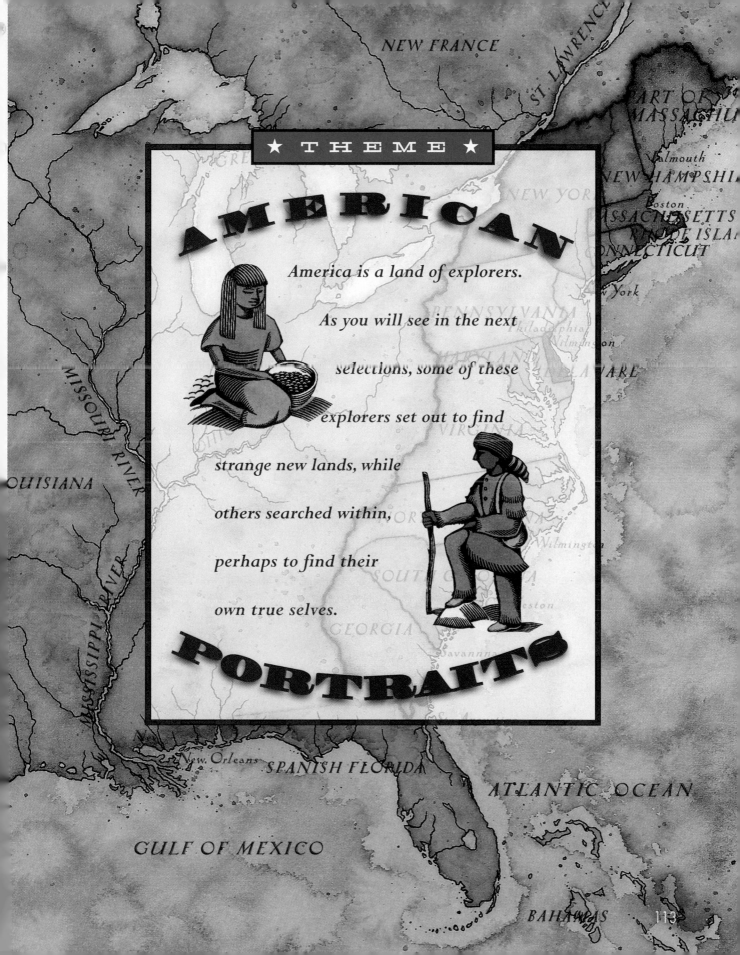

AMERICAN

America is a land of explorers.

As you will see in the next

selections, some of these

explorers set out to find

strange new lands, while

others searched within,

perhaps to find their

own true selves.

PORTRAITS

NEW FRANCE

ATLANTIC OCEAN

GULF OF MEXICO

SPANISH FLORIDA

New Orleans

LOUISIANA

MISSISSIPPI RIVER

MISSOURI RIVER

VIRGINIA

GEORGIA

SOUTH CAROLINA

BAHAMAS

AMERICAN

PORTRAITS

BOOKSHELF

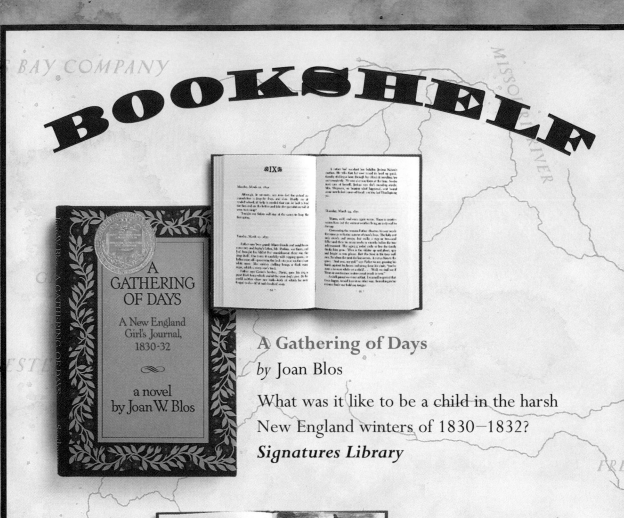

A Gathering of Days

by Joan Blos

What was it like to be a child in the harsh
New England winters of 1830–1832?

Signatures Library

What's the Big Idea, Ben Franklin?

by Jean Fritz

A light-hearted look at one of the most
talented men in American history.

Signatures Library

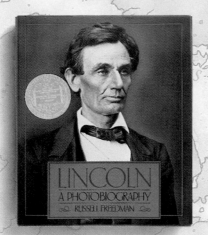

Lincoln: A Photobiography

by Russell Freedman

Photographs and drawings depict the life of Abraham Lincoln and the many faces of the American Civil War.

Newbery Medal

The House of Dies Drear

by Virginia Hamilton

The family's enormous old house in a southern Ohio town was once a station on the Underground Railroad. It contains many secrets—and many dangers.

ALA Notable Book

North American Indian Survival Skills

by Karen Liptak

To survive in the wilderness, early North American Indians used the resources of the land to build shelters, find food, and make clothing.

BY **MICHAEL DORRIS**

ILLUSTRATED BY **FABRICIO VANDEN BROECK**

R·N·I·N·G
G·I·R·L

WHO WERE THE PEOPLE WATCHING COLUMBUS WHEN HE FIRST CAME ASHORE IN NORTH AMERICA? WHAT WERE THEIR NAMES? WHAT WERE THEIR DAILY LIVES LIKE?

FOLLOW TWO CHILDREN NAMED MORNING GIRL AND STAR BOY FOR A GLIMPSE INTO THOSE LIVES, INCLUDING WHAT IT MAY HAVE BEEN LIKE TO WATCH COLUMBUS COMING ASHORE.

The name my family calls me is Morning Girl because I wake up early, always with something on my mind. Mother says it's because I dream too hard, and that I don't relax even in sleep. Maybe she's right—in my dreams I'm always doing things: swimming or searching on the beach for unbroken shells or figuring out a good place to fish. I open my eyes as soon as the light calls through the smoke hole in the roof, sift the ideas that have come to me in the night and decide which one to follow first.

I don't tell this to anyone because they might misunderstand, but I like the aloneness of the early morning. I try to step gently on the path so that the sounds I make will blend into the rustle of the world. Father taught me how to swim on land, careful as a turtle. You'll see more if you're quiet, he told me. Things don't hide or wait for you to pass. And, it's more polite.

Another thing: if the day starts before you do, you never catch up. You spend all your time running after what you should have already done, and no matter how much you hurry, you never finish the race in a tie. The day wins.

I tried once to explain all this to my little brother, but he just blinked at me, asked me who said it was a race in the first place? See, he likes the darkness best, especially when there are no clouds and no moon. Sometimes he shakes me until I look as he points out the patterns he sees in the sky, the tracks made of white sand. He's sure what we see is part of another island, even bigger than the one where we live or than the one that appears in a pond when the water is very smooth. He thinks we're like birds floating above that sky island, very, very high.

I don't know how my brother came to see everything so upside down from me. For him, night is day, sleep is awake. It's as though time is split between us, and we only pass by each other as the sun rises or sets. Usually, for me, that's enough.

Mother promises that someday my brother and I will be friends, like she and her brother Sharp Tooth finally got to be. She whispers when she tells stories of how my uncle acted when he was a boy—how twice he laughed at her when she got into trouble or how he told a lie and never untied it, ever, with the truth. She became very still, closed her eyes, and took a deep breath at that memory, but then she shook her head, looked into me the way only she can do, and said that she used to believe she'd never forget what he had done; but look, she has. And now Sharp Tooth is exactly the brother she wants, the person in the whole world who remembers important things from when she was a young girl, who remembers Grandfather when he was alive and before he grew old.

I don't answer what I think: that *my* brother is different from *hers*. Because my brother is her son, Mother doesn't know him as others do. As I do. When he's away from her sight, he eats too much. When she isn't there to hear him, he doesn't understand how to be quiet. And who knows what he does all night while the rest of us are asleep?

Just before dawn today I woke and found him sitting on the edge of my mat, watching me with big eyes.

"What's the matter?" I asked him. My voice was not soft. He wouldn't let me be alone even at night.

"Nothing," he said. "What do you mean? You're always complaining."

"I'm not the one who stares like a duck," I answered. "I'm not the one who can't stay asleep like a normal person."

"Ghosts," Father sighed from his hammock. "My house is filled with ghosts. They talk to each other all night. I'll have to build a new house. I'll live there in peace. It will be wonderful."

"Oh yes. I'll come with you." Mother's voice was unhappy as a fish pulled into the air from the sea. "Let's escape from such cruel ghosts who will not let people have their rest."

I could have explained that it was my brother's fault, but it would have done no good. Father would only have made more jokes and Mother would have said, "We'll listen later, Morning Girl."

I stood up, squeezed the stiffness from the back of my neck, and gave my brother a parting frown that I hoped would leave him very worried. That did no good, either, for he was already back on his own mat, curled into a comfortable position, pretending to be dreaming. His eyes were closed tightly, and his mouth was smiling.

Outside, at least, belonged to me, since no one else was around. I could do anything, go anywhere. I could walk or run, I could climb or swim, I could watch the ocean or slip into the mango grove, keep very quiet until the birds forgot I was there and began to talk to one another again.

The day welcomed me, brushed my hair with its breeze, greeted me with its songs. I raised my arms high and stretched. I let the rich scent of the large red flowers color my thoughts, and the perfume gave me an idea of how to use my special time. I would search for the most beautiful blossoms and weave them together into necklaces for Father and Mother. If I hurried I could finish before they rose for the second time, and they would find my gifts waiting at the entrance to our house.

As I was working, my mind rushed ahead to what I knew was sure to happen. Mother would come outside first, see the necklaces, and go back in to get Father. Then they would return to the doorway together, him rubbing his eyes and grumbling until he noticed what lay at his feet.

"Look at this," he would cry, as if he were completely surprised, and Mother would press her hands together and say, "How unusual! How well made!"

"Where could these amazing necklaces have come from?" Mother and Father would ask each other as they placed my flowers around their necks.

And they would still be wearing them, still be happy with me, when finally, late in the morning, long after everyone else, my brother woke up.

STAR BOY

You know how it is when you're on the beach on a white sunny morning and you shut your eyes tight? What you see isn't exactly dark, at least not dark the way it's dark when you're inside your house at night and you can't make anything out, when every noise is a question you can't answer. What you see with your eyes closed during the day is something different. It's like deep water, a pond that's draped with shade. I don't know what makes it happen—the fins of tiny fish, or their eyes, the sparkle of agates—but there are lights moving down there, something to watch. It's the same on a night when there's no moon and you look straight into the sky: the more you watch, the more you see. Grains of white sand, it looks like, and sometimes one drops so fast you can hardly follow it before it's lost.

What I don't like is nothing. I don't mean I like everything, because I don't. I don't like it when my sister wakes me up. I don't like to eat fish with too many bones. I don't like those hungry bugs so small you don't know they're there until they bite you. But mostly I don't like . . . nothing. You know: *nothing*. I don't like it when there's nothing to hear, nothing to taste, nothing to touch, especially when there's nothing to see. Those times, I don't know where I am. The first night I woke up and noticed that everyone was invisible, I held perfectly still and disappeared. I became nothing, too, and I didn't know how to get back. Finally I talked to myself, whispered a little song my father sings when he speaks to the birds, excusing himself for bothering them. I rubbed the tip of my thumb against the tip of my fingers. I touched my tongue to my lips and tasted salt from the ocean, and I waited that way until the day remembered us, and returned.

"Why are you awake so early?" my mother asked me that morning. "Are you becoming the same kind of flower as your sister, the kind that bends to the east and calls the sun?"

I didn't like being anything like my sister, who in fact is called Morning Girl because she gets up before everyone else, so I told a different story.

"I don't need sleep anymore," I said.

"That's too bad." My mother shook her head and smoothed my hair flat. "How will you dream if you don't sleep? How will you hear yourself?"

I thought about this problem.

"Maybe you're a bat," my mother suggested, smiling at me, "and will dream all day while the rest of us work. How lucky for you."

I thought of bats and how they race through the dark sky fast as late summer rain. I thought of how the wind would feel against my skin if I could fly.

"It's true," I said. "I *will* sleep today."

"And hang upside down from the limb of a tree?" asked Morning Girl, who always listened to what anyone said even though it had nothing to do with her. "I want to see that. Maybe I'll poke you with a stick."

"And maybe during the night I'll land in your hair," I told her. "Maybe I'll build a nest."

"Bats don't make nests," she pointed out, but still she raised her hand to her head at the idea.

"Maybe I'm a new kind of bat."

"What is it about the night that you like?" my mother asked, to stop the argument—but not just for that reason. She was truly interested and always listened closely to what I said. Now she stopped cleaning a manioc root and looked at me.

"I like . . . ," I began, and thought back to the white sand scattered on the sky's black beach. "I like the stars. I like to look down at them."

"You don't look *down* at the sky," Morning Girl contradicted. "You look *up*."

"Maybe not if you're a bat," my father said, his voice very serious. His eyes were still closed, and so it seemed as though his words came from nowhere. We couldn't tell if he was joking or not. "But no one is asking the right question," he continued. "Why *don't* bats sleep at night? Perhaps they like the same things as this Star Boy does."

Star Boy.

That was the first time I heard my new name. Star Boy. Before that I was called "Hungry" because that's what I was most of the time. I liked "Star Boy" much better. No one spoke as we all listened, tested the weight of the words.

Star Boy.

My mother smiled. "Who is talking?" she asked at last. "Who has found such a good question? Who has thought of such a fine name for my son?"

"It is the father of a bat," said my father. "The father of a morning flower. It is the husband of the mother of a bat and a flower. It is a man who is surrounded by people who talk when others are trying to sleep. I think I must be in the wrong family, since I am the only one who knows the value of rest. I think—"

My mother looked at Morning Girl and me with her eyebrows raised, then slipped a piece of clean fruit between my father's lips to stop his words. We all watched while he chewed. He still did not open his eyes.

"No," he said after he swallowed. "This is not the wrong family. There is only one person who knows where to find fruit so sweet, only one person with fingers so gentle."

My mother lowered her eyes, but she was pleased. "Why do bats like the dark?" she asked me, returning to our conversation. "Tell us, Star Boy."

When she used my new name I knew it was now mine for good, and at that moment I decided that I would become an expert, a person who would be asked questions about the night and who would know the answers.

"Because it's big," I said. "Because there are special things to see if you watch closely. Because in it you can be dreaming even if you're awake. Because someone must remember the day while others sleep and call it when it's time for the sun to come home."

My father opened his eyes at last, propped himself on his elbows, and nodded.

"Star Boy," he said.

MORNING GIRL

Dawn made a glare on the ocean, so I splashed through the shallow surf and dived without looking. I felt the hair lift from around my head, felt a school of tiny fish glide against my leg as I swam underwater. Then, far in the distance, I heard an unfamiliar and frightening sound. It was like the panting of some giant animal, a steady, slow rhythm, dangerous and hungry. And it was coming closer.

I forgot I was still beneath the surface until I needed air. But when I broke into the sunlight, the water sparkling all around me, the noise turned out to be nothing! Only a canoe! The breathing was the dip of many paddles! It was only *people* coming to visit, and since I could see they hadn't painted themselves to appear fierce, they must be friendly or lost.

I swam closer to get a better look and had to stop myself from laughing. The strangers had wrapped every part of their bodies with colorful leaves and cotton. Some had decorated their faces with fur and wore shiny rocks on their heads. Compared to us, they were very round. Their canoe was short and square, and, in spite of all their dipping and pulling, it moved so slowly. What a backward, distant island they must have come from. But really, to laugh at guests, no matter how odd, would be impolite, especially since I was the first to meet them. If I was foolish, they would think they had arrived at a foolish place.

"I won't make a mistake," I told She Listens.[1] "I won't be too good, and I won't say too much because I might choose the wrong words."

I kicked toward the canoe and called out the simplest thing. "Hello!"

---

[1] Morning Girl pretends to talk to a younger sister called "She Listens."

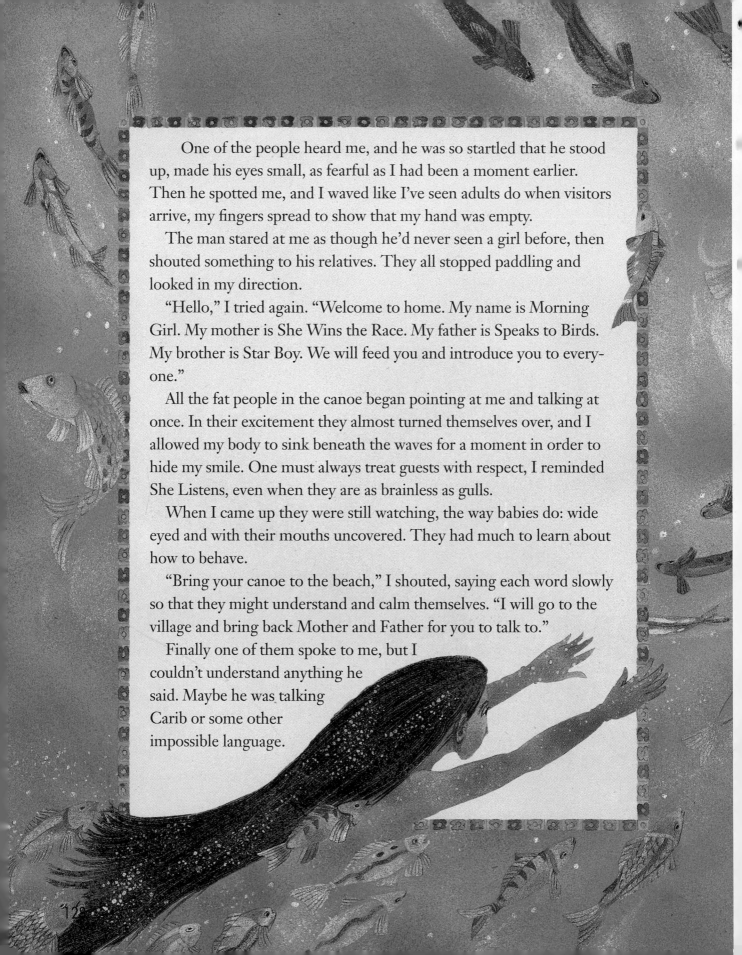

One of the people heard me, and he was so startled that he stood up, made his eyes small, as fearful as I had been a moment earlier. Then he spotted me, and I waved like I've seen adults do when visitors arrive, my fingers spread to show that my hand was empty.

The man stared at me as though he'd never seen a girl before, then shouted something to his relatives. They all stopped paddling and looked in my direction.

"Hello," I tried again. "Welcome to home. My name is Morning Girl. My mother is She Wins the Race. My father is Speaks to Birds. My brother is Star Boy. We will feed you and introduce you to every-one."

All the fat people in the canoe began pointing at me and talking at once. In their excitement they almost turned themselves over, and I allowed my body to sink beneath the waves for a moment in order to hide my smile. One must always treat guests with respect, I reminded She Listens, even when they are as brainless as gulls.

When I came up they were still watching, the way babies do: wide eyed and with their mouths uncovered. They had much to learn about how to behave.

"Bring your canoe to the beach," I shouted, saying each word slowly so that they might understand and calm themselves. "I will go to the village and bring back Mother and Father for you to talk to."

Finally one of them spoke to me, but I couldn't understand anything he said. Maybe he was talking Carib or some other impossible language.

But I was sure that we would
find ways to get along together.
It never took that much time,
and acting out your thoughts with
your hands could be funny. You had
to guess at everything and you made
mistakes, but by midday I was certain we
would all be seated in a circle, eating steamed fish and giving each
other presents. It would be a special day, a memorable day, a day
full and new.

I was close enough to shore now for my feet to touch bottom,
and quickly I made my way to dry land. The air was warm against my
shoulders, and there was a slight breeze that disturbed the palm fronds
strewn on the ground. I squeezed my hair, ran my hands over my arms
and legs to push off the water, and then stamped on the sand.

"Leave your canoe right here," I suggested in my most pleasant
voice. "It will not wash away, because the tide is going out. I'll be back
soon with the right people."

The strangers were drifting in the surf, arguing among themselves,
not even paying attention to me any longer. They seemed very worried,
very confused, very unsure what to do next. It was clear that they hadn't
traveled much before.

I hurried up the path to our house, but not before She Listens
reminded me to take the white conch shell from the seaweed where I
had left it. As I dodged through the trees, I hoped I hadn't done anything to make the visitors leave before I got back, before we learned
their names. If they were gone, Star Boy would claim that they were
just a story, just my last dream before daylight. But I didn't think that
was true. I knew they were real.

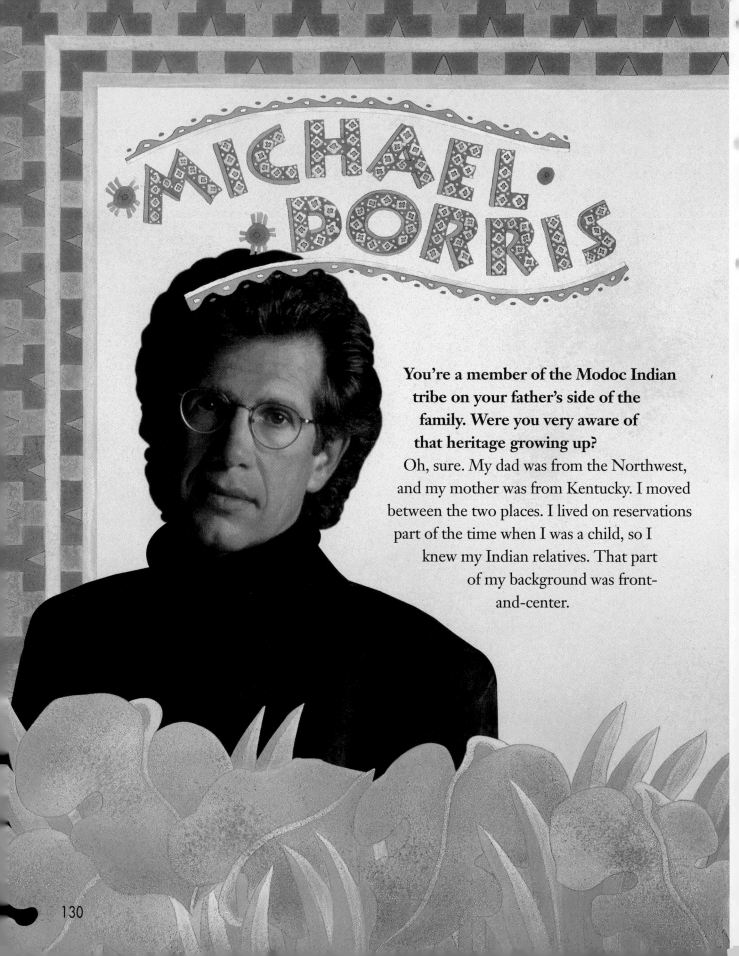

MICHAEL·DORRIS

You're a member of the Modoc Indian tribe on your father's side of the family. Were you very aware of that heritage growing up?

Oh, sure. My dad was from the Northwest, and my mother was from Kentucky. I moved between the two places. I lived on reservations part of the time when I was a child, so I knew my Indian relatives. That part of my background was front-and-center.

Was being both Indian and white an easy mix for you?

I think it's always complicated for a child to be outside the mainstream. For one thing, it forces you to listen more closely. It's a great background for a writer, though.

When you were growing up in the 1950s and 1960s, Indians were portrayed as stereotypes on television and in the movies. Did that bother you?

Not really, because those "Indians" were very different from the Indians I knew in real life. I hope things have changed, but I'm not so sure. I think that even today Indians are shown as being different. People think: *They talk to animals; they know the future; they can do things that other people can't do.* It's as though they should be put on a pedestal or put in a museum. In any case, it's all pretty hard to live up to.

The Taino Indians from *Morning Girl* left no written record, so how did you do the research for the book?

My wife and I had researched our adult book called *Crown of Columbus*, so some of the work was already done. I used my own experience as an anthropologist. I used what I had observed about small societies. And I went to the Caribbean so I could imagine the scenes.

Two of your daughters are about the age of your readers. How do they react to you as a writer of children's books?

They're tough readers. Polite, but tough. They don't hesitate to tell me when they don't like something.

You were a big reader when you were a kid, weren't you?

Oh, yes. The thing about reading is that it puts you in charge. You can stop and start, you can reread something, and you can imagine what the characters and places look like. When you read, you're a participant in the story. When you're watching television, you're not.

This Land Is My Land

George Littlechild

When I was a boy I was taught the song "This land is your land, this land is my land." When I got older I thought it was very strange to be singing about the ownership of the land. Whose land was this? Did it belong to anyone? The first people in this land were the Indians. We prefer to be called First Nations or First Peoples, because this was our homeland first.

North America is a very large continent. Add Central America and South America and together they make up the whole Western Hemisphere. This painting reminds us that all this land was once Indian land.

Response Corner

WRITE A REPORT

Batmania

Do Morning Girl and Star Boy have the correct facts about bats? Learn more about bats' nighttime and daytime habits. Work with a small group to create a report about your findings. Share your report with the rest of your classmates.

EXTEND THE STORY

Funny Fellows

Morning Girl laughs when she first sees Columbus and his men. She thinks they must come from a "backward, distant island." Extend the story by adding a paragraph telling more about the ways in which the men seem backward to Morning Girl.

CREATE A DRAWING

This Land Is Your Land

George Littlechild's painting is made up of simple pictures that represent the land we call America. Create your own drawing using pictures that represent America to you. Then explain your drawing to your classmates.

What Do You Think?

- How are Morning Girl and Star Boy alike? How are they different?

- Have your thoughts or feelings changed about the landing of Columbus after reading the story and the commentary on the painting? Why or why not?

- Do you think Morning Girl did the right thing when she greeted Columbus and his crew? Why or why not?

The Log of Christopher Columbus

SELECTIONS BY STEVE LOWE   ILLUSTRATED BY ROBERT SABUDA

INTRODUCTION

Years before Columbus set sail to change the course of history, he wrote these words in a favorite geography book: "The end of Spain and the beginning of India are not far distant but close, and it is evident that this sea is navigable in a few days with a fair wind." While others believed this too, Columbus was determined to prove it.

Columbus had the dream of sailing west to India, but not the money. Turned down once by King John of Portugal and once at the court of Spain, he made a last appeal to Ferdinand and Isabella: Pay my expenses, then name me Admiral of the not-so-wide ocean, and I will bring you back the gold of India.

In the spring of 1492 the king and queen agreed.

With his reputation at stake, Columbus set about the task of proving what he believed. A fair wind, he thought, might be had off the western coast of Africa, far south of the Azores. There in the Canaries, he guessed, were the westward currents that would send his small fleet to Marco Polo's fabulously rich Indies in less than thirty days.

By the time the *Niña*, the *Pinta*, and the *Santa María* had covered all the miles Columbus believed separated Europe from India, he was still a week away from land. He used no maps, no instrument but a compass. He lied about the distance traveled to angry sailors who no longer trusted him. He pushed the crew westward, dreading that he might have passed land at night. He offered a reward to whoever spotted land first, then threatened punishment if the sighting proved false. He even began to wonder if he imagined land where there was only horizon. Then, after sailing thirty-three days without sight of land, Christopher Columbus kept three frightened crews from mutiny for two more days—the time it took to follow migrating birds to the moonlit beach of a new world.

No one knows how many brave mariners never returned from attempts to cross the Atlantic before Columbus. What we do know is that in 1492–1493, a crew of ninety led by Christopher Columbus left Europe, made contact with a new continent to the west, and returned. We know this because Columbus wrote a daily log. Although the original log is missing today, copies of it were made in the sixteenth century. So the words you read here are as close to Columbus's own as we will ever have.

—STEVE LOWE
SUMMER 1991

Spring and summer 1492

Based on the information that I had given Your Highnesses about the land of India . . . Your Highnesses decided to send me, Christopher Columbus, to the regions of India, to see the princes there and the peoples and the lands.

I left Grenada on Saturday, the twelfth day of the month of May in the same year of 1492 and went to the town of Palos, which is a seaport. There I fitted out three vessels, very suited to such an enterprise. I left the said port well supplied with a large quantity of provisions and with many seamen on the third day of the month of August in the said year, on a Friday, half an hour before sunrise. I set my course for the Canary Islands of Your Highnesses, which are in the Ocean Sea, from there to embark on a voyage that will last until I arrive in the Indies. . . . I decided to write down everything I might do and see and experience on this voyage, from day to day, and very carefully.

Thursday September 6, 1492

Shortly before noon I sailed from the harbor at Gomera and set my course to the west.

Sunday September 9, 1492

This day we completely lost sight of land, and many men sighed and wept for fear they would not see it again for a long time. I comforted them with great promises of lands and riches. To sustain their hope and dispel their fears of a long voyage, I decided to reckon fewer leagues than we actually made. I did this that they might not think themselves so great a distance from Spain as they really were. For myself I will keep a confidential accurate reckoning.

Saturday September 15, 1492

I sailed to the west day and night for 81 miles, or more. Early this morning I saw a marvelous meteorite fall into the sea 12 or 15 miles to the southwest. This was taken by some people to be a bad omen, but I calmed them by telling of the numerous occasions that I have witnessed such events. I have to confess that this is the closest that a falling star has ever come to my ship.

Monday September 17, 1492

I held my course to the west and made, day and night, 150 miles or more, but I only logged 141 miles. . . . I saw a great deal of weed today—weed from rocks that lie to the west. I take this to mean that we are near land. . . . Everyone is cheerful, and the *Pinta*, the fastest sailing vessel, went ahead as fast as it could in order to sight land.

Tuesday September 18, 1492

. . . I have sailed for 11 days under a full sail, running ever before the wind. . . .

Wednesday September 19, 1492

The wind of last night has left us. . . . It is my desire to go directly to the Indies and not get sidetracked with islands that I shall see on the return passage, God willing. The weather is good.

Thursday September 20, 1492

Today I changed course for the first time since departing Gomera because the wind was variable and sometimes calm. . . . Very early this morning three little birds flew over the ship, singing as they went, and flew away as the sun rose. This was a comforting thought, for unlike the large water birds, these little birds could not have come from far off.

Friday September 21, 1492

Today was mostly calm. . . . The sea is as smooth as a river. . . .

Sunday September 23, 1492

I saw a dove, a tern, another small river bird, and some white birds. . . . The crew is still grumbling about the wind. When I get a wind from the southwest or west it is inconstant, and that, along with a flat sea, has led the men to believe that we will never get home.

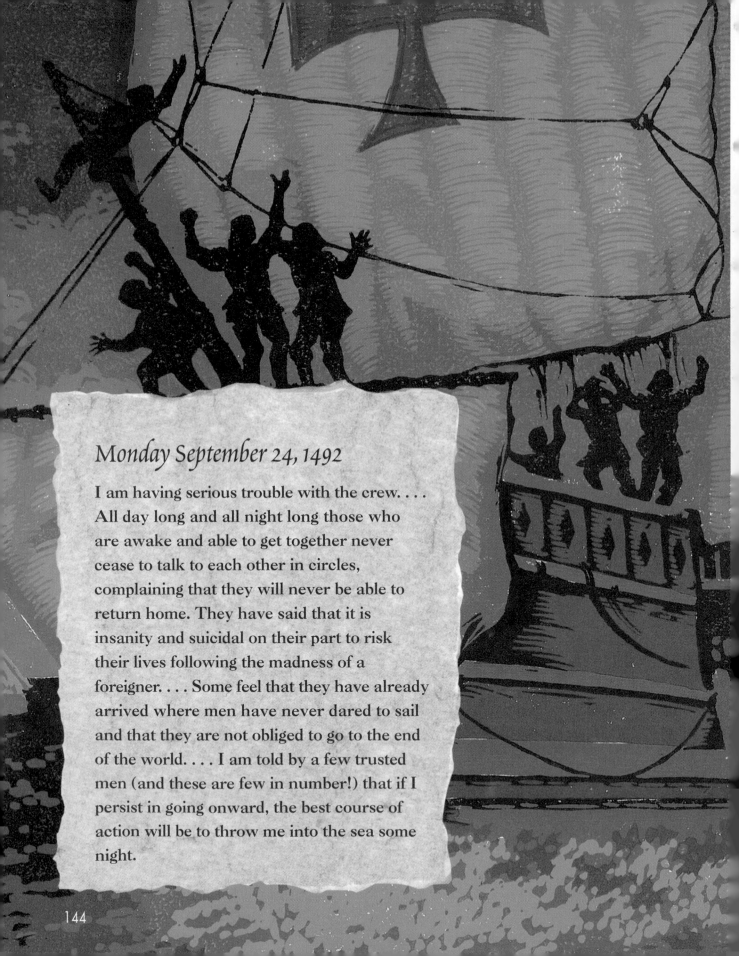

Monday September 24, 1492

I am having serious trouble with the crew. . . .
All day long and all night long those who
are awake and able to get together never
cease to talk to each other in circles,
complaining that they will never be able to
return home. They have said that it is
insanity and suicidal on their part to risk
their lives following the madness of a
foreigner. . . . Some feel that they have already
arrived where men have never dared to sail
and that they are not obliged to go to the end
of the world. . . . I am told by a few trusted
men (and these are few in number!) that if I
persist in going onward, the best course of
action will be to throw me into the sea some
night.

Tuesday September 25, 1492

At sunset Martin mounted the stern of the *Pinta* and with great joy called to me that he saw land and claimed the reward. When I heard this stated so positively, I fell to my knees to give thanks to Our Lord. . . . My people did the same thing, and the *Niña*'s crew all climbed the mast and rigging, and all claimed that it was land.

Wednesday September 26, 1492

After sunrise I realized that what we all thought was land last evening was nothing more than squall clouds, which often resemble land. I returned to my original course of west in the afternoon, once I was positive that what I had seen was not land. Day and night I sailed 93 miles, but recorded 72. The sea was like a river and the air sweet and balmy.

Monday October 1, 1492

It rained very hard this morning. . . . My personal calculation shows that we have come 2,121 miles. I did not reveal this figure to the men because they would become frightened, finding themselves so far from home, or at least thinking that they were that far.

Sunday October 7, 1492

This morning we saw what appeared to be land to the west, but it was not very distinct. Furthermore, no one wished to make a false claim of discovery, for I had ordered that if anyone make such a claim and, after sailing three days, the claim proved to be false, the . . . reward promised by the Catholic Sovereigns would be forfeited, even if afterwards he actually did see it. Being warned of this, no one aboard the *Santa María* or *Pinta* dared call out "Land, land."

. . . Joy turned to dismay as the day progressed, for by evening we had found no land and had to face the reality that it was only an illusion.

Thursday October 11, 1492

About 10 o'clock at night, while standing on the sterncastle, I thought I saw a light to the west. It looked like a little wax candle bobbing up and down. . . . I am the first to admit that I was so eager to find land that I did not trust my own senses, so I called for Pedro Gutiérrez, the representative of the King's household, and asked him to watch for the light. After a few moments, he too saw it.

Friday October 12, 1492

The moon, in its third quarter, rose in the east shortly before midnight. . . . Then, at two hours after midnight, the *Pinta* fired a cannon. . . . I hauled in all sails but the mainsail and lay-to till daylight. The land is about 6 miles to the west.

Friday October 12, 1492

At dawn . . . I went ashore in the ship's boat. I unfurled the royal banner. After a prayer of thanksgiving I ordered the captains of the *Pinta* and the *Niña* . . . to bear faith and witness that I was taking possession of this island for the King and Queen. . . . To this island I gave the name *San Salvador*. . . .

No sooner had we concluded the formalities of taking possession of the island than people began to come to the beach. . . . They are very well-built people . . . their eyes are large and very pretty. . . . Many of the natives paint their faces . . . others paint their whole bodies. . . . They are friendly. . . .

Tuesday November 27, 1492

As I went along the river it was marvelous to see the forests and greenery, the very clear water, the birds, and the fine situation, and I almost did not want to leave the place. I told the men with me that, in order to make a report to the Sovereigns of the things they saw, a thousand tongues would not be sufficient to tell it, nor my hand to write it, for it looks like an enchanted land.

Words from the Illustrator

Robert Sabuda

I grew up in Michigan, in the country. When I started drawing, everything had an outdoor theme. By the time I was in fifth grade, my identity was that of the kid who could draw. Some teacher was always saying, "Go get Bobby Sabuda to make a bulletin board." My interest in history came along later.

Doing the research for *The Log of Christopher Columbus* took longer than making the drawings. No one knows exactly what Columbus's three ships looked like, but the Peabody Museum near Boston had a model of a ship from that time period that is thought to be very similar to Columbus's. I based my pictures of the ships on that. The costumes were easier to research—I was able to use common reference materials.

As for the drawings themselves, those come from my own imagination. I'm able to draw what I see in my mind's eye. Sometimes, as I'm reading a manuscript, I see the illustrations almost as if I'm watching them on television in my head.

If You Were There in 1492

by **Barbara Brenner**

illustrated by Raphaelle Goethals

Take an especially good look at Spain on the map.

Spain is part of what is still called the Iberian Peninsula. In 1492 the Iberian Peninsula looked pretty much the way it does today—like a lady's head. Portugal is a mask on the face. The skinny neck looks as if it had broken off from Africa. Between the two pieces is the Rock of Gibraltar, poking out from the sea. (You would have called it the Pillar of Hercules in 1492.) The lady's nose and mouth are in the Atlantic Ocean, which on the old maps is called the Ocean Sea. The back of her head is washed by the Mediterranean Sea. Behind and above the head are other places whose names we know as countries today: France, Italy, Germany, England.

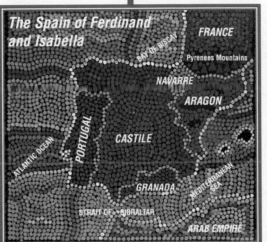

Spain controlled almost all of the Iberian peninsula, and beyond.

In those days, Spain was divided into two kingdoms, Aragon and Castile. Queen Isabella governed Castile, and King Ferdinand was the ruler of the territories of Aragon. But since these two monarchs had married each other, their two kingdoms had been wedded, too.

If you lived in the port city of Palos, Spain, that year you could have seen the ships coming in and going out. You could have watched the goods from other parts of the world arriving—the silks and spices, the sugar and the slaves. You would have seen Spain's products—the wool and leather, the iron and velvet, the raisins and dates—being put aboard. You might have seen people dressed in the colorful costumes of their native countries. You could have smelled the spices.

153

What you would not have been able to see or smell were the ideas in the air. The

King Ferdinand

year 1492 was a time of new ideas. Explorers, writers, astronomers, artists, scientists, and musicians were all bursting with them. Ideas traveled like birds. They flew from country to country, bringing excitement with them.

If you lived in Spain or Portugal, you would have been living in one of the "hot spots" of history. It was where the exploring fever had reached its height. In 1492 the coast

154

cities of Spain and Portugal were busy. Every day that the winds were good, ships left ports with romantic names like Palos and Cádiz, Lisbon and Cartagena. Guided by the maps and the star charts produced by the mapmakers, they sailed to Africa and the Middle East and down the coast of Africa. Spain alone had a thousand merchant ships. In all the countries of Europe, exploring was in the air. But in Spain and Portugal in 1492, it had become almost a mania.

Queen Isabella

RESPONSE

Across the Ocean Blue

With a partner, trace Columbus's journey on a globe or a map. Use details from the log to find where he set out on his journey and where he may have come ashore. Follow his route by "sailing" to places written about in the log.

Don't Look Back

All through the journey, Columbus encouraged his fearful and homesick crew. Reread the log entry for September 9, 1492, and write a short speech that Columbus might have given. Give your speech to a group of classmates.

CORNER

Natural Treasures

What were some of the natural treasures European explorers found in the New World? Work with a partner to research plants and animals that are native to North and South America. Then create a collage using pictures, drawings, and real items.

What Do You Think?

- What were the most important ideas that you learned about Columbus's voyage from his log entries?

- If you were there in 1492, would you have signed on as a member of Columbus's crew? Why or why not?

- Would our world be different today if Columbus had never made his voyage or if he had turned back? Explain your answer.

ART & LITERATURE

The characters in this theme are seekers. Some seek new lands, while others seek a better society. The central figure in the painting is George Washington. What can you learn about George Washington from this American portrait? How do you think the painter felt about George Washington?

Washington Crossing the Delaware

by Emanuel Gottlieb Leutze

Emanuel Gottlieb Leutze was born in Germany in 1816 and moved to Philadelphia as a child. Washington Crossing the Delaware, *one of the most famous paintings in American art, shows a scene from the American Revolution. How might a photograph of Washington's real crossing compare with this painting?*

Oil on canvas, 1851
The Metropolitan Museum of Art, New York, NY

WHERE WAS PATRICK HENRY ON THE 29TH OF MAY?

by Jean Fritz

illustrated by Margot Tomes

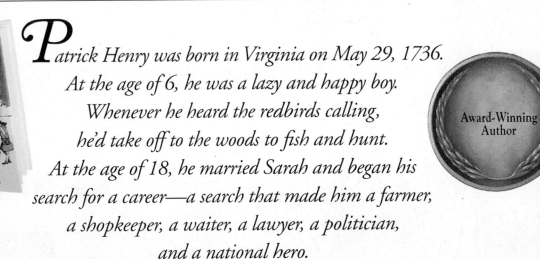

Patrick Henry was born in Virginia on May 29, 1736. At the age of 6, he was a lazy and happy boy. Whenever he heard the redbirds calling, he'd take off to the woods to fish and hunt. At the age of 18, he married Sarah and began his search for a career—a search that made him a farmer, a shopkeeper, a waiter, a lawyer, a politician, and a national hero.

Award-Winning Author

Patrick attended court as often as possible. He liked to watch a lawyer run his opposition up a tree. He liked to listen to him roll out his words, the way his Uncle Langloo did on Election Day. The more he listened, the more he thought he might like to have a try at it himself. After all, he was twenty-four years old now; he no longer had a farm or a store or even a house. He had to try *something*. So he got a few books and began studying on his own.

This was the winter of 1760, about the same time as young seventeen-year-old Thomas Jefferson met him at a houseparty and was struck by Patrick's "passion for fiddling, dancing and pleasantry." But Patrick read at least two heavy law books that winter and in the middle of April he hung up a sign at John Shelton's tavern. *Patrick Henry,* the sign said, *Attorney at Law.* Patrick had been to Williamsburg, the capital of Virginia; he'd been examined by three prominent lawyers and he'd been issued a license to practice law. (He had also been told that he needed to study some more.)

In his first year Patrick represented 60 clients (many of them relatives) in 176 cases but the cases didn't amount to much and he collected less than half of what was owed him. Much of the time he had so little to do, he'd ride into the piney woods for a week or more of hunting—"sleeping under a tent," according to Thomas Jefferson, "wearing the same shirt the whole time." Then likely as not, he'd go directly to court in his greasy leather breeches and a pair of saddle bags on his arm.

What Patrick Henry needed to prove himself as a lawyer was a big case at one of the quarter sessions of court when the whole county would take an interest.

At the December session in 1763 Patrick had his chance. There was an argument between a group of preachers (or parsons, as they were called) and the people, but in one sense it was an argument between the people of Virginia and England. For a long time England had been so busy fighting wars that she had left America relatively free to manage her own affairs. But now the French and Indian War was over, a new king was on the throne, and there were rumors that England had a plan to rule the colonies more strictly. With the Parsons' Case, it looked as if England had already started. The case went back to a year when the tobacco crop in Virginia failed. Instead of selling for the normal rate of 2 cents a pound, tobacco was so scarce, it sold for 6 cents. This should have been good news for the parsons because, according to law, they were paid in tobacco, but this year the people felt they couldn't afford it. So they passed a new law which allowed them to pay the parsons in cash at the 2 cent rate. The parsons took their case to the king; the king vetoed the law and now a group of parsons were suing the people for damages and back pay. And Patrick Henry was representing the people.

On the day of the trial Patrick was uneasy. Not only were there more spectators than he'd ever seen at the courthouse, there were two men that he wished were not there. The first was his Uncle Patrick who was one of the parsons. Patrick met his uncle at his carriage when he arrived at the courthouse and asked him if he wouldn't turn his carriage around.

He had never spoken in public, Patrick explained, and his uncle's presence would overawe him. Besides, he might say something about the parsons that his uncle wouldn't like. So wouldn't he please just go home? His uncle complied.

But Patrick couldn't ask the same of his father. Colonel John Henry was the presiding justice of the day and all through the trial he'd be sitting on a bench in front of the courtroom, right before Patrick's eyes.

Actually Colonel Henry was as uneasy as his son. He prayed that Patrick, who had failed in so many things, would not be an embarrassment today. But when Patrick stood up to argue the case, he was stooped, awkward, unable to look at the audience. When he spoke, he fumbled for words, halted, started sentences, stopped them as if he'd forgotten where he was going.

Colonel Henry sank down in his chair. He studied his hands. He looked out the window. Patrick's friends in the courtroom stared at the floor. What on earth had Patrick done with his voice, they asked themselves. Why didn't he *send* it?

Then all at once something seemed to come over Patrick. He stopped thinking about the people in the courtroom and about his father looking out the window and he began thinking about the King of England and how he could, if he wanted, change the character of the cheerful, independent world that Patrick lived in. Patrick Henry straightened up, he threw back his head, and sent his voice out in anger. How did the king know how much Virginians could pay their parsons? he asked. What right did he have to interfere? Patrick was rolling his words out now like his Uncle Langloo. He was doing things with his voice that he had never known he could do—lowering it, raising it not only to fit his emotions but in such a way as to stir the emotions of everyone in the courtroom. The crowd sat transfixed. So did Colonel Henry. And why not? Here was Patrick Henry, a poor country lawyer, turning himself into an orator right before their eyes.

He talked for an hour. What about the parsons? he asked. Were they feeding the hungry and clothing the naked as the Scriptures told them to? No, he said. They were getting the king's permission to grab the last hoecake from the honest farmer, to take the milk cow from the poor widow.

When Patrick had finished, the jury took just five minutes to reach a decision. They could not deny the parsons all damages since a previous court had ruled they had to be paid something, but after hearing Patrick, they allowed the parsons so much less than they had asked for that the parsons demanded a retrial. They were refused.

The people in the courthouse were beside themselves with excitement at Patrick's success. As soon as court was adjourned, they raised him to their shoulders and carried him around the courtyard, hip-hip-hooraying him all the while. As for Colonel Henry, when asked about his son's performance, he smiled. He'd been pleasantly surprised, he said.

It was a good thing for America, as it turned out, that Patrick Henry became an orator at the same time that England was unfolding her new plan. Taxation was England's next step. Although Americans had always managed their own money, suddenly in 1765 the English government, without any kind of by-your-leave from America, slapped down a stamp tax on the colonies. It had provisions for taxing 55 separate items and Patrick Henry was ready to fight every one of them.

On May 29th, 1765, Patrick became twenty-nine years old. He and Sarah had four children now and were living in a four-room house on top of a hill in Louisa County. And on the 29th of May, what was he doing?

Well, he was bawling out the king again. He had become a member of the House of Burgesses, Virginia's governing body, only nine days before and now he was standing up in his buckskin breeches before the finest men of Virginia, using such bold language that at one point there was a cry of "Treason!" But Patrick went right on reeling off resolutions. Later these resolutions were printed and sent out through the colonies, giving other Americans courage to oppose the taxation. Indeed, there was so much opposition to the Stamp Tax that after a year the king repealed it.

But England did not give up the idea of taxation nor did Patrick give up talking. In 1773, when England decided to enforce a tax on tea, Patrick went right to the floor of the House. He was so spellbinding that in the middle of one speech the spectators rushed from the gallery to the cupola of the capitol to pull down the English flag. The members of the House, noticing the commotion, thought there was a fire and ran for safety.

OUR DEAR MOTHER'S ROOM

Patrick and Sarah had six children now and were back in Hanover County in an eighteen-room house set on a thousand acres. Patrick was a public figure. When he went out, he wore a black suit or perhaps his peach-blossom-colored one, silver buckled shoes, and a tie wig which he was said to twirl around his head when he was excited.

Yet his private life contained much sadness. After the birth of their sixth child, Sarah lost her mind, turning on her husband and her own children in such a way that until she died in 1775 she had to be confined to her room. Unfortunately the years of Sarah's illness were also the critical years for the country and again and again Patrick was obliged to leave home. During one of her most severe spells he was with George Washington in Philadelphia, attending the Continental Congress.

On March 23rd, 1775, just a few weeks after Sarah's death, Patrick delivered his most famous speech at St. John's Church in Richmond, Virginia. By this time everyone knew who Mr. Henry was; they had all heard of his passion for liberty and of the extraordinary quality of his voice. There were those who swore that Patrick Henry could not even announce that it was a cold evening without inspiring awe. So of course on March 23rd St. John's Church was filled to overflowing—people standing in the aisles, in doorways, sitting on window ledges.

Patrick Henry was angry not only at the king who was disregarding America's petitions, insisting on taxation, and preparing for war, but he was also angry at those people in America who still wanted to be friendly to the king and keep peace. Patrick stood up and pushed his glasses back on his head which was what he did when he was ready to use his fighting words.

"Gentlemen may cry peace, peace," he thundered, "but there is no peace . . . Is life so dear or peace so sweet, as to be purchased at the price of chains and slavery?" Patrick bowed his body and locked his hands together as if he, himself, were in chains. Then suddenly he raised his chained hands over his head.

"Forbid it, Almighty God!" he cried. "I know not what course others may take but as for me—" Patrick dropped his arms, threw back his body and strained against his imaginary chains until the tendons of his neck stood out like whipcords and the chains seemed to break. Then he raised his right hand in which he held an ivory letter opener. "As for me," he cried, "give me liberty or give me death!" And he plunged the letter opener in such a way it looked as if he were plunging it into his heart.

The crowd went wild with excitement. One man, leaning over the balcony, was so aroused that he forgot where he was and spit tobacco juice into the audience below. Another man jumped down from the window ledge and declared that when he died, he wanted to be buried on the very spot that Patrick Henry had delivered those words. (And so he was, 25 years later.)

The next year war came and Virginia volunteers marched off to battle with *Liberty or Death* embroidered on their shirtfronts. As for Patrick Henry, the people elected him governor.

On May 29th, 1777, he was elected for the second time. He was forty-one years old now, living in the luxurious palace where the royal governors had lived for 55 years. And he was busy, so busy that if a nice spring day came along, he wouldn't even have heard a redbird call.

EXCERPT FROM PATRICK HENRY'S SPEECH TO THE SECOND VIRGINIA CONVENTION

There is no retreat but in submission and slavery! Our chains are forged! Their clanking may be heard on the plains of Boston! The war is inevitable—and let it come! I repeat it, sir, let it come!

It is in vain,[1] sir, to extenuate[2] the matter. Gentlemen may cry peace, peace—but there is no peace. The war is actually begun! The next gale that sweeps from the North will bring to our ears the clash of resounding arms! Our brethren are already in the field! Why stand we here idle? What is it that gentlemen wish? What would they have? Is life so dear, or peace so sweet, as to be purchased at the price of chains and slavery? Forbid it, Almighty God! I know not what course others may take; but as for me, give me liberty, or give me death!

---

[1] in vain: without success
[2] extenuate: partially excuse

PRIDE OF THE COURT

Imagine that you are Colonel John Henry, Patrick's father. Write a letter to Patrick after his big day in your courtroom. Share your feelings with your son about his performance in court.

RESPONSE

PATRIOT PARTY

Thomas Jefferson saw that young Patrick Henry had a "passion for fiddling, dancing, and pleasantry." Work with a small group to discover a song or dance popular in Patrick Henry's time. Present your discovery to the class in a creative way.

HENRY FOR GOVERNOR

Make a campaign poster for Patrick Henry's run for governor of Virginia. Give details about him in a way that will get people's attention. You may wish to include a catchy slogan on your poster. Display your campaign poster in the classroom.

CORNER

♛

WHAT DO YOU THINK?

🏛 How does Patrick Henry change from the beginning of the story to the end?

🏛 What is one important thing that you learned about Patrick Henry?

🏛 How was Patrick Henry's performance like an actor's on stage? What was one difference?

FLAGS
IN AMERICAN HISTORY

The Viking flag of Leif Ericson was the first flag in North America, in the 1000s.

The Spanish flag carried by Columbus in 1492, *above,* combined the arms of Castile and Leon. Columbus's own flag, *below,* bore the initials F and Y for Ferdinand and Isabella (Ysabel).

from *The World Book Encyclopedia*

The *Stars and Stripes* is the most popular name for the red, white, and blue national flag of the United States. No one knows where this name came from, but we do know the origin of several other names. Francis Scott Key first called the United States flag the *Star-Spangled Banner* in 1814 when he wrote the poem that became the national anthem (see **Star-Spangled Banner**). William Driver, a sea captain from Salem, Mass., gave the name *Old Glory* to the U.S. flag in 1824 (see **Driver, William**).

The Stars and Stripes stands for the land, the people, the government, and the ideals of the United States, no matter when or where it is displayed.

First United States flags

At the start of the Revolutionary War, Americans fought under many flags. The first flag to represent all the colonies was the *Continental Colors*, also called the *Cambridge, or Grand Union, Flag.* This flag, on which the British flag appeared at the upper left, was the unofficial American flag from 1775 to 1777.

After the Declaration of Independence, the British flag was no longer appropriate as part of the U.S. flag. On June 14, 1777, the Continental Congress resolved that "the Flag of the united states be 13 stripes alternate red and white, and the Union be 13 stars white in a blue field representing a new constellation."

No one knows for sure who designed this flag, or who made the first one. But soon after the flag was adopted, Francis Hopkinson, a delegate to the Continental Congress, claimed that he had designed it. Most scholars accept this claim.

In 1870, William J. Canby claimed that his grandmother, Betsy Ross, had made the first United States flag. Betsy Ross was a Philadelphia seamstress who made flags during the Revolutionary War. But most historians do not support the claim that Betsy Ross made the first United States flag (see **Ross, Betsy**).

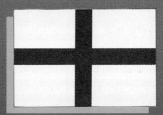

The English flag of John Cabot, *above*, flew in Canada in 1497. The British flag, *below*, adopted in 1606, flew over the British colonies in North America, beginning with Jamestown, 1607.

The Continental Colors served as America's first national flag from 1775 to 1777.

The flag of 1777 had no official arrangement for the stars. The most popular design had alternating rows of 3, 2, 3, 2, and 3 stars. Another flag with 13 stars in a circle was rarely used.

The flag of 1795 had 15 stripes, as well as 15 stars, to stand for the 15 states.

The colors. The Continental Congress left no record to show why it chose red, white, and blue as the colors for the flag. But, in 1782, the Congress of the Confederation chose these same colors for the newly designed Great Seal of the United States. The resolution on the seal listed meanings for the colors. *Red* is for hardiness and courage, *white* for purity and innocence, and *blue* for vigilance, perseverance, and justice.

The stripes in the flag stand for the thirteen original colonies. The stripes were probably adopted from the flag of the Sons of Liberty, which had five red and four white stripes (see **Sons of Liberty**). The British Union Jack was added to show that the colonists did not at first seek full independence.

The stars. The resolution passed by Congress in 1777 stated that the flag should have 13 stars. But Congress did not indicate how the stars should be arranged. The most popular arrangement showed the stars in alternating rows of three, two, three, two, and three stars. Another version had 12 stars in a circle with the 13th star in the center. A flag with 13 stars in a circle is often associated with the period. However, there is little evidence that such a design was used.

Changes in the United States flag

By 1794, two new states had joined the Union. Congress decided to add two stars and two stripes to the flag. It ordered a 15-stripe flag used after May 1, 1795. The stars appeared in five rows, three in a row. Americans carried this flag in the War of 1812.

Five more states had come into the Union by 1817. Congress did not want the flag to have 20 stars and 20 stripes, because it would be too cluttered. Peter Wendover, a representative from New York, proposed a flag of 13 stripes, with a star for each state. Congress accepted the idea, because it could then change the stars easily. On April 4, 1818, it set the number of stripes at 13 again. It ordered a new star to be added to the flag on the July 4th after a state joined the Union.

The flag of 1818 went back to 13 stripes, and had 20 stars for the 20 states. One design had four rows of five stars each. The Great Star Flag, *below*, formed the 20 stars in a large star.

Today's 50-star United States flag

The 48-star flag served as the national flag the longest of any flag, from 1912 to 1959.

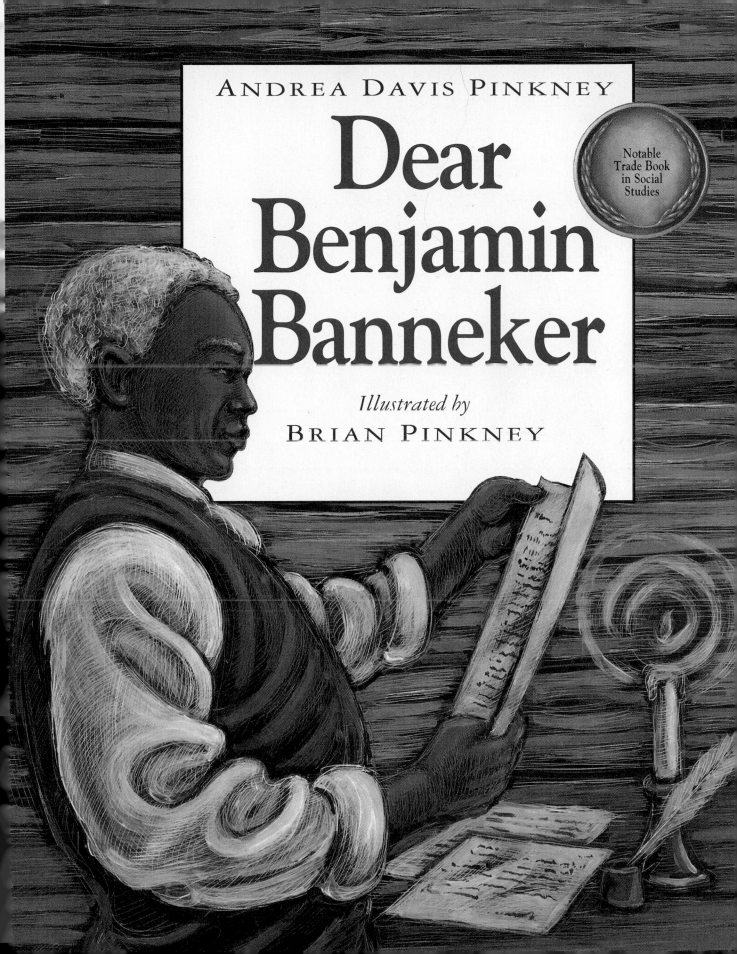

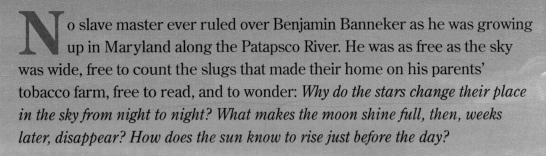

No slave master ever ruled over Benjamin Banneker as he was growing up in Maryland along the Patapsco River. He was as free as the sky was wide, free to count the slugs that made their home on his parents' tobacco farm, free to read, and to wonder: *Why do the stars change their place in the sky from night to night? What makes the moon shine full, then, weeks later, disappear? How does the sun know to rise just before the day?*

Benjamin's mother, Mary, grew up a free woman. His daddy, Robert, a former slave, gained his freedom long before 1731 when Benjamin was born. Benjamin Banneker had official papers that spelled out his freedom.

But even as a free person, Benjamin had to work hard. When Benjamin grew to be a man, he discovered that to earn a decent living he had little choice but to tend to the tobacco farm his parents left him, a grassy hundred acres he called Stout.

Benjamin worked long hours to make sure his farm would yield healthy crops. After each harvest, Benjamin hauled hogshead bundles of tobacco to sell in town. The work was grueling and didn't leave him much time for finding the answers to his questions about the mysterious movements of the stars and cycles of the moon.

But over the course of many years, Benjamin managed to teach himself astronomy at night while everyone else slept.

There were many white scientists in Benjamin's day who taught themselves astronomy and published their own almanacs. But it didn't occur to them that a black man—free or slave—could be smart enough to calculate the movements of the stars the way Benjamin did.

Benjamin wanted to prove folks wrong. He knew that he could make an almanac as good as any white scientist's. Even if it meant he would have to stay awake most nights to do it, Benjamin was determined to create an almanac that would be the first of its kind.

In colonial times, most families in America owned an almanac. To some, it was as important as the Bible. Folks read almanacs to find out when the sun and moon would rise and set, when eclipses would occur, and how the weather would change from season to season. Farmers read their almanacs so they would know when to seed their soil, when to plow, and when they could expect rain to water their crops.

Beginning in 1789, Benjamin spent close to a year observing the sky every night, unraveling its mysteries. He plotted the cycles of the moon and made careful notes.

The winter of 1790 was coming. In order to get his almanac printed in time for the new year, Benjamin needed to find a publisher quickly. He sent his calculations off to William Goddard, one of the most well-known printers in Baltimore. William Goddard sent word that he wasn't interested in publishing Benjamin's manuscript. Benjamin received the same reply from John Hayes, a newspaper publisher.

Benjamin couldn't find a publisher who was willing to take a chance on him. None seemed to trust his abilities. Peering through his cabin window at the bleak wintry sky, Benjamin's own faith in his almanac began to shrivel, like the logs burning in his fireplace.

Finally, in late 1790, James Pemberton learned of Benjamin Banneker and his almanac. Pemberton was the president of the Pennsylvania Society for the Abolition of Slavery, a group of men and women who fought for the rights of black people. Pemberton said Benjamin's almanac was proof that black people were as smart as white people. He set out to help Benjamin get his almanac published for the year 1791.

With Pemberton's help, news about Benjamin and his almanac spread across the Maryland countryside and up through the channels of the Chesapeake Bay. Members of the abolitionist societies of Pennsylvania and Maryland rallied to get Benjamin's almanac published.

But as the gray days of December grew shorter and colder, Benjamin and his supporters realized it was too late in the year 1790 to publish Benjamin's astronomy tables for 1791. Benjamin would have to create a new set of calculations for an almanac to be published in 1792.

Benjamin knew many people would use and learn from his almanac. He also realized that as the first black man to complete such a work, he'd receive praise for his accomplishment. Yet, Benjamin wondered, what good would his almanac be to black people who were enslaved? There were so many black people who wouldn't be able to read his almanac. Some couldn't read and were forbidden to learn. Others, who could read, had masters who refused to let them have books. These thoughts were never far from Benjamin's mind as he worked on his 1792 almanac.

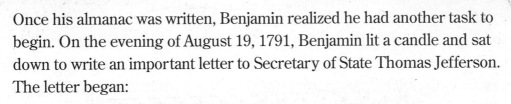

Once his almanac was written, Benjamin realized he had another task to begin. On the evening of August 19, 1791, Benjamin lit a candle and sat down to write an important letter to Secretary of State Thomas Jefferson. The letter began:

> *Maryland, Baltimore County,*
> *Near Ellicott's Lower Mills August 19th. 1791.*
> *Thomas Jefferson Secretary of State.*
>
> *Sir, I am fully sensible of the greatness of that freedom*
> *which I take with you on the present occasion; a liberty*
> *which Seemed to me Scarcely allowable, when I reflected*
> *on the distinguished, and dignifyed station in which you*
> *Stand; and the almost general prejudice and prepossession*
> *which is so previlent in the world against*
> *those of my complexion.*

Years before, in 1776, Thomas Jefferson wrote the Declaration of Independence, a document that said "all men are created equal." But Thomas Jefferson owned slaves. How, Benjamin wondered, could Thomas Jefferson sign his name to the declaration, which guaranteed "life, liberty and the pursuit of happiness" for all? The words Thomas Jefferson wrote didn't match the way he lived his life. To Benjamin, that didn't seem right.

Benjamin knew that all black people could study and learn as he had—if only they were free to do so. Written on the finest paper he could find, Benjamin's letter to Thomas Jefferson said just that. His letter reminded Thomas Jefferson that before he came to the United States from England, he—a white man—had been a slave under British rule. He went on to say:

> Sir how pitiable is it to reflect, that altho you were so fully convinced of the benevolence of the Father of mankind, and of his equal and impartial distribution of those rights and privileges which he had conferred upon them, that you should at the Same time counteract his mercies, in detaining by fraud and violence so numerous a part of my bretheren under groaning captivity and cruel oppression, that you should at the Same time be found guilty of that most criminal act, which you professedly detested in others, with respect to yourselves.

Along with his letter, Benjamin enclosed a copy of his almanac.

Eleven days later, Benjamin received a reply from Thomas Jefferson. In his letter, Jefferson wrote that he was glad to get the almanac and that he agreed with Benjamin, black people had abilities that they couldn't discover because they were enslaved. He wrote:

> Philadelphia, Aug. 30. 1791.

> Sir, I Thank you sincerely for your letter of the 19th instant and for the Almanac it contained. No body wishes more than I do to see such proofs as you exhibit, that nature has given to our black brethren, talents equal to those of the other colors of men, and that the appearance of a want of them is owing merely to the degraded condition of their existence. . . .

Jefferson wrote Benjamin that he wanted things to change. He hoped, in time, that black people would be treated better. He said:

> I can add with truth, that no body wishes more ardently to see a good system commenced for raising the condition both of their body & mind to what it ought to be, as fast as the imbecility of their present existence, and other circumstances which cannot be neglected, will admit.

Benjamin reread the secretary of state's letter several times. Then he folded it carefully and tucked it in one of his astronomy books for safekeeping. Benjamin had spoken his mind in the hope that all people would someday be free.

In December 1791, store owners started selling Benjamin Banneker's Pennsylvania, Maryland, Delaware, and Virginia almanac for the year 1792. Townsfolk from near and far purchased the book. The first edition sold out right away.

Benjamin's almanac contained answers to some of the questions he had asked himself when he was a boy watching the sky. It included cycles of full moons and new moons, times of sunrise and sunset, tide tables for the Chesapeake Bay, and news about festivals and horse habits.

The success of Benjamin's almanac meant that he was free to leave tobacco farming behind. Benjamin sold most of his land but kept his cabin so that he could spend the rest of his days studying astronomy, asking more questions, and finding the answers.

Benjamin published an almanac every year until 1797. His 1793 almanac included the letter he had written to Thomas Jefferson, along with the secretary of state's reply.

Benjamin didn't live to see the day when black people were given their freedom. But his almanacs and the letter he wrote to Thomas Jefferson showed everybody that all men are indeed created equal.

AN INTERVIEW WITH THE AUTHOR AND THE ILLUSTRATOR: ANDREA DAVIS

How did you first come to hear about Benjamin Banneker?

Andrea Davis Pinkney: I'm from the Chesapeake Bay area where Benjamin Banneker lived, so I grew up hearing about him. When my editor asked if we would do a book about him, it was already on my mind.

Andrea, were you the one who did the research?

Andrea: We both did. We always try to visit the locations where our stories take place. We went to Maryland and rode around the area where Banneker grew up, and we went to the Banneker–Douglass Museum. I was taking notes the whole time.

Brian Pinkney: At the same time, I was doing my own research. I had my sketch pad, and I was collecting anything that had pictures or engravings.

How did you decide what you would put in the book?

Andrea: That was hard. Benjamin Banneker did so many things in his life. He was a clockmaker, a surveyor, an astronomer, a mathematician. We decided we needed to focus on one thing. We chose his letter to Thomas Jefferson, which is something few people know about. We worked everything else around that.

Brian, how do you decide what text to illustrate?

Brian: I work by drawing small sketches first. I draw rectangles for each two-page spread of art. For instance, I might decide that the first spread is going to show Benjamin as a little boy, and I sketch that in. The second will show him in the fields, and so on. Andrea and I work together to match the text to the art spreads.

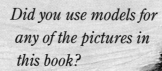

Did you use models for any of the pictures in this book?

PINKNEY *and* BRIAN PINKNEY

Brian: As a matter of fact, I did. In the spread that shows Benjamin in the tobacco fields, my brother-in-law was the model. His relatives were tobacco farmers, so he was able to show me how the tobacco is put into bundles.

What about the costumes—how did you research those?

Brian: The New York Public Library was very helpful.

Andrea: Brian is very careful in his research. He wants to know if a shirt from colonial times had three buttons or four buttons. In the picture in which Thomas Jefferson is writing the letter, the chair he is sitting on is not just any chair—it is Jefferson's chair at Monticello.

Is it difficult for you to work together as a married couple?

Brian: We had to work that out. It's hard for me to take criticism, so when Andrea is looking at my artwork, I ask that she say things in a certain way. Then she doesn't hurt my feelings. For example, "unresolved" is a good word to use for a picture that's not quite right.

Andrea: And I always ask that Brian start his criticism of my writing by saying, "You're off to a great start." We also set up meetings to talk about the work, and we talk about it *only* during those meetings. It's more professional than talking about our books while we're brushing our teeth.

BANNEKER's

ALMANAC,

For the YEAR 1795:

Being the THIRD after LEAP YEAR.

CONTAINING,

(Befides every Thing neceffary in an Almanac,)

A N

Account of the Yellow Fever,

LATELY PREVALENT IN PHILADELPHIA.

WITH

The Nnmber of thofe who DIED, from the Firft of
Auguft till the Ninth of November, 1793.

———————

PHILADELPHIA:

Printed for WILLIAM YOUNG, Bookfeller, No. 52,
the Corner of *Chefnut* and *Second-ftreets.*

ECLIPSES in the YEAR 1795.

THERE will be four eclipfes this year, two of each luminary.

I. Of the Sun, January 20th, invifible in the United States, ☌ at 7h. 20m. P. M. in Lon. 10 S. 1º, ☉ is centrally eclipfed on the meridian at 7h. 26m. in Lon. 111º$\frac{1}{2}$ weft. from the meridian of Baltimore, and Lat. 25$\frac{1}{4}$ north.

II. Is a vifible eclipfe of the Moon, February 3d, at 7h 46m. P. M.

	H	M.	
Beginning,	6	31	Digits eclipfed 7$\frac{1}{2}$ on her fouth limb.
Greateft obfcuration,	7	49	
End,	9	7	
Whole duration,	2	36	

The CENSUS of the feveral STATES, fo far as returns have been made into the office of the Secretary of State.
————No returns being yet received from thofe marked thus *, their numbers are ftated conjecturally, in order to give an idea of the aggregate amount of the whole.

New-Hampfhire,	-	141,885	Maryland, -	319,728
Maffachufetts,	378,787 ⎱ 475,327		Virginia, -	747,610
Maine, -	96,540 ⎰		Kentucky, -	73,677
Rhode-Ifland,	-	68,825	North-Carolina, -	393,751
Connecticut,	-	237,946	* South-Carolina, -	240,000
* Vermont,	-	85,000	Georgia, -	82,548
New-York,	-	340,120	* S. W. territory -	30,000
New-Jerfey,	-	184,139	* N. W. territory, -	5,000
Pennfylvania,	-	434,373		
Delaware,	-	59,094	Total Number	3,919,023

Table of the Federal Money of Accompt, as eftablifhed by Congrefs.

10 Mills make	1 Cent.
10 Cents	1 Dime.
10 Dimes	1 Federal Dollar.
10 Dollars	1 Eagle.

WE TH (Alabama) — P PUL (Alaska) — OF TH (Arizona) — U NI (Arkansas) — DIDD (California) — ST8S (Colorado)

INNOR (Connecticut) — DUR 2 (Delaware) — 4M A (Washington, D.C.) — MOR PUR (Florida) — FEC UNE (Georgia) — NONE (Hawaii)

S TAB (Idaho) — LISH (Illinois) — JUSTIZ (Indiana) — N SURE (Iowa) — DOME (Kansas)

ESTIK (Kentucky) — TRAN (Louisiana) — KWILI (Maine) — T PRO (Maryland) — VIDE 4 (Massachusetts) — TH COM (Michigan)

UN DE (Minnesota) — FENZ (Mississippi) — PRO MOT (Missouri) — TH JEN R (Montana) — L WEL (Nebraska)

FARE N (Nevada) — C CURE (New Hampshire) — TH BLES (New Jersey) — NGS OF (New Mexico) — LIBBER (New York) — T 2 R (North Carolina)

SELVS (North Dakota) — N R POS (Ohio) — TERI T (Oklahoma) — DO R (Oregon) — DANE N (Pennsylvania)

S-TAB (Rhode Island) — LISH (South Carolina) — THIS (South Dakota) — CON STI (Tennessee) — 2 10 (Texas) — 4 TH (Utah)

U NI (Vermont) — TID (Virginia) — ST8S (Washington) — OF AH (West Virginia) — MARE (Wisconsin) — E CUH (Wyoming)

PREAMBLE TO THE CONSTITUTION OF THE UNITED STATES OF AMERICA

W■■■■■

e the People of the United States, in Order to form a more perfect Union, establish Justice, insure domestic Tranquility, provide for the common defence, promote the general Welfare, and secure the Blessings of Liberty to ourselves and our Posterity, do ordain and establish this Constitution for the United States of America.

Preamble, Mike Wilkens, 1987
The beginning of the U.S. Constitution is echoed in car license plates from all fifty states plus the District of Columbia.

RESPONSE CORNER

Life, Liberty, and the Pursuit of Happiness

Benjamin Banneker stood up for his rights. What are some of the rights and privileges of a citizen of the United States? Create a poster that shows some of the best things about being an American.

What Do You Think?

* How did Benjamin Banneker solve his problem of finding a publisher?
* What was the most surprising thing you learned about Benjamin Banneker?
* How was Benjamin Banneker's life different from that of other black people of his time? How was it the same?

WRAP-UP

The characters in this theme lived in the same part of the world, the east coast of North America. But they lived there 300 years apart. Describe how the world changed in that time.

If you could visit either the time of Morning Girl and Christopher Columbus or the time of Patrick Henry and Benjamin Banneker, which would you choose? Why?

ACTIVITY CORNER

Work with a partner to act out and write an interview for *American Portraits Magazine*. Choose a character from the theme as your subject, and then choose who will play the interviewer and who will play the interviewed. Work together to write the final version.

Personal Journeys

What do you see when you look in the mirror? If you are like the people in the next selections, you may see a dream that is waiting to come true, or you may see a type of courage that you never knew you had.

In the Year of the Boar and Jackie Robinson
by Bette Bao Lord

Shirley Temple Wong takes a journey of 10,000 miles to a strange land—the USA.
Signatures Library

Bookshelf

Pride of Puerto Rico
by Paul Robert Walker

Baseball player Roberto Clemente rises from humble beginnings to stardom in the major leagues.
Signatures Library

The Summer of the Swans
by Betsy Byars

Sara sees herself as ugly and is tired of her everyday routine. But when her ten-year-old brother Charlie turns up missing, Sara begins to realize her true worth.
NEWBERY MEDAL

Aldo Peanut Butter
by Johanna Hurwitz

Aldo and his three sisters learn responsibility when they are left in charge of a house and two frisky puppies.

Yang the Third and Her Impossible Family
by Lensey Namioka

Yingmei Yang spends all her time trying to "be American," even changing her name to the more American-sounding Mary. Then Mary learns the value of being true to herself.

HOMESICK
My Own Story

Jean Guttery, who would one day become the celebrated author Jean Fritz, is the daughter of a Christian missionary. That is why Jean, although a citizen of the United States, was born half a world away in Hangkow, China. Jean spent the first twelve years of her life there under the watchful eye of her maidservant, Lin Nai-Nai. Most of what she learned about her native land came from her grandmother's letters or from conversations with American friends such as Andrea and Edward Hull.

But in 1927, China was a land on the brink of civil war. It was a land where most foreigners were no longer welcome. For their own safety, the Guttery and the Hull families set sail on the ocean liner *President Taft*. Jean was finally going home, to learn about America for herself.

Newbery Honor

BY JEAN FRITZ

ILLUSTRATED BY DAVID JOHNSON

On the whole, Andrea and I had a good time on the *President Taft*. In the evenings we often watched movies. In the afternoons we made pigs of ourselves at tea where we had our pick of all kinds of dainty sandwiches, scones, macaroons, chocolate bonbons, and gooey tarts. Actually, I even liked going to bed on shipboard. I'd lie in my bunk and feel the ship's engines throbbing and know that even when I fell asleep I wouldn't be wasting time. I'd still be on the go, moving closer to America every minute.

Still, my "in-between" feeling stayed with me. One evening after supper I took Andrea to the top deck and told her about the feeling. Of course the "in-betweenness" was stronger than ever in the dark with the circle of water rippling below and the night sky above spilling over with stars. I had never seen so many stars. When I looked for a spot where I might stick an extra star if I had one, I couldn't find any space at all. No matter how small, an extra star would be out of place, I decided. The universe was one-hundred-percent perfect just as it was.

And then Andrea began to dance. She had slipped off her shoes and stockings and she was dancing what was obviously an "in-between" dance, leaping up toward the stars, sinking down toward the water, bending back toward China, reaching forward toward America, bending back again and again as if she could not tear herself away, yet each time dancing farther forward, swaying to and fro. Finally, her arms raised, she began twirling around, faster and faster, as if she were trying to outspin time itself. Scarcely breathing, I sat beside a smokestack and watched. She was making a poem and I was inside the poem with her. Under the stars, in the middle of the Pacific Ocean. I would never forget this night, I thought. Not if I lived to be one hundred.

Only when we came to the international date line did my "in-between" feeling disappear. This is the place, a kind of imaginary line in the ocean, where all ships going east add an extra day to that week and all ships going west drop a day. This is so you can keep up with the world turning and make time come out right. We had two Tuesdays in a row when we crossed the line and after that when it was "today" for me, I knew that Lin Nai-Nai was already in "tomorrow." I didn't like to think of Lin Nai-Nai so far ahead of me. It was as if we'd suddenly been tossed on different planets.

On the other hand, this was the first time in my life that I was sharing the same day with my grandmother.

Oh, Grandma, I thought, *ready or not, here I come!*

It was only a short time later that Edward saw a couple of rocks poking out of the water and yelled for us to come. The rocks could hardly be called land, but we knew they were the beginning of the Hawaiian Islands and we knew that the Hawaiian Islands were a territory belonging to the United States. Of course it wasn't the same as one of the forty-eight states; still, when we stepped off the *President Taft* in Honolulu (where we were to stay a couple of days before going on to San Francisco), we wondered if we could truthfully say we were stepping on American soil. I said no. Since the Hawaiian Islands didn't have a star in the flag, they couldn't be one-hundred-percent American, and I wasn't going to consider myself on American soil until I had put my feet flat down on the state of California.

We had a week to wait. The morning we were due to arrive in San Francisco, all the passengers came on deck early, but I was the first. I skipped breakfast and went to the very front of the ship where the railing comes to a point. That morning I would be the "eyes" of the *President Taft*, searching the horizon for the first speck of land. My private ceremony of greeting, however, would not come until we were closer, until we were sailing through the Golden Gate. For years I had heard about the Golden Gate, a narrow stretch of water connecting the Pacific Ocean to San Francisco Bay. And for years I had planned my entrance.

Dressed in my navy skirt, white blouse, and silk stockings, I felt every bit as neat as Columbus or Balboa and every bit as heroic when I finally spotted America in the distance. The decks had filled with passengers by now, and as I watched the land come closer, I had to tell myself over and over that I was HERE. At last.

Then the ship entered the narrow stretch of the Golden Gate and I could see American hills on my left and American houses on my right, and I took a deep breath of American air.

"'Breathes there the man, with soul so dead,'" I cried,

"'Who never to himself hath said,
This is my own, my native land!'"

I forgot that there were people behind and around me until I heard a few snickers and a scattering of claps, but I didn't care. I wasn't reciting for anyone's benefit but my own.

Next for my first steps on American soil, but when the time came, I forgot all about them. As soon as we were on the dock, we were jostled from line to line. Believe it or not, after crossing thousands of miles of ocean to get here, we had to prove that it was O.K. for us to come into the U.S.A. We had to show that we were honest-to-goodness citizens and not spies. We had to open our baggage and let inspectors see that we weren't smuggling in opium or anything else illegal. We even had to prove that we were germ-free, that we didn't have smallpox or any dire disease that would infect the country. After we had finally passed the tests, I expected to feel one-hundred-percent American. Instead, stepping from the dock into the city of San Francisco, I felt dizzy and unreal, as if I were a made-up character in a book I had read too many times to believe it wasn't still a book. As we walked the Hulls to the car that their Aunt Kay had driven up from Los Angeles, I told Andrea about my crazy feeling.

"I'm kind of funny in the head," I said. "As if I'm not really me. As if this isn't really happening."

"Me too," Andrea agreed. "I guess our brains haven't caught up to us yet. But my brains better get going. Guess what?"

"What?"

"Aunt Kay says our house in Los Angeles is not far from Hollywood."

Then suddenly the scene speeded up and the Hulls were in the car, ready to leave for Los Angeles, while I was still stuck in a book without having said any of the things I wanted to. I ran after the car as it started.

"Give my love to John Gilbert," I yelled to Andrea.

She stuck her head out the window. "And how!" she yelled back.

My mother, father, and I were going to stay in a hotel overnight and start across the continent the next morning, May 24, in our new Dodge. The first thing we did now was to go to a drugstore where my father ordered three ice-cream sodas. "As tall as you can make them," he said. "We have to make up for lost time."

My first American soda was chocolate and it was a whopper. While we sucked away on our straws, my father read to us from the latest newspaper. The big story was about America's new hero, an aviator named Charles Lindbergh who had just made the first solo flight across the Atlantic Ocean. Of course I admired him for having done such a brave and scary thing, but I bet he wasn't any more surprised to have made it across one ocean than I was to have finally made it across another. I looked at his picture. His goggles were pushed back on his helmet and he was grinning. He had it all over John Gilbert, I decided. I might even consider having a crush on him—that is, if and when I ever felt the urge. Right now I was coming to the bottom of my soda and I was trying to slurp up the last drops when my mother told me to quit; I was making too much noise.

The rest of the afternoon we spent sight-seeing, riding up and down seesaw hills in cable cars, walking in and out of American stores. Every once in a while I found myself smiling at total strangers because I knew that if I were to speak to them in English, they'd answer in English. We were all Americans. Yet I still felt as if I were telling myself a story. America didn't become completely real for me until the next day after we'd left San Francisco and were out in the country.

My father had told my mother and me that since he wasn't used to our new car or to American highways, we should be quiet and let him concentrate. My mother concentrated too. Sitting in the front seat, she flinched every time she saw another car, a crossroad, a stray dog, but she never said a word. I paid no attention to the road. I just kept looking out the window until all at once there on my right was a white picket fence and a meadow, fresh and green as if it had just this minute been created. Two black-and-white cows were grazing slowly over the grass as if they had all the time in the world, as if they knew that no matter how much they ate, there'd always be more, as if in their quiet munching way they understood that they had nothing, nothing whatsoever to worry about. I poked my mother, pointed, and whispered, "Cows." I had never seen cows in China but it was not the cows themselves that impressed me. It was the whole scene. The perfect greenness. The washed-clean look. The peacefulness. Oh, *now*! I thought. Now I was in America. Every last inch of me.

By the second day my father acted as if he'd been driving the car all his life. He not only talked, he sang, and if he felt like hitching up his trousers, he just took his hands off the wheel and hitched. But as my father relaxed, my mother became more tense. "Arthur," she finally said, "you are going forty-five."

My father laughed. "Well, we're headed for the stable, Myrtle. You never heard of a horse that dawdled on its way home, did you?"

My mother's lips went tight and thin. "The whole point of driving across the continent," she said, "was so we could see the country."

"Well, it's all there." My father swept his hand from one side of the car to the other. "All you have to do is to take your eyes off the road and look." He honked his horn at the car in front of him and swung around it.

At the end of the day, after we were settled in an overnight cabin, my father took a new notebook from his pocket. I watched as he wrote: "May 24. 260 miles." Just as I'd suspected, my father was out to break records. I bet that before long we'd be making 300 miles or more a day. I bet we'd be in Washington, P.A., long before July.

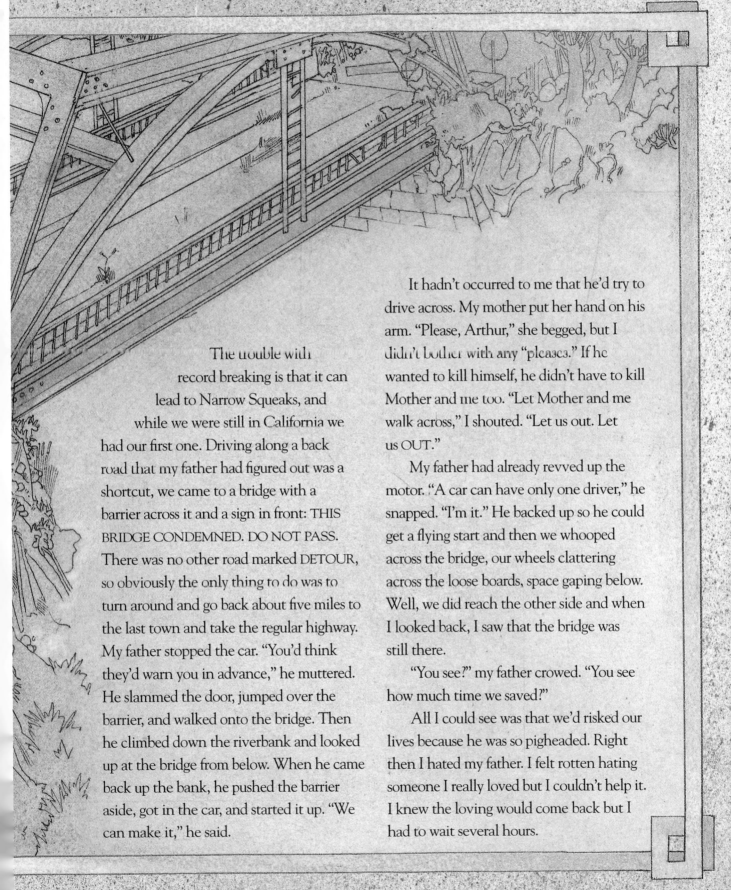

The trouble with record breaking is that it can lead to Narrow Squeaks, and while we were still in California we had our first one. Driving along a back road that my father had figured out was a shortcut, we came to a bridge with a barrier across it and a sign in front: THIS BRIDGE CONDEMNED. DO NOT PASS. There was no other road marked DETOUR, so obviously the only thing to do was to turn around and go back about five miles to the last town and take the regular highway. My father stopped the car. "You'd think they'd warn you in advance," he muttered. He slammed the door, jumped over the barrier, and walked onto the bridge. Then he climbed down the riverbank and looked up at the bridge from below. When he came back up the bank, he pushed the barrier aside, got in the car, and started it up. "We can make it," he said.

It hadn't occurred to me that he'd try to drive across. My mother put her hand on his arm. "Please, Arthur," she begged, but I didn't bother with any "pleases." If he wanted to kill himself, he didn't have to kill Mother and me too. "Let Mother and me walk across," I shouted. "Let us out. Let us OUT."

My father had already revved up the motor. "A car can have only one driver," he snapped. "I'm it." He backed up so he could get a flying start and then we whooped across the bridge, our wheels clattering across the loose boards, space gaping below. Well, we did reach the other side and when I looked back, I saw that the bridge was still there.

"You see?" my father crowed. "You see how much time we saved?"

All I could see was that we'd risked our lives because he was so pigheaded. Right then I hated my father. I felt rotten hating someone I really loved but I couldn't help it. I knew the loving would come back but I had to wait several hours.

223

There were days, however, particularly across the long, flat stretches of Texas, when nothing out-of-the-way happened. We just drove on and on, and although my father reported at the end of the day that we'd gone 350 miles, the scenery was the same at the end as at the beginning, so it didn't feel as if we'd moved at all. Other times we ran into storms or into road construction and we were lucky if we made 200 miles. But the best day of the whole trip, at least as far as my mother and I were concerned, was the day that we had a flat tire in the Ozark Mountains. The spare tire and jack were buried in the trunk under all our luggage, so everything had to be taken out before my father could even begin work on the tire. There was no point in offering to help because my father had a system for loading and unloading which only he understood, so my mother and I set off up the mountainside, looking for wild flowers.

"Watch out for snakes," my mother said, but her voice was so happy, I knew she wasn't thinking about snakes. As soon as I stepped out of the car, I fell in love with the day. With the sky—fresh, blotting-paper blue. With the mountains, warm and piney and polka-dotted with flowers we would never have seen from the window of a car. We decided to pick one of each kind and press them in my gray geography book which I had in the car. My mother held out her skirt, making a hollow out of it, while I dropped in the flowers and she named

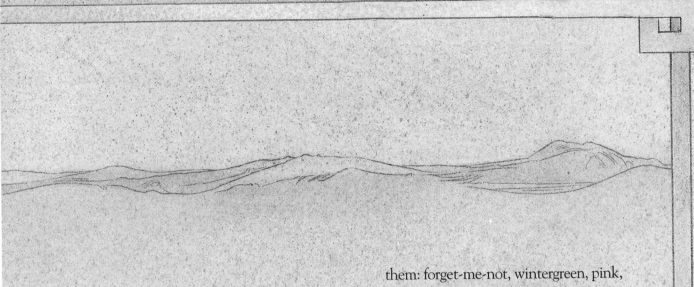

them: forget-me-not, wintergreen, pink, wild rose. When we didn't know the name, I'd make one up: pagoda plant, wild confetti, French knot. My mother's skirt was atumble with color when we suddenly realized how far we'd walked. Holding her skirt high, my mother led the way back, running and laughing. We arrived at the car, out of breath, just as my father was loading the last of the luggage into the trunk. He glared at us, his face streaming with perspiration. "I don't have a dry stitch on me," he said, as if it were our fault that he sweat so much. Then he looked at the flowers in Mother's skirt and his face softened. He took out his handkerchief and wiped his face and neck and finally he smiled. "I guess I picked a good place to have a flat tire, didn't I?" he said.

The farther we went, the better mileage we made, so that by the middle of June we were almost to the West Virginia state line. My father said we'd get to Washington, P.A., the day after the next, sometime in the afternoon. He called my grandmother on the phone, grinning because he knew how surprised she'd be. I stood close so I could hear her voice.

"Mother?" he said when she answered. "How about stirring up a batch of flannel cakes?"

"Arthur!" (She sounded just the way I knew she would.) "Well, land's sakes, Arthur, where are you?"

"About ready to cross into West Virginia."

My grandmother was so excited that her words fell over each other as she tried to relay the news to my grandfather and Aunt Margaret and talk over the phone at the same time.

The next day it poured rain and although that didn't slow us down, my mother started worrying. Shirls Avenue, my grandparents' street, apparently turned into a dirt road just before plunging down a steep hill to their house and farm. In wet weather the road became one big sea of mud which, according to my mother, would be "worth your life to drive through."

"If it looks bad," my mother suggested, "we can park at the top of the hill and walk down in our galoshes."

My father sighed. "Myrtle," he said, "we've driven across the Mohave Desert. We've been through thick and thin for over three thousand miles and here you are worrying about Shirls Avenue."

The next day the sun was out, but when we came to Shirls Avenue, I could see that the sun hadn't done a thing to dry up the hill. My father put the car into low, my mother closed her eyes, and down we went, sloshing up to our hubcaps, careening from one rut to another, while my father kept one hand down hard on the horn to announce our arrival.

By the time we were at the bottom of the hill and had parked beside the house, my grandmother, my grandfather, and Aunt Margaret were all outside, looking exactly the way they had in the calendar picture. I ran right into my grandmother's arms as if I'd been doing this every day.

"Welcome home! Oh, welcome home!" my grandmother cried.

I hadn't known it but this was exactly what I'd wanted her to say. I needed to hear it said out loud. I was home.

GOLDEN GATE BRIDGE

MAY 31, 1937 **10** CENTS

AS JEAN FRITZ AND HER FAMILY WERE SAILING INTO SAN FRANCISCO BAY, GREAT PLANS WERE BEING MADE TO BUILD AN ENGINEERING MARVEL ACROSS IT—THE GOLDEN GATE BRIDGE.

Golden Gate Bridge, World's Longest Span, Opens May 28

The Golden Gate Bridge is designed to connect the city of San Francisco on the south, with the counties on the north where many San Franciscans live and where much of the city's food is grown. From tower to tower the central span of the bridge stretches 4,200 ft.—the longest span on earth. It took four years to build and cost $35,000,000, which will be recovered, if at all, in 50¢ tolls. It contains more steel (100,000 tons) than any similar structure.

GOLDEN GATE BRIDGE, WORLD'S LONGEST SPAN, OPENS MAY 28

The Golden Gate Bridge is designed to connect the city of San Francisco on the south, with the counties on the north where many San Franciscans live and where much of the city's food is grown. From tower to tower the central span of the bridge stretches 4,200 ft.—the longest span on earth. It took four years to build and cost $35,000,000, which will be recovered, if at all, in 50 yrs. It contains more steel (100,000 tons) than any similar structure.

Work on the bridge began in 1933. Engineers first sunk two piers, one close to the southern shore and the other about 1,100 ft. out from the San Francisco shore. Sharp controversy marked the placing of the southern pier, a Stanford seismologist claiming that it stood on a geologic fault, the sound possible place in event of earthquake. But Chief Engineer Strauss argued the critic down and the two 746-ft. towers which you see at left were reared. Designed for beauty as well as strength, they taper to the top in set-back style.

Between the towers were strung two cables each 36½ in. thick and together containing 80,000 miles of steel wire. The picture above shows one of the twenty completed cables, with two workmen adding the last strands. The finished cables were wound with more wire, so tightly that the one in the picture at right appears to be doubled in total.

Suspended from the cables is a six-lane roadway. Because the Golden Gate is a great channel of commerce, the roadway had to be 220 ft. above high water level. Even so, the great Canadian Pacific liners which go to the Orient have had to shorten their masts.

For the safety of workmen on the bridge Chief Engineer Strauss strung a huge net under the bridge. On Feb. 17, a platform broke loose and ripped through the net, carrying ten men to their deaths. But even with this tragic accident the death toll was less than on most bridges of comparable size.

THE WORLD'S MOST SPECTACULAR BRIDGE SITE

Work on the bridge began in 1933. Engineers first sank two piers, one close to the northern shore and the other about 1,100 ft. out from the San Francisco shore. Sharp controversy marked the placing of the southern pier, a Stanford seismologist claiming that it stood on a geologic fault, the worst possible place in event of earthquake. But Chief Engineer Strauss argued the critic down and the two 746-ft. towers which you see at the left [1] were reared. Designed for the beauty as well as strength, they taper to the top in setback style. Between the towers were strung two cables each 36 1/2 in. thick and together containing 80,000 miles of steel wire. The picture above [2] shows one of the nearly completed cables, with two workmen adding the last strands. The finished cables were wound with more wire, so tightly that the one in the picture at right [3] appears to be sheathed in metal.

Suspended from the cables is a six-lane roadway. Because the Golden Gate is a great channel of commerce, the roadway had to be 220 ft. above high water level. Even so, the great Canadian Pacific liners which go to the Orient have had to shorten their masts.

For the safety of workmen on the bridge Chief Engineer Strauss borrowed an idea from trapeze artists and strung a huge net under the bridge. On Feb. 17, a platform broke loose and ripped through the net, carrying ten men to their deaths. But even with this tragic accident the death toll was less than on most bridges of comparable size.

The World's Most Spectacular Bridge Site

Spanning the mile-wide entrance to San Francisco Bay, the Golden Gate Bridge occupies probably the most spectacular bridge site in the world. You are looking from inside the harbor toward the open sea. In the foreground is the northern end of the city of San Francisco, [4] showing a landing field along the shore, a yacht basin, and a dilapidated colonnade *(bottom, center)*, left standing from the Panama-Pacific Exposition of 1915. On the further shore are the hills of Marin County, behind which lie prosperous suburbs, orchards, truck farms, and sheep ranches. The northern approach to the bridge is a tunnel through the hills. Out of the picture to the east is one of the world's most beautiful harbors, spanned by the longer but less impressive Transbay Bridge which opened last year. The Golden Gate Bridge is so designed that if it should be destroyed by an enemy fleet it would sink to the bottom of the channel and not bottle up the harbor.

> **From tower to tower the central span of the bridge stretches 4,200 ft.— the longest span on earth.**

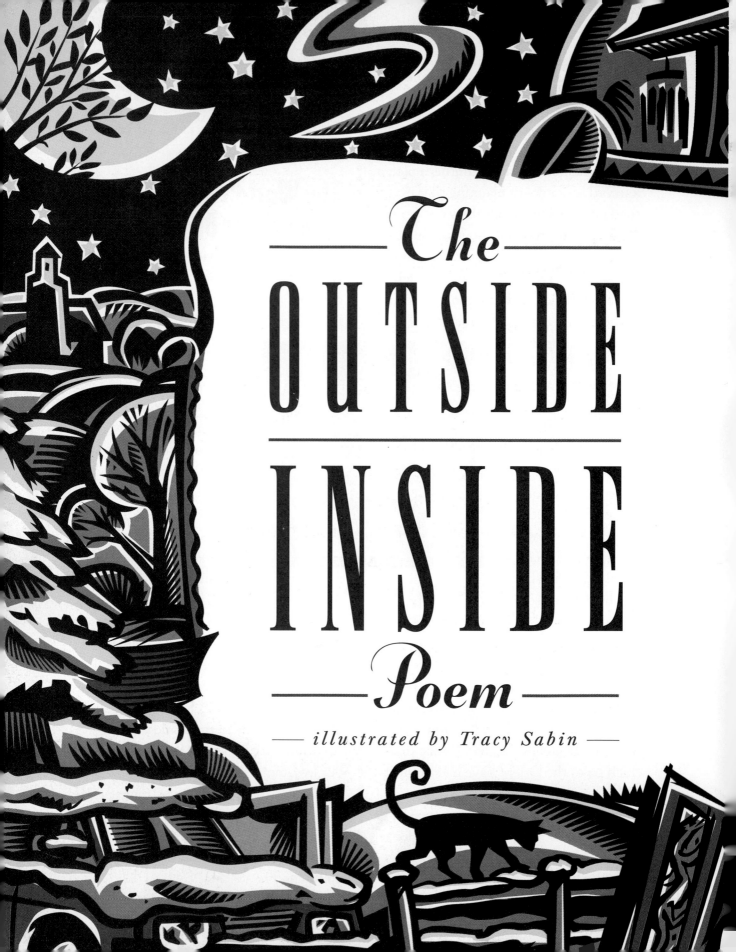

The OUTSIDE INSIDE Poem

— illustrated by Tracy Sabin —

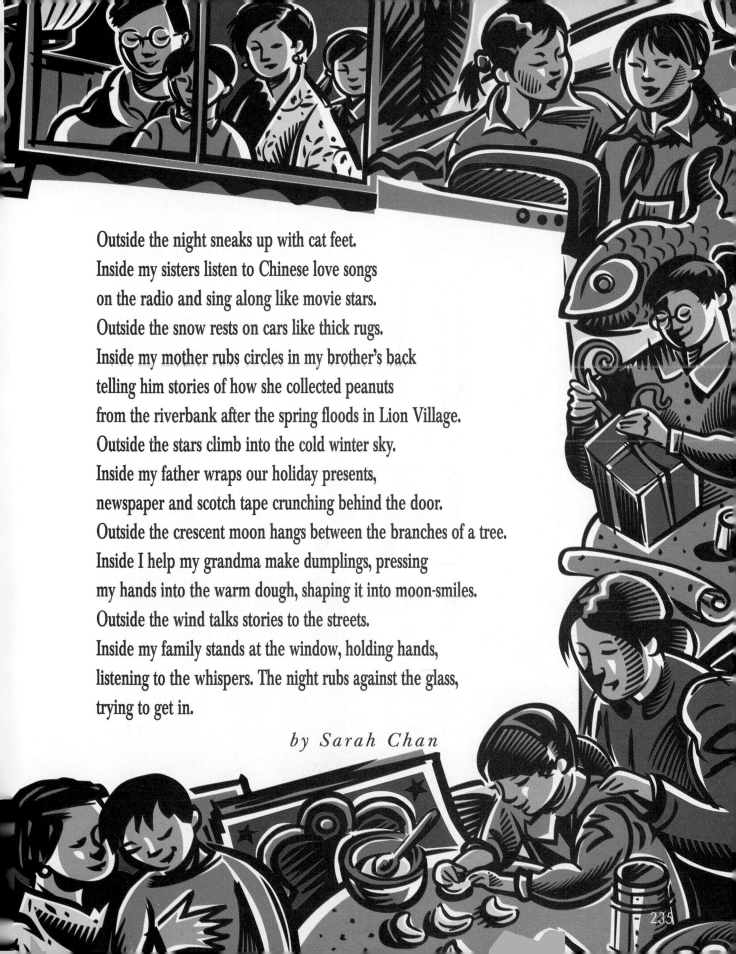

Outside the night sneaks up with cat feet.
Inside my sisters listen to Chinese love songs
on the radio and sing along like movie stars.
Outside the snow rests on cars like thick rugs.
Inside my mother rubs circles in my brother's back
telling him stories of how she collected peanuts
from the riverbank after the spring floods in Lion Village.
Outside the stars climb into the cold winter sky.
Inside my father wraps our holiday presents,
newspaper and scotch tape crunching behind the door.
Outside the crescent moon hangs between the branches of a tree.
Inside I help my grandma make dumplings, pressing
my hands into the warm dough, shaping it into moon-smiles.
Outside the wind talks stories to the streets.
Inside my family stands at the window, holding hands,
listening to the whispers. The night rubs against the glass,
trying to get in.

by Sarah Chan

What Does the Watch Read?

Work with a partner to research the international date line. Where is it located? How and why was it set up? Then write and exchange word problems about what time it is in different parts of the world when it is 8:00 A.M. in San Francisco.

RESPONSE

MAKE A MAP

America the Beautiful

Jean Fritz traveled by car from the California coast to her grandmother's home in Pennsylvania. Make and decorate a map that shows some of the beauty of America that she might have seen along the way. Display your map in the classroom.

What Do You Think?

- How did Jean feel about going to America? Give details from her story to explain your answer.

- Imagine that you were Jean. How might you feel about your journey from the "outside" to the "inside," from China to America?

- How different might Jean's first reaction to America have been if she had seen the Golden Gate Bridge?

CORNER

Inside/Outside

What is happening, at the exact same moment, inside and outside your school? Work with a partner to think about answers to this question. Then create a poem in which you take turns writing lines—first a line about what is happening inside and then a line about what is happening outside. Practice and perform a choral reading of your poem.

237

MARY
McLEOD
BETHUNE

Dream Maker

by Mary Satchell

The campus of Bethune-Cookman College, Daytona Beach, Florida

CHARACTERS

MARY MCLEOD BETHUNE

BERTHA MITCHELL,
Mary's friend and secretary

ROSE KEMP, *college freshman*

ALICE JACKSON,
student at Kindell Institute

REV. WATKINS,
principal of Kindell Institute

BOY
GIRL } *students in class*

STUDENTS,
six or more, as desired

240

Dr. Mary McLeod Bethune,
founder of Bethune-Cookman College

Scene 1

TIME: *1954; Graduation Day and the Fiftieth Anniversary of*
Bethune-Cookman College.

SETTING: MARY BETHUNE's *office at Bethune-Cookman College in*
Daytona Beach, Florida. Desk and chair are placed downstage, center. A
phone, letter opener, and two or three stacks of mail are on desk. At left is a
small bookcase filled with books. Two chairs are opposite desk, a small table is
near exit at right.

AT RISE: MARY BETHUNE *sits at desk, opening and reading telegrams and letters.*
BERTHA MITCHELL *enters, carrying maroon cap and gown, and pauses near table.*

BERTHA *(Scolding mildly):* Why, Mary Bethune, how can you work at a time like
this? The graduation exercises will begin in little more than an hour. *(Places cap*
and gown on table) The seniors are already lining up in front of the auditorium.

MARY *(Continuing to open mail):* This isn't work, Bertha. I'm having the time of
my life reading these beautiful messages from my friends all over the world.
It's hard to believe that we've been running this college for 50 years.

BERTHA *(Coming to stand near desk):* We're going to have lovely weather for
today's graduation. There's not a cloud in sight.

MARY *(Putting down letter opener):* I gave some thought to having this year's program outside, but then I remembered what happened on our thirty-fifth anniversary.

BERTHA: Wasn't that the year Mrs. Eleanor Roosevelt came down to be our guest speaker?

MARY *(Nodding and leaning back in her chair):* How could I forget! We had hundreds of chairs set up on the campus lawn, and the moment Mrs. Roosevelt stood up to speak, it started raining.

BERTHA: What *I'll* never forget is how you walked to Mrs. Roosevelt's side and held an umbrella over her head while she gave her entire address.

MARY *(Mischievously):* She didn't see me glaring at the audience, daring them to move from their seats. *(She and BERTHA laugh.)*

BERTHA: I can laugh about that rainy graduation day now, but I certainly didn't feel like laughing then.

MARY *(Reminiscing):* I was thinking back to the year you started working as my secretary. Booker T. Washington paid his first visit to our school that same year. It was in 1908.

BERTHA (*Sitting in chair*): I remember it very well, Mary.

MARY: I'm afraid you didn't have much faith in me or my dreams in those days. (*Chuckling*) You were embarrassed because we had only one building to show Mr. Washington.

BERTHA (*Laughing at herself*): And that wasn't even finished. (*With broad sweep of her arm*) If only Mr. Washington could see it today: a four-year college with nineteen buildings! (ROSE KEMP *appears at exit, hesitates.*)

MARY (*Motioning* ROSE *to enter*): Don't stand there looking as if you're meeting the enemy, young lady. Everyone's welcome here. (ROSE *enters, appearing uncomfortable as she clutches a notepad.*)

ROSE (*Hesitantly*): Mrs. Bethune, my name is Rose Kemp, and I'd like to interview you this afternoon, if I may.

MARY (*Amused*): Who sent you, Rose? From the look on your face, you didn't come here on your own.

ROSE (*Eagerly*): I volunteered for this assignment, Mrs. Bethune. You see, I'm a freshman, and I want to make the campus newspaper staff, but the editor says I don't have what it takes to be a reporter.

MARY (*Indignantly*): I'm glad you didn't let yourself be discouraged by that kind of talk.

ROSE: I thought if I could get an interview with you, the editor might change his mind.

BERTHA (*Standing up*): Excuse me, Mrs. Bethune, but in a little while you'll have to start greeting your guests.

MARY: Surely we can make time for something as important as a young student's future. *(Smiles at* ROSE*)* I think Rose and I may have a lot in common. We both have the spirit to show others what we can do.

BERTHA *(Reluctantly):* Very well. Only fifteen or twenty minutes, though, please, Mrs. Bethune, or your entire schedule will be ruined.

MARY: Much can be done in fifteen minutes. *(Kindly)* Now, Rose, if you keep your questions short and to the point, I'm sure we'll both make our deadlines.

Dr. Bethune in her office, 1943

BERTHA *(Resigned):* I should have known better than to say anything. You've never refused to give any student your time.

MARY: This is what I've lived and worked for all these years, Bertha. I can't stop now. *(*BERTHA *exits. To* ROSE, *humorously)* I can always tell when my assistant is annoyed with me. She calls me *Mrs. Bethune.* *(*ROSE *laughs and relaxes.)* Sit down, Rose, and ask whatever you wish. I'm always ready to talk. *(*ROSE *sits on edge of chair and holds her pen poised over pad.)*

ROSE: How did you get started as a teacher, Mrs. Bethune?

MARY: That question could take all day to answer. I didn't want to be a teacher, not at first.

ROSE *(Surprised and interested):* Really? What did you want to be?

MARY: I wanted to be a missionary, Rose. And do you know, I think I got my heart's desire. *(With mounting excitement)* Let me tell you something of my adventure, Rose. And we won't worry about the time, just now. *(*ROSE *begins to write, as curtain closes.)*

Photograph of early student body

Scene 2

TIME: *1899*

SETTING: *Classroom at Kindell Institute in Sumter, South Carolina.* MARY MCLEOD BETHUNE's *desk and chair are up left, opposite two or three rows of her students' old-fashioned desks. A wastebasket and lectern stand beside* MARY's *desk, which has books and globe on it. Exit is right.*

AT RISE: ALICE JACKSON *somberly enters, carrying books, which she puts inside her desk. She goes to* MARY's *desk and plays with the globe absently, slowly spinning it as she leans against the desk.* MARY *enters unnoticed, and studies the girl before speaking.*

MARY (*Brightly*): Why, Alice, you're certainly the early bird today. The rest of your family must still be at the breakfast table. (*Takes off shawl and drapes it over back of her chair*)

ALICE (*Glancing curiously at* MARY): I don't have a family, Mrs. Bethune. My parents died a long time ago. I live at the Children's Home.

MARY (*Sadly*): Goodness, you're only a young girl, and you talk as if you're older than I am.

ALICE: But it's true. (*Sadly*) I wish I did have a family like the other children here at school.

MARY *(Putting hand on* ALICE's *shoulder):* Alice, I think you should count your blessings. Why, you're far more fortunate than many of your classmates.

ALICE *(Shaking head):* How can you say that, Mrs. Bethune?

MARY: You have a very large family at the Children's Home. There are people at that orphanage who love and care for you just as parents do. If you look at it that way, every boy and girl at the Children's Home is really your brother and sister.

ALICE: I hadn't thought of it like that. (ALICE *turns back to globe and spins it.)*

Portrait of Mary McLeod Bethune, painted by Betsy Graves, 1943-44

MARY: That globe was given to me when I graduated from Scotia Seminary years ago. *(Enthusiastically)* I've kept it since as a reminder of how big and wonderful this world is.

ALICE *(Mockingly):* It looks very tiny to me, Mrs. Bethune. *(Puts finger on one spot of globe)* See? I can cover up a whole island with just one of my fingers.

MARY *(Amused):* You know this globe is only on a very small scale, Alice. Of course, we all know that in reality, our world is extremely large, and you mustn't forget it. Never limit your future or your dreams.

ALICE *(Moving from desk):* Mrs. Bethune, I used to dream of being adopted and having a mother and father of my own. *(Wistfully)* We would live in our own house; I'd have clothes as nice as the other girls at school. I waited a long time for someone to come to the orphanage and take me home. *(Looks down at her shoes)* But nobody ever came.

MARY *(Putting her arm around* ALICE's *shoulder):* Perhaps you should change your dream a little. *I* did, when I was about twenty years old. You see, I didn't really want to be a schoolteacher.

ALICE *(Shyly):* You're the best teacher I ever had, Mrs. Bethune.

MARY: When I hear one of my students say that, I'm glad I had to change my dream of being a missionary. Teachers get the chance to help so many people.

ALICE *(Shyly):* I hope someday I can help a lot of people. *(Other students enter, carrying books. They greet* MARY, *take seats, and put books in desks.* ALICE *goes to her seat.* MARY *goes to her desk and sits.)*

MARY *(Cheerfully):* Good morning, everyone. We're going to begin our class a little differently today. I'd like you to talk about your secret dreams—what you would *really* like to be when you grow up. Who wants to start? *(Silence. Finally,* BOY *raises his hand.)* Yes?

An early eighth and ninth grade class

BOY: I want to be a preacher like our principal, Reverend Watkins.

GIRL *(Smirking)*: Humph! You're too bad to be a minister. *(All laugh.)*

MARY *(Reproachfully)*: I don't want to hear any more of that. *(Glances casually at class, then lets her eyes rest on* ALICE*)* Alice, what's your secret dream?

ALICE *(Caught offguard)*: Well . . . *(Very softly)* I want to be a nurse.

STUDENTS *(From opposite side of the class; ad lib)*: Talk louder, Alice. We can't hear you. *(Etc.)*

ALICE *(Loudly and defiantly)*: I want to be a nurse.

MARY *(Gently, firmly)*: Then it's settled, Alice. That's what you will be.

ALICE: But I live at the Children's Home, Mrs. Bethune. How could I ever get to nursing school?

MARY *(Decisively, leaving her desk)*: We'll talk about that as soon as I get back. Excuse me for a moment, class. *(Exits rapidly)*

BOY *(Threateningly, turning to* GIRL*)*: So I'm too bad to be a preacher, am I? *(He gets a slingshot from his desk.)*

STUDENTS *(Ad lib)*: I dare you. Leave her alone! *(Etc.)*

GIRL *(Fearfully)*: You'd better not do that! I'll tell Mrs. Bethune! *(*MARY *re-enters, briskly;* BOY *quickly hides slingshot.* REV. WATKINS *enters, follows* MARY *to her desk. Class quickly quiets down.)*

MARY (*Standing behind desk*): Class, I asked Reverend Watkins to tell you a little about his life, especially his youth. *(To* REV. WATKINS*)* Reverend, we'd like to hear about your childhood, and how you came to be a school principal. *(Sits at desk)*

WATKINS (*Standing at lectern; to* MARY*):* Thank you, Mrs. Bethune. *(To class)* Good morning, boys and girls. *(Gives a little bow)*

STUDENTS *(Together):* Good morning, Reverend Watkins.

WATKINS: I didn't expect to be making a speech so early, but I'm always glad to talk to our students. *(Takes off glasses, wipes them with handkerchief, then puts them on again)* Mrs. Bethune tells me you've been talking about your plans for the future. My future seemed pretty dismal when I was your age. *(Sighs)* You see, I was an orphan, and I lived at the Children's Home right here in town. (ALICE, *shocked, leans forward.*) But I wanted to be something in life, to get an education, and to help others.

ALICE: You must have been adopted by rich people who could send you away to college.

WATKINS *(Smiling):* That was my secret dream for over twelve years, Alice. However, nobody ever came to adopt me, either rich or poor. I stayed at the Children's Home till I was old enough to go out on my own. I took any job I could get to finish college.

ALICE *(With awe):* You came from the Children's Home, Reverend Watkins, and yet your dreams came true?

WATKINS *(Assertively):* I *made* my dreams come true, young lady, and so can all of you.

MARY *(Graciously):* Thank you. You've been a great help to us, Reverend Watkins.

WATKINS: Please invite me again, and next time, I'll spend more time with you. *(Bowing to* MARY*)* And before I go, I think the class would like to ask you about *your* secret dream, Mrs. Bethune. *(Turns to class)* Isn't that right? *(Students nod their heads and clap their hands.)*

MARY *(Flustered):* I didn't expect the tables to be turned this way. *(Laughs lightly)* Yet I suppose it's only fair.

BOY: Mrs. Bethune, I'll bet you want to be a principal like Rev. Watkins.

MARY: You're getting warm, but not quite. What I really want to do is establish a college one day. My son Albert, Jr. is just an infant, but I want to see him in a good college when he's old enough. And I want to see every other youngster get the same opportunity.

WATKINS *(Sincerely):* I have no doubt that you will build your college, Mrs. Bethune. It's just a matter of time. My only regret is that you'll be leaving us someday.

MARY: My husband said there may be some opportunity for us in Florida. A new railroad's being built on the east coast of the state, and we plan to visit there soon.

WATKINS: I wish you well, Mrs. Bethune. Some of my friends live in Daytona Beach. I hope you'll find time to look them up.

MARY: It will be my pleasure, Reverend Watkins. *(With fervor)* Wherever my journey may lead me, I'm sure I'll spend the rest of my days in helping students like these to have happier and better lives. *(Curtain)*

The renowned Bethune-Cookman College Concert Choir

Scene 3

TIME: *1954*

SETTING: *Same as in Scene 1.*

AT RISE: MARY *sits, holding mortarboard and graduation robe.* ROSE *holds notepad.*

MARY: So then, Rose, my family and I moved here to Daytona Beach, and I opened my tiny school in 1904. (ROSE *jots down some notes.)* There were only five students at the time. In 1923, my school for girls was combined with a boys' school, Cookman Institute of Jacksonville.

ROSE *(Proudly):* And now Bethune-Cookman College has over 1,300 students.

MARY *(Smiling radiantly):* Yes. So you see, Rose, my life has been a grand adventure, and I honestly can say that it still is an adventure.

ROSE *(Scribbling rapidly on notepad):* That's a beautiful quote to end my feature article with, Mrs. Bethune. *(With great enthusiasm)* This is going to be one of the best stories ever printed in our college newspaper.

MARY: I'm eager to read it. *(Shakes a finger at* ROSE) Just you be sure to quote me correctly and get all the facts straight.

ROSE: Oh, I will! I can't afford to make any mistakes. It will give me the chance I need. My career in journalism may depend on how this article turns out.

MARY: Nonsense, your career *and* your future would hardly depend on one little incident. What you become depends largely on what you *do,* hour after hour, day after day, year after year. (MARY *picks up robe.*)

ROSE: Please let me help you with that, Mrs. Bethune. (*Helps* MARY *put on robe*)

MARY: Thank you, my dear. (*Facing* ROSE) Now that we have only a few moments left together, I'll ask you a question, Rose. You've asked me so many.

ROSE (*Flippantly*): Fire away!

MARY: Just what is your secret dream?

ROSE (*A bit defensively*): Why would you want to know that, Mrs. Bethune?

MARY: I always get around to asking that of every young person I meet. Give me an answer quickly. (BERTHA *enters right.*)

BERTHA (*Anxiously*): The program's about to begin. All the seniors are in line and ready to march into the auditorium. Please hurry, Mary. Everyone's waiting for you.

MARY: I'll be there in a moment, Bertha. (BERTHA *exits, and "Pomp and Circumstance" begins to play softly offstage.*)

ROSE: (*Evasively*): We don't have time to talk any longer, Mrs. Bethune. The music has started.

MARY *(Persistently):* Oh yes, we do, Rose. I won't budge until you tell me.

ROSE *(Relenting):* All right. I really dream of publishing my own weekly newspaper.

MARY: Promise me you won't stop until you reach your goal.

ROSE *(Vowing solemnly):* I promise that, one day, I'll have my own newspaper. *(Strains of graduation music grow louder.)*

MARY *(Adjusting mortarboard):* Now, it's time to go. We'll meet again at this same place three years from today, Rose. I'll present you the college newspaper editor's award at your graduation. Is that a deal?

ROSE *(Happily):* Yes, Mrs. Bethune. It's a deal! *(They exit.* MARY, *with head high, leads the way. Music grows louder, and continues to end of march. Curtain)*

The End

Mary McLeod Bethune (second row, left) joins graduates on their way to commencement exercises.

Her Dreams

a poem by ELOISE GREENFIELD
painting by MR. AMOS FERGUSON
from the book UNDER THE SUNDAY TREE

In her dreams
there are sometimes trees
on which hang ornaments
as tall as she
she lifts her arms
to touch them
if she can stretch
high enough to
claim them
they will become
the jewelled moments
of her life.

Response Corner

WRITE A SPEECH

Reach for the Stars!

Write a speech that Mary McLeod Bethune might have given at the graduation ceremony talked about in the play. Remember that it is the fiftieth anniversary of Bethune-Cookman College. Deliver your speech as if you were Mary McLeod Bethune.

PREPARE A REPORT

A Visit with Washington

Research the life and work of another great African American, Booker T. Washington. Prepare a report to share what you learn about Washington. Make a poster showing the information, or write a short biographical sketch.

BETHUNE - COOKMAN
COLLEGE

Her Dreams Came True

With a small group of classmates, talk about the "jeweled moments" of Mary McLeod Bethune's life. Then take turns telling what would be "a dream come true" for each of you.

✏ How is Mary McLeod Bethune an example of Reverend Watkins's message that you can make your dreams come true?

✏ Has this play changed the way you feel about your education? Explain your response.

✏ Do you think that either Mrs. Bethune or the narrator of "Her Dreams" believes that wishing can make dreams come true? Explain your response.

257

Personal journeys can lead people to new places or to discoveries about themselves. The cars in the painting *East River Drive* are traveling in the same direction. However, the lives of the people in the cars are most likely moving in very different directions. What thoughts about personal journeys do you have when you look at this painting?

Art & Literature

East River Drive
by Yvonne Jacquette

Yvonne Jacquette has painted many views of cities, called cityscapes. East River Drive shows a street in New York City that runs along the East River. Imagine that you are looking down on this scene from a tall building. You can see that the lights of the cars form a line that gently curves from the top of the painting to the bottom, helping you to imagine the flow of traffic.

258

Pastel on gray laid paper, 18¾" x 23"
The Metropolitan Musem of Art, New York, NY

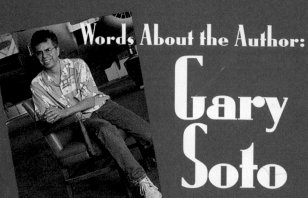

Words About the Author:
Gary Soto

"I think I'm very childlike," says Gary Soto. "I like the *youth* in my poetry. For me that's really important."

It was Gary's youthful outlook on life that led him to start writing stories for young people in addition to poetry. He likes writing short stories because he doesn't have to keep notes. Instead, he says, "When I get an idea for a short story, I pounce on it right away, to keep it from disappearing."

Most of his stories are about experiences he had growing up. He believes he can write best about the things he knows. The kinds of fun that he had appear in many of his stories. Things that were not fun are there too, such as chopping cotton and cutting grapes under the hot California sun. In Gary Soto's stories, you can share in these experiences too.

by Gary Soto

el-a-Pound lane Ride

illustrations by

Jacqueline Rogers

Araceli slipped the rubber band off the morning newspaper. One eye closed, she shot it across the living room at her sleeping cat, Asco, who didn't stir.

"You lazy thing," Araceli muttered, smiling and pushing her long hair behind her ears. Araceli was a slightly built twelve-year-old, skin the color of brown sugar, eyes shiny with triangles of light. She could wiggle a little of her tongue in the gap between her front teeth.

She unfolded the newspaper and glanced at the front page. She grimaced at a photo of a car wreck on Highway 99. It was winter in California's San Joaquin Valley; cold air burned like ice pressed against a warm cheek, and sometimes the fog and rain caused cars to slide off the freeway and buckle like aluminum cans.

But this morning Araceli didn't care about the front page. Her friend Carolina had called last night with more exciting news: she had heard about some airplane rides at Chandler Airfield for almost nothing. More than anything Araceli wanted to fly in an airplane. Everyone she knew had gone up in a plane and come down like an angel. Her mother and father had flown to Hawaii for their tenth wedding anniversary. Her grandfather flew to Reno once a month. Her cousin, who was the manager of a rock group, spent more time airborne between pillowy clouds than on the black asphalt of Los Angeles, his hometown. Her brother, Eddie, a junior in high school and the drum major for the Roosevelt High School marching band, had flown to New York to be in the Macy's Parade. Even her baby cousin, Carlos, had flown from Los Angeles to Guadalajara, shaking a yellow rattle for hours, he was so happy.

Settling into the couch Araceli scoured the paper for news of the plane rides. Toward the back of the paper near the gardening section, wedged between the black-and-white ads for tri-tips and lawn mowers, her eye caught the one-column story: the American Legion was offering nickel-a-pound airplane rides to benefit the Children's Hospital.

"Finally," Araceli beamed, rereading the story two more times. "I'm going to fly!" She spread her arms like wings and flew into the kitchen, where she fixed herself a bowl of cornflakes and made some coffee. Instead of milk, Araceli poured coffee laced with a splash of cream over her cereal, a concoction she'd learned about from her grandmother. She liked the taste of hot coffee over soggy cornflakes—and she liked the idea that she was grown up enough to drink coffee.

Her father came into the kitchen looking for the newspaper. His hair was tousled, and his eyes glazed from a hard sleep.

"Morning, Dad," Araceli greeted him, not looking up from the comics. She automatically handed him the sports section.

"Morning, sugar," he said groggily, taking the section and staggering to the kitchen counter, where he poured coffee into his Raiders cup. He took the paper and coffee into the living room.

Araceli rinsed her bowl at the sink and straightened the newspaper. She knew she had to be extra good because she was going to beg her dad to take her to Chandler Airfield. She danced into the living room and asked, "Dad, do you want another cup of coffee?"

Still reading his newspaper, her father held out his half-empty cup. She took it to the kitchen and carefully measured out the hot black brew from their Mr. Coffee, poured in a dash of half-and-half, and brought the cup back to him.

"Dad," Araceli said, after he'd pursed his lips and sipped his coffee with a quiet slurp. "Dad, we should do something special this weekend."

Having turned to the front section of the paper, her father was reading about the freeway accident. "Yeah, you can clean up your room. Mom will be home this evening." Araceli's mother was on a retreat in the mountains with other women from church.

"It's clean already."

"Clean it some more." A smile played at the corners of her father's mouth. He was kidding her.

"No, Dad, I want to go flying."

Her father put down the paper and gave Araceli a

baffled look. He touched her forehead and asked playfully, "Do you have a fever?"

"Dad," she wheedled. "Dad, they have this thing where you can pay a nickel for every pound you weigh and then you get to fly."

"You're gonna make me poor."

"I'm not fat." She knew she was halfway to convincing her father.

"Well, tell me more about this plane ride," her father said.

"We're helping the world," Araceli explained. "The money goes to Children's Hospital. Think of all the babies we will save if we go and get on the plane. The American Legion will be able to buy all these machines, and then everybody will be OK."

Her father laughed. "How much do you weigh? They're gonna make a fortune off you."

"Every little bit helps."

"You're funny," her father said. "I'm going to shave. We'll go—*ahorita*.[1]"

"All right!" Araceli yelled, jumping up and down and twirling so that her nightie flared.

Araceli went into the bathroom and, still wearing her flannel nightgown printed with horses, stood on the cold scale. She weighed 68 pounds. She stood on tiptoe, hoping it would make her weigh less. The needle twitched, but her weight remained the same.

---

[1]right now

Father and daughter dressed for the day. "It's gonna rain buckets, I think," Araceli's father said, stepping out onto the porch.

The wind was shaking the top of the elm in front of their house. The sky was as gray as cement. The neighbor's chimney was sending up billows of smoke that immediately broke apart in the wind.

They settled into the Honda and drove west toward Chandler Airfield, which was at the edge of town. Araceli's father turned on the headlights and swished the wipers to clear the mist from the windshield. The heater warmed their feet.

"Are you sure you want to fly?" he asked. He wasn't teasing her now. He peered through the windshield at the dark sky. A few drops of rain blurred the glass.

"I'm not scared," Araceli said, smiling stiffly at her father. She worked her tongue into the gap between her front teeth. She wanted to fly; she was determined to do it.

As they approached the airfield, they spotted a single-engine airplane taking off. It seemed effortless: a short run on the airstrip, and then it was up, up, up.

The mist had become a soft, slanting rain. Araceli and her father got out of the car and—hand-in-gloved-hand, their jacket hoods over their heads—hurried across the parking lot to the long line of people waiting to fly.

After a few minutes in line her father said, "I don't know, sugar."

"Come on, Dad. It's not that long."

"Not long? There's only two planes and all these people."

To the west, a feather of blue was showing between the dark clouds.

"See, it might even clear up," Araceli argued, pointing to that faraway blue sky.

A few people in line gave up and raced back to their cars. The line stepped ahead like a centipede. Araceli's father, shuddering from the cold, suggested, "I have an idea. You can wait in the car and I'll wait in line. We'll take turns every ten minutes." He looked down at his watch. "It's fifteen to twelve."

Araceli nodded. "Fair enough."

She raced back to the car, leaping over puddles, and immediately flicked on the heater. She held her hands up to the vents and sneezed.

She stayed in the car for exactly eight minutes and then raced back to the line. She was surprised how wet her father looked. The hood of his jacket was plastered to his head, and his eyeglasses were so splattered with rain that he couldn't see her clearly enough to recognize her. She had to tug on his arm to get his attention.

"Dad, it's me."

"Sugar, it's really starting to come down," he said.

"It's not that bad."

"It is. The man said they might cancel the flights."

"Come on, Dad."

A large family in front of them gave up, in spite of tantrums from two of the children. They hurried back to their station wagon, and suddenly Araceli was almost to the gate.

"You go. I'll wait for you," her father said.

"Come on, Dad," Araceli insisted.

"I weigh too much," he chuckled. "I didn't bring the checkbook."

At that moment Araceli's friend, Carolina, walked slowly out of the gate clinging to her father's arm. They had just landed with the latest load of passengers.

"Carolina," Araceli shouted through cupped hands. "How was it?"

Carolina looked in Araceli's direction but didn't say anything. Her eyes seemed shiny, as if she had gotten a lot of rain in them.

"What's wrong with her?" Araceli asked her father.

"Maybe she's sick. I'm getting cold."

"I'm not cold," Araceli lied. "In fact, I'm hot." She undid the top button of her jacket.

When they were finally next in line, her father turned to Araceli and said, "You can change your mind."

"No way," she said. She hopped up on the scale and smiled at her weight: 74 pounds, wet clothes and all. "See, Dad, I'm not fat."

Her father paid and was given a stub that declared his donation to be tax deductible.

"Hold on," Araceli heard her father say, but the advice that followed was eaten by the wind. A man ushered her to the airplane, where a man, woman, and boy sat waiting. Araceli climbed on board next to the boy. She was glad to get out of the rain and wind, but she was shocked by how small the compartment was. There was hardly room for her to move her feet. Even the airplane's windshield was small, like a little picture frame.

"Buckle your seat belts," the pilot said.

Araceli strapped herself in and smiled. She stopped smiling as the engine began to roar. The noise was deafening. She held her gloved hands over her ears and saw that the other passengers were doing the same. They were large, couch-potato types, and they all smelled of wet wool. She wondered how much it had cost that family to fly, and then she wondered if the airplane could get off the ground with all that weight.

"This is going to be fun," she said over the roar of the engine.

The boy looked doubtfully at Araceli.

The airplane maneuvered onto the runway. Araceli leaned forward between the mother and father opposite her. She wanted to get a peek at the pilot turning knobs, flicking switches, and adjusting levers. She saw him pull back the throttle, and the airplane began to fishtail down the runway.

The plane seemed to move slowly, and for the first time Araceli worried that they might crash. She wished that these heavy people were not on board. She was upset by the thought that, if the plane crashed, she would be squashed like a bug under their weight.

Araceli closed her eyes and tried to get a sense of when the airplane left the ground. She wanted to memorize this sensation. She wanted to write in her diary later, "I was off the ground, and it was cool."

But when she opened her eyes, she discovered that they were still rolling down the runway. She screamed, "Come on, get us in the air."

The boy and his parents looked at Araceli. They looked like turtles, slow, with unblinking eyes. The pilot didn't turn his head.

The airplane bumped twice on the runway, and then they were airborne, the wings tipping left, then right, as the airplane climbed.

I'm flying, Araceli thought. She made the sign of the cross and muttered, "I'm not scared."

The airplane dipped and rocked, and Araceli's face slammed into the boy's shoulder. He turned and looked at Araceli but didn't say a word.

"Hold on to your hats," the pilot said calmly. "Winds are out of the northwest."

The airplane vibrated and shuddered, and everyone except the pilot screamed when it bumped through an air pocket. Araceli made the sign of the cross a second time as she closed her eyes to pray. When she opened her eyes, blinking slowly because it all seemed like a dream, she saw a patch of blue in the distance. She thought she might be in heaven, until she smelled the wet coats of the couch potatoes. This is not heaven, she thought.

The plane rocked again, and the left wing dipped. Araceli recalled the roller coaster she'd ridden in Santa Cruz, a big wooden structure called the Big Dipper. She had been nine at the time and foolish—so foolish that when the roller coaster sped earthward, she had closed her eyes and screamed. The wind had ripped the gum out of her wide-open mouth and tore a dollar bill from her fingers.

But now she was four thousand feet above her hometown. She was twelve, not nine, and still she was scared.

The turtle-faced boy and his parents mumbled among themselves. They fumbled with their seat belts, and the father, leaning into the pilot's shoulder, asked, "These doors got locks?"

The pilot laughed, "No, of course not," and gripped the controls as the plane shuddered. "There's nothing to worry about."

Araceli wondered if the airplane was equipped with parachutes. She looked around. She saw only an old orange T-shirt. If only I could find some string, she thought. I could make my own parachute.

When the airplane banked right, Araceli slid into the corner. The pilot pointed out landmarks: the Fresno Convention Center, the water tower, Kearny Park. The stadium stood out in the distance, its lights on as evidence of taxpayers' money being wasted. He spotted a wreck on Highway 99.

The pilot pointed with his gloved hand, but Araceli couldn't see the landmarks from the back of the plane. She stared at the back of the woman's jacket and began to feel better. She thought that if they crashed, she would be cushioned by this family's big jackets. She would survive the crash and tell about it on TV.

Araceli once again saw a patch of blue sky. She pointed a finger and screamed over the engine noise to the pilot, "Can't you fly over there?"

"What?" he yelled back.

"Don't you think it's better over there?" The blue patch was slowly filling with gray clouds. "Never mind." She fell back in her seat, chewed on a fingernail, and crossed herself for the third time.

They circled once and then returned for landing. Araceli began to pray in earnest as the airplane kept wiggling and dropped suddenly.

"Hold on," the pilot warned. His sunglasses had slid crookedly across his face.

The airplane landed safely, and Araceli was glad that she got away with just a few jolts. She couldn't hear because the sound of the engine continued to play over and over in her ears.

She jumped from the cockpit without thanking the pilot or even glancing at her traveling companions, who were shaking out their stiff legs. She raced to her father and hugged him, hard.

"How was it, sugar?" he asked, drinking coffee from a Styrofoam cup.

"Great! I love flying." She tried to climb into his arms, but her father took her by the hand and walked her back to the car. She was glad when the car got going and the heater blew hot air on her cold toes. She took off her socks and shoes and saw that her toes were wrinkled, as if she had stayed in the bathtub too long.

They returned home to find Araceli's mother doing aerobics to oldies music.

"Hi, Mom, I went flying," Araceli yelled. She threw her arms around her mother's waist and said, "I missed you."

Her mother turned down the volume on the stereo. "You went flying?"

"Yeah, it was a special thing. We were helping children who are sick."

"You weren't scared?"

"Of course not!"

She explained the nickel-a-pound airplane rides and the beautiful sensations of flying. She didn't tell her mother about the burly family of three.

Araceli took a hot bath and lounged around the house, occasionally hugging her father, then her mother, then Asco. She even smiled at her brother, who had come home wet as a duck after playing football with his friends.

As she watched TV Araceli gripped the arms of the chair. When a United Airlines commercial came on, she changed the channel. She didn't want to think about flying—she wanted to think about being on the ground.

She ate dinner and went to bed early. Nestled safely in bed she said some more prayers and thought about the rain in Carolina's eyes. They were tears, she realized, and then, to her surprise, Araceli began to cry big, hot, nickel-sized tears. Flying was no fun at all.

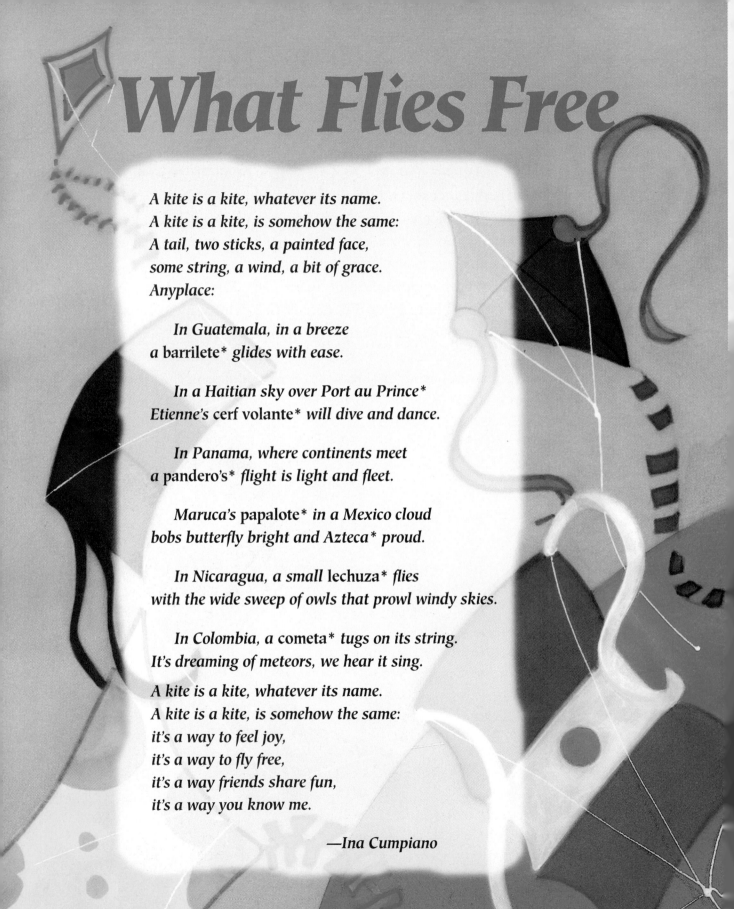

What Flies Free

A kite is a kite, whatever its name.
A kite is a kite, is somehow the same:
A tail, two sticks, a painted face,
some string, a wind, a bit of grace.
Anyplace:

In Guatemala, in a breeze
a barrilete* glides with ease.

In a Haitian sky over Port au Prince*
Etienne's cerf volante* will dive and dance.

In Panama, where continents meet
a pandero's* flight is light and fleet.

Maruca's papalote* in a Mexico cloud
bobs butterfly bright and Azteca* proud.

In Nicaragua, a small lechuza* flies
with the wide sweep of owls that prowl windy skies.

In Colombia, a cometa* tugs on its string.
It's dreaming of meteors, we hear it sing.

A kite is a kite, whatever its name.
A kite is a kite, is somehow the same:
it's a way to feel joy,
it's a way to fly free,
it's a way friends share fun,
it's a way you know me.

—Ina Cumpiano

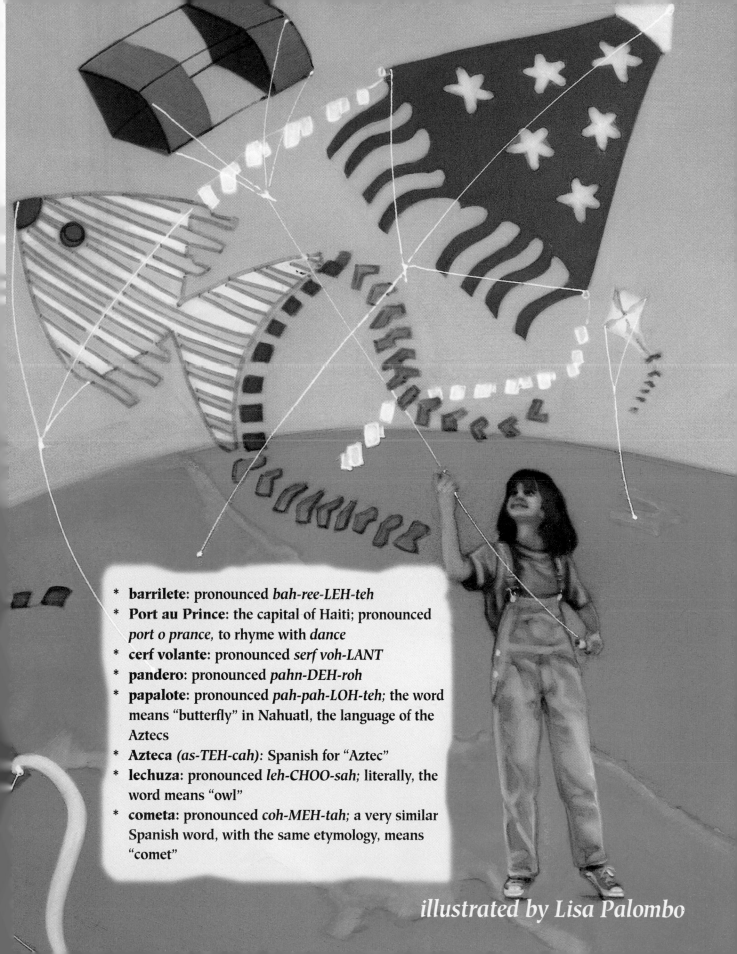

* **barrilete**: pronounced *bah-ree-LEH-teh*
* **Port au Prince**: the capital of Haiti; pronounced *port o prance*, to rhyme with *dance*
* **cerf volante**: pronounced *serf voh-LANT*
* **pandero**: pronounced *pahn-DEH-roh*
* **papalote**: pronounced *pah-pah-LOH-teh;* the word means "butterfly" in Nahuatl, the language of the Aztecs
* **Azteca** *(as-TEH-cah)*: Spanish for "Aztec"
* **lechuza**: pronounced *leh-CHOO-sah;* literally, the word means "owl"
* **cometa**: pronounced *coh-MEH-tah;* a very similar Spanish word, with the same etymology, means "comet"

illustrated by Lisa Palombo

RESPONSE

Fly for Almost Free

Araceli saw an advertisement in the newspaper for the nickel-a-pound plane ride. Write a radio ad for such an offer. Make sure you include information about *who*, *what*, *when*, *where*, *why*, and *how* in your ad. Then broadcast it to your classmates.

Can You Spare a Nickel?

Work with other students to figure out the cost of a group plane ride. Write your weights on slips of paper. Gather the slips and find the total weight. Then find your group's cost based on a nickel a pound.

CORNER

Go Hang a Kite!

Araceli wanted to fly as freely as a kite, but the weather and her fears weighed her down. Don't let this happen to you! Design and make a colorful kite to hang from the ceiling of your classroom.

What Do You Think?

- Why does Araceli want to fly? Why does she change her mind about flying?

- Would you have gone on the plane in the rain? Explain your response.

- In what way do Araceli and the narrator of "What Flies Free" have the same view of flying? How does Araceli's view change?

279

Christopher

a newspaper article by Warren Perley

Boy pilot resumes historic

MONTREAL (UPI) — Fortified with a meal of two hamburgers and "a tiger in his heart," 11-year-old Christopher Marshall resumed his quest Monday to become the youngest person to retrace Charles Lindbergh's solo trans-Atlantic flight.

Christopher, accompanied by former "Top Gun" Navy pilot Randy Cunningham, took off from Dorval Airport in a Mooney 252, single-engine aircraft during a mid-afternoon rain shower.

"I'm really happy and not nervous," the boy said when asked his feelings about facing possible head-winds of up to 100 mph over the icy North Atlantic. "If anything happened over the Atlantic, we'd have to ditch in the water. But we have lots of emergency equipment. I'm a little bit impatient for this trip."

Cunningham, 46, a decorated Vietnam War ace who commanded the elite "Top Gun" Navy fighter pilot school, is accompanying Christopher on the 3,650-mile journey, which started last Thursday in San Diego and is supposed to end this week in Paris.

Christopher, clad in a blue flight suit with his name sewn on the chest, does the flying, propped up by two foam cushions allowing him to see out the windshield.

When asked if he felt like Christopher's babysitter, Cunningham replied: "We're buddies. He's a good little guy. He's got a tiger in his heart. We get along real fine."

The flight plans called for a stop overnight in either Wabush, Labrador, about 700 miles northeast of Montreal, or a community near Frobisher Bay, about 1,200 miles northeast of Montreal.

They will continue Tuesday to Greenland and will stop overnight Tuesday in Iceland before flying on to Scotland and Paris. If all goes well, they could arrive as soon as Wednesday at Lebourget, the Paris airfield where Lindbergh landed in

Marshall  EXTRA

trans-Atlantic crossing

Seven private pilots have been lost over Greenland and Iceland this year, Canadian aviation officials say.

The plane the boy is flying is a $240,000, four-seater Mooney equipped with thermal survival suits in case it is forced to ditch in the ocean. It also has two life rafts, beacons, flares, emergency food rations and mosquito netting.

By the time the journey ends in Paris, Christopher will have flown roughly the same route that Lindbergh took when he piloted the Spirit of St. Louis from a San Diego aircraft plant to France 61 years ago.

Christopher, who starts the fifth grade in September at Oceano, Calif., said he got the idea to make the trip two months ago "to show kids across America that they can achieve their dreams."

1927. Lindbergh's flight was the first by a solo pilot across the Atlantic and was greeted by wild celebrations in Paris and followed by banner headlines in newspapers throughout the world.

Christopher's endurance, the weather and headwinds are the three factors which will affect the pace of the journey, Cunningham said.

"My job is to take care of Chris and to prove that aviation is safe," Cunningham said. "I'm not going to go out there and put us in hazard."

CHRISTOPHER MARSHALL
UP, UP & AWAY

by Claudia Cangilla McAdam from *Cricket* magazine

When he was born, doctors thought Christopher
Marshall would never walk. But in the fifteen years
since then, Christopher has proven he can do just
about anything he puts his mind to—including setting
world records.

NEW YORK . . .

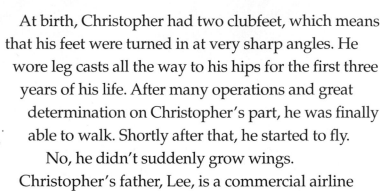

At birth, Christopher had two clubfeet, which means that his feet were turned in at very sharp angles. He wore leg casts all the way to his hips for the first three years of his life. After many operations and great determination on Christopher's part, he was finally able to walk. Shortly after that, he started to fly.

No, he didn't suddenly grow wings. Christopher's father, Lee, is a commercial airline pilot, and when his son was very young, he began taking him up in a private plane. "His dad brought home a huge paper layout of a 727, which he spread out on the floor," says Christopher's mother, Gail. "Christopher loved to study the layout. At age four, he could tell you what every button and switch on the plane was for." By age seven, Christopher was taking flying lessons.

In the summer of 1987, the young pilot from Oceano, California, became a world-record setter. At age ten, he was the youngest person ever to fly coast to coast across the United States—and back again.

Because a pilot has to be at least sixteen in order to solo, his instructor flew with him. But Christopher, propped up by three pillows so he could see, handled the controls himself the entire time.

He believes that the best part of the flight was flying through severe thunderstorms over Mississippi. "I thought the storms were a lot of fun," he says. "The plane bounced so much, it was like a roller-coaster ride. I wanted to keep on going, but my instructor told me I should land the plane before we got hurt."

In 1988, Christopher set another record when, at age eleven, he became the youngest pilot to fly across the Atlantic Ocean.

The choice of copilot for Christopher's transatlantic flight was easy. He asked his real-life hero, Randy "Duke" Cunningham, to join him on the record-setting trip. Randy, who is one of America's most decorated combat pilots, flew over three hundred missions during the Vietnam War. He also flew the MiG stunt planes in the movie *Top Gun*.

The flight across the Atlantic was more than 3,600 miles. Before Christopher took off from New York, his single-engine plane was checked out and loaded up with survival gear in case he and Randy had to make an emergency water landing. The gear included an inflatable boat, dry suits, and extra food.

With a smile and a wave of his hand, Christopher left New York. He stopped in Montreal, Canada, for fueling, and then headed for Greenland. After landing long enough to refuel at Farewell on the southern tip of Greenland, Christopher and Randy took off on the next leg of their journey.

...TO PARIS

"After we took off, we flew for a while and then passed a little island," Christopher says. "Then we flew about 275 miles farther out."

Over the deep waters of the Atlantic, terror struck the young pilot. "Suddenly, I noticed that the oil pressure was going down, and the oil temperature was going up." Christopher and Randy were horrified to see oil spraying out of the hood. They would have to make an emergency landing!

"I whipped down at 235 miles per hour," Christopher recalls. "We flew fifty feet off the ground, and the water was blue with icebergs sticking up all over the place." He remembers thinking, What if we have to go down? I don't know how I'm going to get into my dry suit, and how will I get the boat out? Copilot Cunningham said that he'd never been so scared—not even in his combat missions over Vietnam.

Cunningham took over and managed to land on the tiny island of Kulusuk, about 275 miles off the southeast coast of Greenland. Fifteen people were living there, and they took the pilots into their homes. "I was in Paris waiting for them," Christopher's mother says, "and no one knew where they were. I was thinking maybe they were down in the ocean." She was frantic. Reporters kept calling her for news of the plane, and she had none.

On Kulusuk, Christopher discovered that the mechanic who checked out the plane in Greenland had forgotten to replace the oil dipstick—a human error that could have cost two lives.

The two pilots stayed overnight with their new friends, and the next day, with a new dipstick in place, Christopher took off again.

Christopher hopped the plane from Greenland to Iceland to Scotland and finally to Paris where he was greeted by a cheering crowd. His mother was overjoyed to see him. "When we pulled up, I had all these goose bumps," Chris says.

Setting records isn't the most important thing to Christopher. His earlier record for being the youngest to fly across the United States no longer stands, but he doesn't mind. "Records are meant to be broken," he says.

What *is* important to him is flying. It always has been. Christopher's father says that aviation isn't a job, it's a way of life. "You've got to love it to do it," he says, and Christopher has proven that he does indeed love it. When other kids were reading nursery rhymes, he was reading his father's flight plans.

He knew very early what he wanted to do with his life. Now his biggest thrill is to watch the earth drop away on takeoffs as he soars a mile or more into the sky. "I like the feeling of going fast," he says. His next goal is to fly around the world.

Christopher's hobby isn't a cheap one. Flying lessons are expensive, and his month-long trip around the globe will cost at least half a million dollars. Christopher must rely on getting businesses to sponsor him. He also helps to meet expenses through the sale of T-shirts and through special dinners and other fund-raising events.

When he is old enough, Christopher would like to be a commercial airline pilot like his dad and serve in the navy reserve. He says that he'll work hard to reach his goals. His advice to his friends and all other kids is very simple: "Go for it! The sky's the limit!"

HATCHET

by Gary Paulsen
illustrated by John Rosato

Brian is flying 7,000 feet above the Canadian wilderness on the way to visit his father. He is enjoying his first flight in a small plane, until the unthinkable happens.

Newbery Honor

The pilot sat large, his hands lightly on the wheel, feet on the rudder pedals. He seemed more a machine than a man, an extension of the plane. On the dashboard in front of him Brian saw dials, switches, meters, knobs, levers, cranks, lights, handles that were wiggling and flickering, all indicating nothing that he understood and the pilot seemed the same way. Part of the plane, not human.

When he saw Brian look at him, the pilot seemed to open up a bit and he smiled. "Ever fly in the copilot's seat before?" He leaned over and lifted the headset off his right ear and put it on his temple, yelling to overcome the sound of the engine.

Brian shook his head. He had never been in any kind of plane, never seen the cockpit of a plane except in films or on television. It was loud and confusing. "First time."

"It's not as complicated as it looks. Good plane like this almost flies itself." The pilot shrugged. "Makes my job easy." He took Brian's left arm. "Here, put your hands on the controls, your feet on the rudder pedals, and I'll show you what I mean."

Brian shook his head. "I'd better not."

"Sure. Try it . . ."

Brian reached out and took the wheel in a grip so tight his knuckles were

white. He pushed his feet down on the pedals. The plane slewed suddenly to the right.

"Not so hard. Take her light, take her light."

Brian eased off, relaxed his grip. The burning in his eyes was forgotten momentarily as the vibration of the plane came through the wheel and the pedals. It seemed almost alive.

"See?" The pilot let go of his wheel, raised his hands in the air and took his feet off the pedals to show Brian he was actually flying the plane alone. "Simple. Now turn the wheel a little to the right and push on the right rudder pedal a small amount."

Brian turned the wheel slightly and the plane immediately banked to the right, and when he pressed on the right rudder pedal the nose slid across the horizon to the right. He left off on the pressure and straightened the wheel and the plane righted itself.

"Now you can turn. Bring her back to the left a little."

Brian turned the wheel left, pushed on the left pedal, and the plane came back around. "It's easy." He smiled. "At least this part."

The pilot nodded. "All of flying is easy. Just takes learning. Like everything else. Like everything else." He took the controls back, then reached up and rubbed his left shoulder. "Aches and pains—must be getting old."

Brian let go of the controls and moved his feet away from the pedals as the pilot put his hands on the wheel. "Thank you . . ."

But the pilot had put his headset back on and the gratitude was lost in the engine noise and things went back to Brian looking out the window at the ocean of trees and lakes. The burning eyes did not come back, but memories did, came flooding in. The words. Always the words.

Divorce.

The Secret.

Fights.

Split.

The big split. Brian's father did not understand as Brian did, knew only that Brian's mother wanted to break the marriage apart. The split had come and then the divorce, all so fast, and the court had left him with his mother except for the summers and what the judge called "visitation rights." So formal. Brian hated judges as he hated lawyers. Judges that leaned over the bench and asked Brian if he understood where he was to live and why. Judges who did not know what had really happened. Judges with the caring look that meant nothing as lawyers said legal phrases that meant nothing.

In the summer Brian would live with his father. In the school year, with his mother. That's what the judge said after looking at papers on his desk and listening to the lawyers talk. Talk. Words.

Now the plane lurched slightly to the right and Brian looked at the pilot. He was rubbing his shoulder again and there was the sudden smell of body gas in the plane. Brian turned back to avoid embarrassing the pilot, who was obviously in some discomfort. Must have stomach troubles.

So this summer, this first summer when he was allowed to have "visitation rights" with his father, with the divorce only one month old, Brian was heading north. His father was a mechanical engineer who had designed or invented a new drill bit for

> ## "All of flying is easy. Just takes learning. Like everything else."

oil drilling, a self-cleaning, self-sharpening bit. He was working in the oil fields of Canada, up on the tree line where the tundra started and the forests ended. Brian was riding up from New York with some drilling equipment—it was lashed down in the rear of the plane next to a fabric bag the pilot had called a survival pack, which had emergency supplies in case they had to make an emergency landing—that had to be specially made in the city, riding in a bushplane with the pilot named Jim or Jake or something who had turned out to be an all right guy, letting him fly and all.

Except for the smell. Now there was a constant odor, and Brian took another look at the pilot, found him rubbing the shoulder and down the arm now, the left arm, letting go more gas and wincing. Probably something he ate, Brian thought.

His mother had driven him from the city to meet the plane at Hampton where it came to pick up the drilling equipment. A drive in silence, a long drive in silence. Two and a half hours

of sitting in the car, staring out the window just as he was now staring out the window of the plane. Once, after an hour, when they were out of the city she turned to him.

"Look, can't we talk this over? Can't we talk this out? Can't you tell me what's bothering you?"

And there were the words again. Divorce. Split. The Secret. How could he tell her what he knew? So he had remained silent, shook his head and continued to stare unseeing at the countryside, and his mother had gone back to driving only to speak to him one more time when they were close to Hampton.

She reached over the back of the seat and brought up a paper sack. "I got something for you, for the trip."

Brian took the sack and opened the top. Inside there was a hatchet, the kind with a steel handle and a rubber handgrip. The head was in a stout leather case that had a brass-riveted belt loop.

"It goes on your belt." His mother spoke now without looking at him.

> "Look, can't we talk this over? Can't we talk this out? Can't you tell me what's bothering you?"

There were some farm trucks on the road now and she had to weave through them and watch traffic. "The man at the store said you could use it. You know. In the woods with your father."

Dad, he thought. Not "my father." My dad. "Thanks. It's really nice." But the words sounded hollow, even to Brian.

"Try it on. See how it looks on your belt."

And he would normally have said no, would normally have said no that it looked too hokey to have a hatchet on your belt. Those were the normal things he would say. But her voice was thin, had a sound like something thin that would break if you touched it, and he felt bad for not speaking to her. Knowing what he knew, even with the anger, the hot white hate of his anger at her, he still felt bad for not speaking to her, and so to humor her he loosened his belt and pulled the right side out and put the hatchet on and rethreaded the belt.

"Scootch around so I can see."

He moved around in the seat, feeling only slightly ridiculous.

She nodded. "Just like a scout. My little scout." And there was the tenderness in her voice that she had when he was small, the tenderness that she had when he was small and sick, with a cold, and she put her hand on his forehead, and the burning came into his eyes again and he had turned away from her and looked out the window, forgotten the hatchet on his belt and so arrived at the plane with the hatchet still on his belt.

Because it was a bush flight from a small airport there had been no security and the plane had been waiting, with the engine running when he arrived and he had grabbed his suitcase and pack bag and run for the plane without stopping to remove the hatchet.

So it was still on his belt. At first he had been embarrassed but the pilot had said nothing about it and Brian forgot it as they took off and began flying.

More smell now. Bad. Brian turned

again to glance at the pilot, who had both hands on his stomach and was grimacing in pain, reaching for the left shoulder again as Brian watched.

"Don't know, kid . . ." The pilot's words were a hiss, barely audible. "Bad aches here. Bad aches. Thought it was something I ate but . . ."

He stopped as a fresh spasm of pain hit him. Even Brian could see how bad it was—the pain drove the pilot back into the seat, back and down.

"I've never had anything like this . . ."

The pilot reached for the switch on his mike cord, his hand coming up in a small arc from his stomach, and he flipped the switch and said, "This is flight four six . . ."

And now a jolt took him like a hammerblow, so forcefully that he seemed to crush back into the seat, and Brian reached for him, could not understand at first what it was, could not know.

And then knew.

Brian knew. The pilot's mouth went rigid, he swore and jerked a short

series of slams into the seat, holding his shoulder now. Swore and hissed, "Chest! Oh God, my chest is coming apart!"

Brian knew now.

The pilot was having a heart attack. Brian had been in the shopping mall with his mother when a man in front of Paisley's store had suffered a heart attack. He had gone down and screamed about his chest. An old man. Much older than the pilot.

Brian knew.

The pilot was having a heart attack and even as the knowledge came to Brian he saw the pilot slam into the seat one more time, one more awful time he slammed back into the seat and his right leg jerked, pulling the plane to the side in a sudden twist and his head fell forward and spit came. Spit came from the corners of his mouth and his legs contracted up, up into the seat, and his eyes rolled back in his head until there was only white.

Only white for his eyes and the smell became worse, filled the cockpit, and all of it so fast, so incredibly fast that Brian's mind could not take it in at first. Could only see it in stages.

The pilot had been talking, just a moment ago, complaining of the pain. He had been talking.

Then the jolts had come.

The jolts that took the pilot back had come, and now Brian sat and there was a strange feeling of silence in the thrumming roar of the engine—a strange feeling of silence and being alone. Brian was stopped.

He was stopped. Inside he was stopped. He could not think past what he saw, what he felt. All was stopped. The very core of him, the very center of Brian Robeson was stopped and stricken with a white-flash of horror, a terror so intense that his breathing, his thinking, and nearly his heart had stopped.

Stopped.

Seconds passed, seconds that became all of his life, and he began to know what he was seeing, began to understand what he saw and that was worse, so much worse that he wanted to make his mind freeze again.

He was sitting in a bushplane roaring seven thousand feet above the northern wilderness with a pilot who had suffered a massive heart attack and who was either dead or in something close to a coma.

He was alone.

In the roaring plane with no pilot he was alone.

Alone.

For a time that he could not understand Brian could do nothing. Even after his mind began working and he could see what had happened he could do nothing. It was as if his hands and arms were lead.

Then he looked for ways for it not to have happened. Be asleep, his mind screamed at the pilot. Just be asleep and your eyes will open now and your hands will take the controls and your feet will move to the pedals—but it did not happen.

The pilot did not move except that his head rolled on a neck impossibly loose as the plane hit a small bit of turbulence.

The plane.

Somehow the plane was still flying. Seconds had passed, nearly a minute, and the plane flew on as if nothing had happened and he had to do something, had to do something but did not know what.

Help.

He had to help.

He stretched one hand toward the pilot, saw that his fingers were trem-

bling, and touched the pilot on the chest. He did not know what to do. He knew there were procedures, that you could do mouth-to-mouth on victims of heart attacks and push their chests—C.P.R.—but he did not know how to do it and in any case could not do it with the pilot, who was sitting up in the seat and still strapped in with his seatbelt. So he touched the pilot with the tips of his fingers, touched him on the chest and could feel nothing, no heartbeat, no rise and fall of breathing. Which meant that the pilot was almost certainly dead.

"Please," Brian said. But did not know what or who to ask. "Please . . ."

The plane lurched again, hit more turbulence, and Brian felt the nose drop. It did not dive, but the nose went down slightly and the down-angle increased the speed, and he knew that at this angle, this slight angle down, he would ultimately fly into the trees. He could see them ahead on the horizon where before he could see only sky.

He had to fly it somehow. Had to fly the plane. He had to help himself. The pilot was gone, beyond anything he

301

could do. He had to try and fly the plane.

He turned back in the seat, facing the front, and put his hands—still trembling—on the control wheel, his feet gently on the rudder pedals. You pulled back on the stick to raise the plane, he knew that from reading. You always pulled back on the wheel. He gave it a tug and it slid back toward him easily. Too easily. The plane, with the increased speed from the tilt down, swooped eagerly up and drove Brian's stomach down. He pushed the wheel back in, went too far this time, and the plane's nose went below the horizon and the engine speed increased with the shallow dive.

Too much.

He pulled back again, more gently this time, and the nose floated up again, too far but not as violently as before, then down a bit too much, and up again, very easily, and the front of the engine cowling settled. When he had it aimed at the horizon and it seemed to be steady, he held the wheel where it was, let out his breath—which he had been holding all this time—and tried to think what to do next.

It was a clear, blue-sky day with fluffy bits of clouds here and there and he looked out the window for a moment, hoping to see something, a town or village, but there was nothing. Just the green of the trees, endless green, and lakes scattered more and more thickly as the plane flew—where?

He was flying but did not know where, had no idea where he was going. He looked at the dashboard of the plane, studied the dials and hoped to get some help, hoped to find a compass, but it was all so confusing, a jumble of numbers and lights. One lighted display in the top center of the dashboard said the number 342, another next to it said 22. Down beneath that were dials with lines that seemed to indicate what the wings were doing, tipping or moving, and one dial with a needle pointing to the number 70, which he thought—only thought— might be the altimeter. The device that told him his height above the ground.

Or above sea level. Somewhere he had read something about altimeters but he couldn't remember what, or where, or anything about them.

Slightly to the left and below the altimeter he saw a small rectangular panel with a lighted dial and two knobs. His eyes had passed over it two or three times before he saw what was written in tiny letters on top of the panel. TRANSMITTER 221 was stamped in the metal and it hit him, finally, that this was the radio.

The radio. Of course. He had to use the radio. When the pilot had—had been hit that way (he couldn't bring himself to say that the pilot was dead, couldn't think it), he had been trying to use the radio.

Brian looked to the pilot. The headset was still on his head, turned sideways a bit from his jamming back into the seat, and the microphone switch was clipped into his belt.

Brian had to get the headset from the pilot. Had to reach over and get the headset from the pilot or he would not be able to use the radio to call for help. He had to reach over . . .

His hands began trembling again. He did not want to touch the pilot, did not want to reach for him. But he had to. Had to get the radio. He lifted his hands from the wheel, just slightly, and

303

held them waiting to see what would happen. The plane flew on normally, smoothly.

All right, he thought. Now. Now to do this thing. He turned and reached for the headset, slid it from the pilot's head, one eye on the plane, waiting for it to dive. The headset came easily, but the microphone switch at the pilot's belt was jammed in and he had to pull to get it loose. When he pulled, his elbow bumped the wheel and pushed it in and the plane started down in a shallow dive. Brian grabbed the wheel and pulled it back, too hard again, and the plane went through another series of stomach-wrenching swoops up and down before he could get it under control.

When things had settled again he pulled at the mike cord once more and at last jerked the cord free. It took him another second or two to place the headset on his own head and position the small microphone tube in front of his mouth. He had seen the pilot use it, had seen him depress the switch at his belt, so Brian pushed the switch in and blew into the mike.

He heard the sound of his breath in the headset. "Hello! Is there anybody listening on this? Hello . . ."

He repeated it two or three times and then waited but heard nothing except his own breathing.

Panic came then. He had been afraid, had been stopped with the terror of what was happening, but now panic came and he began to scream into the microphone, scream over and over.

> **H**e heard the sound of his breath in the headset. "Hello! Is there anybody listening on this? Hello. . ."

"Help! Somebody help me! I'm in this plane and don't know . . . don't know . . . don't know . . ."

And he started crying with the screams, crying and slamming his hands against the wheel of the plane, causing it to jerk down, then back up.

But again, he heard nothing but the sound of his own sobs in the microphone, his own screams mocking him, coming back into his ears.

The microphone. Awareness cut into him. He had used a CB radio in his uncle's pickup once. You had to turn the mike switch off to hear anybody else. He reached to his belt and released the switch.

For a second all he heard was the *whusssh* of the empty air waves. Then, through the noise and static he heard a voice.

"Whoever is calling on this radio net, I repeat, release your mike switch—you are covering me. You are covering me. Over."

It stopped and Brian hit his mike switch. "I hear you! I hear you. This is me . . . !" He released the switch.

"Roger. I have you now." The voice was very faint and breaking up. "Please state your difficulty and location. And say *over* to signal end of transmission. Over."

Please state my difficulty, Brian thought. God. My difficulty. "I am in a plane with a pilot who is—who has had a heart attack or something. He is—he can't fly. And I don't know how to fly. Help me. Help . . ." He turned his mike off without ending transmission properly.

There was a moment's hesitation before the answer. "Your signal is breaking up and I lost most of it. Understand . . . pilot . . . you can't fly. Correct? Over."

Brian could barely hear him now, heard mostly noise and static. "That's right. I can't fly. The plane is flying now but I don't know how much longer. Over."

". . . lost signal. Your location please. Flight number . . . location . . . ver."

"I don't know my flight number or location. I don't know anything. I told you that, over."

He waited now, waited but there was nothing. Once, for a second, he thought he heard a break in the noise, some part of a word, but it could have been static. Two, three minutes, ten minutes, the plane roared and Brian listened but heard no one. Then he hit the switch again.

"I do not know the flight number. My name is Brian Robeson and we left Hampton, New York, headed for the Canadian oil fields to visit my father and I do not know how to fly an airplane and the pilot . . ."

He let go of the mike. His voice was starting to rattle and he felt as if he might start screaming at any second.

He took a deep breath. "If there is any-body listening who can help me fly a plane, please answer."

Again he released the mike but heard nothing but the hissing of noise in the headset. After half an hour of listening and repeating the cry for help he tore the headset off in frustration and threw it to the floor. It all seemed so hopeless. Even if he did get somebody, what could anybody do? Tell him to be careful?

All so hopeless.

He tried to figure out the dials again. He thought he might know which was speed—it was a lighted number that read 160—but he didn't know if that was actual miles an hour, or kilometers, or if it just meant how fast the plane was moving through the air and not over the ground. He knew airspeed was different from groundspeed but not by how much.

Parts of books he'd read about flying came to him. How wings worked, how the propellor pulled the plane through the sky. Simple things that wouldn't help him now.

Nothing could help him now.

An hour passed. He picked up the headset and tried again—it was, he knew, in the end all he had—but there was no answer. He felt like a prisoner, kept in a small cell that was hurtling through the sky at what he thought to be 160 miles an hour, headed—he didn't know where—just headed some-where until . . .

There it was. Until what? Until he ran out of fuel. When the plane ran out of fuel it would go down.

Period.

When the plane ran out of fuel it would go down. Period.

Or he could pull the throttle out and make it go down now. He had seen the pilot push the throttle in to increase speed. If he pulled the throttle back out, the engine would slow down and the plane would go down.

Those were his choices. He could wait for the plane to run out of gas and fall or he could push the throttle in and make it happen sooner. If he waited for the plane to run out of fuel he would go farther—but he did not know which way he was moving. When the pilot had jerked he had moved the plane, but Brian could not remember how much or if it had come

back to its original course. Since he did not know the original course anyway and could only guess at which display might be the compass—the one reading 342—he did not know where he had been or where he was going, so it didn't make much difference if he went down now or waited.

Everything in him rebelled against stopping the engine and falling now. He had a vague feeling that he was wrong to keep heading as the plane was heading, a feeling that he might be going off in the wrong direction, but he could not bring himself to stop the engine and fall. Now he was safe, or safer than if he went down—the plane was flying, he was still breathing.

When the engine stopped he would go down.

So he left the plane running, holding altitude, and kept trying the radio. He worked out a system. Every ten minutes by the small clock built into the dashboard he tried the radio with a simple message: "I need help. Is there anybody listening to me?"

In the times between transmissions he tried to prepare himself for what he knew was coming. When he ran out of fuel the plane would start down. He guessed that without the propellor pulling he would have to push the nose down to keep the plane flying—he thought he may have read that somewhere, or it just came to him. Either way it made sense. He would have to push the nose down to keep flying speed and then, just before he hit, he would have to pull the nose back up to slow the plane as much as possible.

It all made sense. Glide down, then slow the plane and hit.

Hit.

He would have to find a clearing as he went down. The problem with that was he hadn't seen one clearing since

they'd started flying over the forest. Some swamps, but they had trees scattered through them. No roads, no trails, no clearings.

Just the lakes, and it came to him that he would have to use a lake for landing. If he went down in the trees he was certain to die. The trees would tear the plane to pieces as it went into them.

He would have to come down in a lake. No. On the edge of a lake. He would have to come down near the

edge of a lake and try to slow the plane as much as possible just before he hit the water.

Easy to say, he thought, hard to do.

Easy say, hard do. Easy say, hard do. It became a chant that beat with the engine. Easy say, hard do.

Impossible to do.

He repeated the radio call seventeen times at the ten-minute intervals, working on what he would do between transmissions. Once more he reached over to the pilot and touched him on the face, but the skin was cold, hard cold, death cold, and Brian turned back to the dashboard. He did what he could, tightened his seatbelt, positioned himself, rehearsed mentally again and again what his procedure should be.

When the plane ran out of gas he should hold the nose down and head for the nearest lake and try to fly the plane kind of onto the water. That's how he thought of it. Kind of fly the plane onto the water. And just before it hit he should pull back on the wheel and slow the plane down to reduce the impact.

Over and over his mind ran the picture of how it would go. The plane running out of gas, flying the plane onto the water, the crash—from pictures he'd seen on television. He tried to visualize it. He tried to be ready.

But between the seventeenth and eighteenth radio transmissions, without a warning, the engine coughed, roared violently for a second and died. There was sudden silence, cut only by the sound of the windmilling propellor and the wind past the cockpit.

Brian pushed the nose of the plane down and threw up.

Going to die, Brian thought. Going to die, gonna die, gonna die—his whole brain screamed it in the sudden silence.

Gonna die.

He wiped his mouth with the back of his arm and held the nose down. The plane went into a glide, a very fast glide that ate altitude, and suddenly there weren't any lakes. All he'd seen since they started flying over the forest was lakes and now they were gone. Gone. Out in front, far away at the horizon, he could see lots of them, off to the right and left more of them, glittering blue in the late afternoon sun.

But he needed one right in front. He desperately needed a lake right in front of the plane and all he saw through the windshield were trees, green death trees. If he had to turn—if he had to turn he didn't think he could keep the plane flying. His stomach tightened into a series of rolling knots and his breath came in short bursts . . .

There!

Not quite in front but slightly to the right he saw a lake. L-shaped, with rounded corners, and the plane was nearly aimed at the long part of the L, coming from the bottom and heading

> **O**ver and over his mind ran the picture of how it would go.

to the top. Just a tiny bit to the right. He pushed the right rudder pedal gently and the nose moved over.

But the turn cost him speed and now the lake was above the nose. He pulled back on the wheel slightly and the nose came up. This caused the plane to slow dramatically and almost seem to stop and wallow in the air. The controls became very loose-feeling and frightened Brian, making him push the wheel back in. This increased the speed a bit but filled the windshield once more with nothing but trees, and put the lake well above the nose and out of reach.

For a space of three or four seconds things seemed to hang, almost to stop. The plane was flying, but so slowly, so slowly . . . it would never reach the lake. Brian looked out to the side and saw a small pond and at the edge of the pond some large animal—he thought a moose—standing out in the water. All so still looking, so stopped, the pond and the moose and the trees,

as he slid over them now only three or four hundred feet off the ground—all like a picture.

Then everything happened at once. Trees suddenly took on detail, filled his whole field of vision with green, and he knew he would hit and die, would die, but his luck held and just as he was to hit he came into an open lane, a channel of fallen trees, a wide place leading to the lake.

The plane, committed now to landing, to crashing, fell into the wide place like a stone, and Brian eased back on the wheel and braced himself for the crash. But there was a tiny bit of speed left and when he pulled on the wheel the nose came up and he saw in front the blue of the lake and at that instant the plane hit the trees.

There was a great wrenching as the wings caught the pines at the side of the clearing and broke back, ripping back just outside the main braces. Dust and dirt blew off the floor into his face so hard he thought there must have been some kind of explosion. He was momentarily blinded and slammed forward in the seat, smashing his head on the wheel.

Then a wild crashing sound, ripping of metal, and the plane rolled to the right and blew through the trees, out over the water and down, down to slam into the lake, skip once on water as hard as concrete, water that tore the windshield out and shattered the side windows, water that drove him back into the seat. Somebody was screaming, screaming as the plane drove down into the water. Someone screamed tight animal screams of fear and pain and he did not know that it was his sound, that he roared against the water that took him and the plane still deeper, down in the water. He saw nothing but sensed blue, cold blue-green, and he raked at the seatbelt catch, tore his nails loose on one hand. He ripped at it until it released and somehow—the water trying to kill him, to end him—somehow he pulled himself out of the shattered front window and clawed up into the blue, felt something hold him back, felt his windbreaker tear and he was free.

Tearing free. Ripping free.

But so far! So far to the surface and his lungs could not do this thing, could not hold and were through, and he sucked water, took a great pull of water that would—finally—win, finally take him, and his head broke into light and he vomited and swam, pulling without knowing what he was, what he was doing. Without knowing anything. Pulling until his hands caught at weeds and muck, pulling and screaming until his hands caught at last in grass and brush and he felt his chest on land, felt his face in the coarse blades of grass and he stopped, everything stopped. A color came that he had never seen before, a color that exploded in his mind with the pain and he was gone, gone from it all, spiraling out into the world, spiraling out into nothing.

Nothing.

Brian opened his eyes and screamed.

For seconds he did not know where he was, only that the crash was still happening and he was going to die, and he screamed until his breath was gone.

Then silence, filled with sobs as he

> # Somebody was screaming, screaming as the plane drove down into the water.

pulled in air, half crying. How could it be so quiet? Moments ago there was nothing but noise, crashing and tearing, screaming, now quiet.

Some birds were singing.

How could birds be singing?

His legs felt wet and he raised up on his hands and looked back down at them. They were in the lake. Strange. They went down into the water. He tried to move, but pain hammered into him and made his breath shorten into gasps and he stopped, his legs still in the water.

Pain.

Memory.

He turned again and sun came across the water, late sun, cut into his eyes and made him turn away.

It was over then. The crash.

He was alive.

The crash is over and I am alive, he thought. Then his eyes closed and he lowered his head for minutes that seemed longer. When he opened them again it was evening and some of the sharp pain had abated—there were many dull aches—and the crash came back to him fully.

Into the trees and out onto the lake.

The plane had crashed and sunk in the lake and he had somehow pulled free.

He raised himself and crawled out of the water, grunting with the pain of movement. His legs were on fire, and his forehead felt as if somebody had been pounding on it with a hammer, but he could move. He pulled his legs out of the lake and crawled on his hands and knees until he was away from the wet-soft shore and near a small stand of brush of some kind.

Then he went down, only this time to rest, to save something of himself. He lay on his side and put his head on his arm and closed his eyes because that was all he could do now, all he could think of being able to do. He closed his eyes and slept, dreamless, deep and down.

There was almost no light when he opened his eyes again. The darkness of night was thick and for a moment he began to panic again. To see, he thought. To see is everything. And he could not see. But he turned his head without moving his body and saw that across the lake the sky was a light gray, that the sun was starting to come up, and he remembered that it had been evening when he went to sleep.

"Must be morning now . . ." He mumbled it, almost in a hoarse whisper. As the thickness of sleep left him the world came back.

He was still in pain, all-over pain. His legs were cramped and drawn up, tight and aching, and his back hurt when he tried to move. Worst was a keening throb in his head that pulsed with every beat of his heart. It seemed that the whole crash had happened to his head.

He rolled on his back and felt his sides and his legs, moving things slowly. He rubbed his arms; nothing seemed to be shattered or even sprained all that badly. When he was nine he had plowed his small dirt bike into a parked car and broken his ankle, had to wear a cast for eight weeks, and there was nothing now like that. Nothing broken. Just battered around a bit.

His forehead felt massively swollen to the touch, almost like a mound out over his eyes, and it was so tender that when his fingers grazed it he nearly cried. But there was nothing he could do about it and, like the rest of him, it seemed to be bruised more than broken.

I'm alive, he thought. I'm alive.

GARY PAULSEN
AUTHOR

Gary Paulsen talks
about writing *Hatchet:*

The idea for *Hatchet* came from things that really happened. One of these took place in Alaska. Two young girls went on a boating trip with their father. The boat began to leak, so he put the girls off on an island, telling them he'd come back as soon as he could. But he became ill, and he couldn't get right back. The girls didn't even have a hatchet! He expected they would be dead by the time he got back. Living on seaweed, and using an old piece of tarp for shelter, the girls somehow survived. I was very interested in that story because I've lived off the land, too. There was a time in my life when I got by with gardening, trapping, and hunting.

Most of the things that happen in the book have happened to me, too. I've been in a forced landing of a small plane, so I know about that kind of fear. I also know what it means to depend on yourself to survive. I wanted to write a book about young people taking care of themselves. I decided to take a city boy, put him in a wild environment, and then see what happened.

When you're writing, there's nothing better than personal experience. When I realized that writing isn't just what I do, but is what I am, things changed for me. Like the storytellers of long ago, I'm the person who puts an animal skin on his back, dances around the fire, and tells what the hunt was like.

RESPONSE ✈ CORNER ✈

WRITE DIRECTIONS

HALLWAY HAZARDS

Work with a partner. Each of you should write down a location in your school that is far from your classroom. Then exchange papers and write specific directions to guide each other from that location to a "safe landing" back in your seats. Read your directions to the class as if you were working in a control tower.

MAKE A PAMPHLET

HOW TO HELP A HEART

Sometimes people who know CPR, or cardiopulmonary resuscitation, are able to help a person having a heart attack. Work with a group to find out more about CPR. Put together a pamphlet that tells when and how CPR should be performed.

A WELL-PACKED SUITCASE

Brian was stranded in the wilderness with only a hatchet to help him survive. If he had known what would happen, what other items might Brian have packed into a small suitcase? Draw and label such a suitcase and its contents.

WHAT DO YOU THINK?

- What are the problems that Brian Robeson faces in this story?

- Do you think a real teenager could actually do what Brian does in the story? Why or why not?

- Do you think Brian will be able to survive in the wilderness? Explain why or why not.

319

In your opinion, which of the main characters in this theme had the most adventurous spirit? Why do you think so?

How are the "dreams" of Jean and Araceli alike? How do their dreams differ from the dream of Mary McLeod Bethune?

Theme Wrap-Up

ACTIVITY CORNER

Work in a small group to create a board game called *Personal Journeys*. Devise and label a board on which players attempt to reach a goal, with rewards and setbacks along the way.

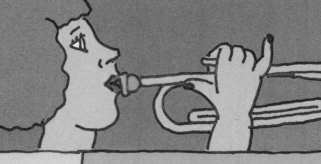

Listen to This!

Pay attention now.

The creative artists (and

would-be artists) in the

next selections all have

something important to

communicate. When

they do, the results can

be historic, inspiring, or—

in one case—hilarious.

321

THEME

Listen to This!

STATE

322

CONTENTS

Beetles, Lightly Toasted
by *Phyllis Reynolds Naylor*

Andy is experimenting with some recipes involving insects. But he wouldn't trick anyone into eating them, would he?

Signatures Library

Bookshelf

Have A Happy...
by *Mildred Pitts Walter*

Chris learns the principles of the African American celebration Kwanzaa, and he uses them to help his struggling family.

Signatures Library

The Singing Man
by Angela Shelf Medearis

Banzar, the youngest of three sons, is forced to leave his West African village because he chooses music over the more practical occupations of his brothers.

NOTABLE TRADE BOOK IN SOCIAL STUDIES

Paper Fun for Kids: 50 Practical Projects for Children of All Ages
by Marion Elliot

Arts and crafts of all kinds require little more than everyday school supplies: scissors, glue, paper, crayons, and so on. These projects are creative and easy to do!

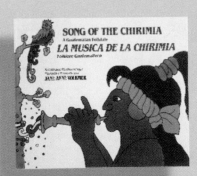

Song of the Chirimia
retold by Jane Anne Volkmer

This Guatemalan folktale tells of a young man's quest to make beautiful music and to win the hand of Princess Moonlight.

NOTABLE TRADE BOOK IN SOCIAL STUDIES

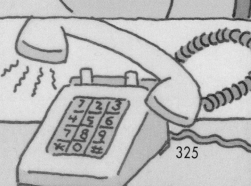

Award-Winning
Author

RADIO FIFTH GRADE

by GORDON KORMAN

illustrated by SANDRA SHAP

RADIO
FIFTH GRADE
Gordon Korman

"Okay, talk."

Winston Churchill sat on the perch in his cage and drew his head further into the orange and green feathers of his neck.

"Well, come on," coaxed Benjy Driver. "You're a parrot. Parrots talk. Look." He held the *Tropical Bird Owners' Manual* right up to the bars of the cage. "It says so right here. 'Parrots talk.'"

"Why show him that?" asked Mark Havermayer. "If he can't talk, he probably can't read, either."

"Four minutes to airtime," put in Brian Murphy, the studio engineer for WGRK Venice, FM 92.5. It was his job to run the radio station for "Kidsview," a Saturday afternoon show put on exclusively by students of Centennial Park School. Fifth-graders Benjy and Mark were co-producers, along with classmate Ellen-Louise Turnbull, the station manager's daughter.

Benjy pointed an accusing finger directly at the parrot's beak. "Did you hear that? The show starts in four minutes! Say something!"

The bird glared back, unblinking and silent.

"Maybe he can't think of anything to say," offered Mark.

Benjy reached up and clutched at his dark brown curls. "This is just great! We're on in four minutes, and the Mascot of the Week is a mute talking parrot!" He turned to Mr. Morenz, Centennial Park's gym teacher, and "Kidsview" staff advisor. "Mr. Morenz, what should we do?"

The teacher was seated with his feet up on the control panel, his chair tilted back on two legs, and his face buried in a thick science-fiction paperback entitled *Vampire Slave Monsters of the Planet Garafraxa*.

"It's your show, Benjy," he said absently, not looking away from his reading. "You kids need the experience of working out problems for yourselves."

The control room door burst open, and in rushed Ellen-Louise, the third co-producer of "Kidsview." "I got the crackers," she said breathlessly, thrusting the box into Benjy's hands.

Benjy stared at the label. "Sour-cream-and-jalapeño flavor? For a bird?"

"Well, they didn't have birdseed flavor, you know," said Ellen-Louise defensively.

"Three minutes," intoned the engineer.

Benjy ripped open the box, took out a brown-speckled cracker, and held it between the bars. In his best imitation of what he thought a parrot should sound like, he squawked, *"Polly want a cracker?"*

Winston Churchill fell on the offering like a starving shark. He wolfed it down in a blur of orange and green feathers and a tiny shower of crumbs.

Mark ignored the feast and looked at Benjy with respect. "That's a halfway decent parrot voice. If you do that on the air, we won't need the bird to talk."

Benjy recoiled in horror. "Wash your mouth out with soap! That's *terrible* journalism! What would Eldridge Kestenbaum think of someone who did that?"

"Eldridge *who*?" put in Murph, the engineer.

"Eldridge Kestenbaum, the greatest man in the history of radio," Benjy explained seriously. "He says it's a broadcaster's duty to give his listeners the absolute truth at all times. He'd die before using a phony parrot voice!"

"But he's not here right now," argued Mark. "You've never even met the guy."

Benjy looked highly insulted. "I have over two hundred hours of his newscasts and specials on tape, and I listen to them every day. I've read his autobiography seventeen times, and that's *after* I spent a year and a half looking for a bookstore that had it. Every second I'm behind that microphone, I feel Eldridge Kestenbaum right there with me."

"Okay," muttered Mark. "Who ever heard of having a radio guy for a hero, anyway? Whatever happened to movie stars, football players, astronauts—?"

"If you guys are finished," interrupted Ellen-Louise, "look at Winston Churchill. The poor bird's just hungry. Give him some more crackers."

"The point is," Benjy explained, "he has to talk for it. If he doesn't talk, he doesn't get one."

"But that's *mean*!" she protested.

The engineer tapped Benjy on the shoulder. "Let's go, Benjy. Time to get into the studio. You're on in two minutes."

"Thanks, Murph." Benjy thrust the cracker box at Mark. "Coax him. Beg him. Threaten him. I expect conversation out of this bird when we do the Mascot of the Week!" Clutching his script, he pushed open the soundproof glass control room door and hurried into the studio. He seated himself at the largest of three broadcast desks and adjusted the hanging microphone so it was about three inches from his mouth.

"Sound check . . . one . . . two . . . three. . . ."

From the control room Murph flashed him a thumbs-up signal. The sound levels were fine.

Meanwhile, Ellen-Louise was pushing cracker after cracker between the bars of Winston Churchill's cage. The bird was enjoying a frenzy of eating, putting away crackers as fast as they appeared.

"But Benjy said—" Mark protested.

"Who listens to Benjy?" she interrupted righteously. "He wants us to blackmail this poor hungry parrot. When Winston has a nice full stomach, he'll talk, just out of gratitude. Isn't that so, Winston?"

The parrot emitted a short squawk, its first sound all day.

"Maybe you're right," said Mark, encouraged. He grabbed a handful of crackers and stuffed them between the bars.

Winston Churchill went wild. He sped up his beak action and all but disappeared inside a blizzard of flying crumbs. Finally with half the box gone, he settled his bright feathers, and looked out at Mark and Ellen-Louise, who were watching intently.

"This is it!" she whispered. "He's going to talk!"

"*Hic!*"

"One minute," announced Murph.

Winston Churchill looked around uneasily. "*Hic! Hic!*"

Mark put his hand over his face. "He's got the hiccups! What'll we do?"

Both sets of eyes traveled to Mr. Morenz, who shrugged automatically and kept on reading.

Alertly Ellen-Louise dashed into the studio and snatched up the water pitcher that was sitting on the desk in front of Benjy.

"Hey, I need that!"

"Winston Churchill has the hiccups!" she tossed over her shoulder, dashing back into the control room.

Benjy turned white. "Oh, no! It's your fault for getting such spicy crackers!"

Mark grabbed the pitcher from Ellen-Louise and filled up the parrot's water tray, spilling enough to create a considerable pool in the bottom of the bird cage.

Instead of drinking, the parrot decided to take a bath. Wings flapping, he splashed and preened and hiccuped, spraying water on the four occupants of the control room.

"Hey, cool him out," ordered Murph. "Ten seconds—five, four, three, two, one—" He hit the tape player, and Mark's voice rang through the studio and radios all over town. "Stay tuned for 'Kidsview,' next on WGRK, FM 92 ½."

Benjy winced. According to Eldridge Kestenbaum, it was unprofessional to say 92 ½ instead of 92.5. But this was Mark's only on-air part in the whole show, and Ellen-Louise insisted he do it his way. Benjy leaned over and spoke into the microphone.

"Good morning, and welcome to 'Kidsview.' I'm your host, Benjamin Driver. Today's show is brought to you by Our Animal Friends, the *family* pet shop, located at the corner of Pamela Street and Conte Boulevard. Remember, there's a new friend waiting for you at Our Animal Friends. Later on we'll be hearing from our Mascot of the Week, Winston Churchill, the talking parrot. And I'm sure he'll have a lot to say." He glanced meaningfully at Mark and Ellen-Louise in the control booth. "But right now we've got the fitness expert of the third grade, Theresa van Zandt, to lead you through your morning workout."

The waiting room door opened, and in marched a thin, blonde, blue-eyed girl in a designer sweatsuit and leg warmers. She refused the chair Benjy offered her, and instead leaned over the broadcast desk to his right. Suddenly she grabbed the microphone and barked, "On the ground—all of you! Twenty push-ups! *Now!* One down, two down— Come on! Touch those noses right to the floor!"

Benjy was staring at her in disbelief when the blue eyes fell on him. "Hey—Benjy! This means you, too! Twenty push-ups! Come on! If it's good enough for our listeners, it's good enough for you!"

Urgently Benjy pointed to himself and shook his head. How could he make the girl realize that this was radio, not television? It wasn't important for anyone except the listeners at home to be exercising. In the control room, Ellen-Louise, Mark, and Murph were watching the goings-on in amazement.

Theresa van Zandt's eyes were burning into Benjy. "You cream puff! You think you're too important to work out? I can already see that spare tire of flab is going to balloon out because you don't exercise!"

Benjy was sweating now. She had him over a barrel. Sure, it would be stupid to do push-ups in the studio, but if he didn't, Theresa would make a big stink and ruin the whole show. What choice did he have? The answer came from *Broadcasting Is My Life,* the autobiography of Eldridge Kestenbaum: "Do *anything* to keep a show on track."

Without hesitation Benjy dropped to the floor and raised himself up with his arms.

"Oh, sloppy, sloppy!" cried Theresa. "Keep your back straight, Benjy!"

Painfully Benjy creaked his way through three push-ups. He was on the point of collapse when Theresa bellowed, "*Get up!* Twenty jumping jacks! Let's go, Benjy! 1–2–3. . . ."

Puffing, Benjy got up to see Mark doubled over with laughter behind the glass. He gritted his teeth as Theresa continued with toe-touches, leg lifts, side bends, and aerobics. *She* hadn't done so much as a deep knee-bend, Benjy noticed bitterly. But she was really pumping herself up, yelling and screaming at the microphone and at Benjy. "Get those knees up! My grandmother's in better shape than you!"

Benjy's clothes were drenched with sweat, and his breath was coming in gasps, each gulp of air burning like fire in his throat. The worst part of all was that, at home, probably not a single person was exercising, and he was the *only one.*

"Nauseating!" she muttered as Benjy slumped behind his desk in exhaustion after the workout was over. He got a standing ovation from the control room. She added, "Now, doesn't that feel good?"

"Oh, yes," croaked Benjy, distracted. He was trying to make sense out of his script. The sweat was dripping off his forehead, making the ink run. He squinted at the paper. "Thank you, Theresa van Zandt, for showing us how much fun good fitness can be." And may your next workout be off a cliff, he wanted to add. He forced that thought from his mind. A host must never show anger toward a guest. Catching his breath, he introduced Frank Singh, who was going to read his essay on the migration of the wildebeest.

Back in the control room the laughter soon faded. Winston Churchill was still hiccuping, even though Mark had thrown his jacket over the cage to convince the bird that night had fallen.

"It always works in the movies," said Mark in a perplexity. "Now what?"

"Leave the coat on there for a while, and maybe he'll go to sleep," shrugged Ellen-Louise. "I'd better

get out there. I'm doing School News after the first commercial."

"You can't leave me alone with this!" Mark protested.

"Murph is here. And Mr. Morenz."

"Carry on," murmured Mr. Morenz. "Just pretend I'm not here."

"That goes double for me," said the engineer with a grin. "Okay, first commercial—now." He hit the button on a large tape player, and the voice of Mr. Whitehead, owner of Our Animal Friends, was heard throughout the studio. During this break, Ellen-Louise went out and seated herself at the desk to Benjy's left.

"How's the bird?" Benjy hissed.

"Not so good. Mark's trying to put him to sleep."

Benjy was horrified. "Put him to sleep? Like kill him?"

She laughed. "You can be so dumb. Real sleep."

"But sleeping's as bad as hiccuping! We need talking!"

"Come on, Benjy. It won't be the end of the world if he doesn't talk."

"Yes it will! Mr. Whitehead is our sponsor—our *only* sponsor! The Mascot of the Week is supposed to be a sure-fire sale. If 'Kidsview' doesn't sell pets for the store, Mr. Whitehead'll drop our show! And no one's going to buy that dumb bird!"

"Maybe somebody will," said Ellen-Louise. "I mean, he's so pretty."

"This is *radio,* Ellen! He could be twenty feet long and have scales, and no one would see him. He has to say something, and fast!"

At that moment, the commercial ended, and Ellen-Louise began her segment. "This is Ellen-Louise Turnbull with School News for WGRK, FM 92 ½."

"That's *point five!*" Benjy hissed. Ellen-Louise was a pretty good broadcaster, but to her, "Kidsview" was just another hobby. She had millions of them—synchronized swimming, horseback riding, piano lessons, and who knew what else. Benjy and Mark had a private joke that she had figured out a way to go without sleep, which was how she managed to get so much accomplished in the same twenty-four hour days everyone else used.

"Four C is writing poems about limestone," Ellen-Louise announced, "and Mr. Calvin is confident that this will be his most successful creative writing project since last year's unit on granite. . . ." Every week, during School News, she described in great detail which classes were working on which topics, which grade was hosting the next assembly, which students were hall monitors and safety patrol members, and so on. Mark had already nicknamed Ellen-Louise's report "The Big Yawn." Even Benjy,

fiercely loyal to the show, had to admit that it wasn't very exciting. But in the words of Eldridge Kestenbaum, "One man's dreary is another man's news."

"Thank you, Ellen-Louise Turnbull, for that fascinating report," said Benjy. "Next is our weekly editorial comment from Arthur Katz."

Arthur was also a member of Benjy's fifth grade class. He strode purposefully out of the waiting room and took the seat to Benjy's right.

"I just read that a new ice age is going to come within the next fifty thousand years," he said with great passion. "Sure, I know what you're thinking. We won't be around in fifty thousand years, so it's no skin off our backs, right? But hold it! The report said *within* fifty thousand years. So it could be forty-five thousand years from now, but it could also be *next week*!"

Benjy's attention was suddenly diverted by a flurry of activity in the control room. In an attempt to cure Winston Churchill's hiccups, Mark had tried to put a paper bag over the bird's head. But the parrot had dodged the bag, and escaped through the open door of his cage. Now he was flapping around the control room, evading capture by Murph and Mark, who were scrambling about, trying to grab him. Mr. Morenz did not glance up from *Vampire Slave Monsters of the Planet Garafraxa*, not even when Winston Churchill made a dive-bombing run at his head.

"What if tomorrow, let's say," Arthur was raving, "it started snowing and just didn't stop? Hey, great—no school. That's everybody's first reaction. But then the snow gets deeper and deeper. Before you know it, it turns into a glacier, and then we're in big trouble, let me tell you! Because every shovel and snowblower in Venice couldn't stop a glacier! We're not prepared!"

Benjy strained to see Murph's time signals through the fracas in the control room, while keeping a cautious eye on Arthur, who was red-faced, shouting into the microphone.

"We all think we're so safe because we've got computers and shopping malls and cable TV! A fat lot of good that stuff will do to a nation of Popsicles! Our scientists should be building giant snow melters, and designing anti-glacier walls that will keep the ice up in Quebec, where it belongs! We're bucking for a big fall here! Remember the dinosaurs? On top of the world one minute—gone the next! Now, what are we going to do about it?"

Benjy waited. Arthur seemed to have more to say, but he just sat seething into the microphone. The seconds ticked by until Benjy realized what was happening.

Dead air!

According to Eldridge Kestenbaum, dead air was the worst thing a radio show could have. Because there was no picture, if you had no sound, either, you had *nothing*.

He had to jump in. "Uh—thank you, Arthur Katz, for—"

"No!" Arthur interrupted hotly. "What are we going to *do*?"

"Well," said Benjy reasonably, "nothing. But now we're all aware of the problem, so—"

"But we need a plan! If we can't stop it, we've got to find someplace else to live! And we need a way to get there through the snow!"

"Well," said Benjy quickly, "it's pretty sunny out today—uh—so far so good. 'Kidsview' will be back with the Mascot of the Week after this message from our sponsor."

Murph put on the tape for the second Our Animal Friends Pet Shop commercial, and Benjy and Ellen-Louise managed to hustle Arthur back into the waiting room. He was still gibbering about the new ice age, and demanding action.

"Get him some water," Benjy ordered briskly.

"No ice cubes," Arthur added.

Benjy returned to the studio just in time to see Mark carrying in Winston Churchill's bird cage. The parrot was once again atop his perch, but still hiccuping.

"We can't put him on the air with hiccups!" Benjy protested.

"Don't worry," said Mark. "I've got one more plan, and this one can't miss."

"Well, hurry up! The commercial's almost over!" Benjy settled himself back in the host's chair, and Mark placed the cage on the right-hand desk, so that the microphone rested up against the bars.

Benjy looked at the bird malevolently. "You're not going to talk, are you? You're going to make me look like an idiot."

"*Hic! Hic!*"

Mark took a paper bag and put it to his lips. He blew it full of air, and held it behind the cage, about three inches from Winston Churchill's glossy green head.

Benjy looked over and took in the scene with a gasp of horror. "Mark—no!"

The commercial ended, and the red *ON AIR* light flashed on, just as Mark smacked the inflated bag with all his might.

Boom!

Winston Churchill toppled off his perch in a dead faint. He landed with a muffled thump, and lay there, a motionless bundle of feathers.

"Oh, no! I've killed him!" blurted out Mark.

Painfully Benjy pointed to the *ON AIR* light. Mark clapped his hand over his mouth.

"Well," said Benjy slowly, "it looks like our Mascot of the Week has decided to take a little nap. And we wouldn't want to wake up a beautiful bird like this. So why don't you come and take a look at him this week at Our Animal Friends, the *family* pet shop? Just ask for Winston Churchill, the talking parrot. And now seems like a good time for a public service message from the City of Venice." He looked imploringly up to the control room.

With a sympathetic smile, Murph put on a tape.

In case of snow emergency, came a cheerful voice, *obey these city bylaws. . . .*

The door of the waiting room burst open to reveal Arthur Katz, wild-eyed. "Snow emergency? Where?"

Ellen-Louise sprinted up to the cage. "Winston! Speak to me!"

"He doesn't speak to anybody," said Benjy in disgust.

The bird opened one eye and gave him a baleful look.

Mark heaved a sigh. "He's alive! I didn't kill him! And look—his hiccups are gone!"

Benjy snatched desperately at his curly dark hair. "Okay, clear the studio. Let's finish the show."

About the Illustrator SANDRA SHAP

Sandra Shap began her career in art college in London, England, at the age of sixteen. She now lives and works in New York City. Her colorful and sometimes comical artwork can be seen in many different places – including fashion magazines, advertisements, and illustrated children's books.

MEET GORDON KORMAN

Gordon Korman was born in Canada in 1963. He got an early start in publishing when a seventh-grade English assignment ended up as a 120-page book! "The characters sort of became real people to me," he says. "And they more or less wrote the book for me."

His classmates enjoyed the book so much that he decided to find a publisher for it. Two years later his first book, *This Can't Be Happening at Macdonald Hall!,* was published. He was just fourteen years old. Since then, he's written a book each summer, even while he attended college at New York University.

Korman wants his books to tell about kids' problems and concerns but also to contain a lot of humor. He says the most important thing in a book is to present characters who seem real and have believable relationships: "My books are the kind of stories I wanted to read and couldn't find when I was ten, eleven, and twelve."

As demonstrated in *Radio Fifth Grade,* Korman likes to place young characters in difficult situations to show how well they can handle themselves. "Whatever an adult can do, somewhere in the world there's a sixteen-year-old who can do it just as well," Korman says. "And that's important because a kid around twelve is just starting to find out that he can do certain things as well as his parents or his teachers."

RESPONSE CORNER

PARROT TALK

Work in one of three groups to interview a local Audubon Society member or a pet shop worker about parrots. Each group should interview a different person. Ask questions about how parrots learn to talk. Share what you learn from your interview with the rest of your classmates.

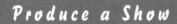

Produce a Show

ON THE AIR

Work with a small group to produce a "Kidsview" show for your class. Talk about how you could change some of the parts of the story. Tape-record your show, and share it with your classmates.

HICCUP HINTS

Winston Churchill has a bad case of the hiccups. What do you do to get rid of the hiccups? Write a how-to paragraph telling the steps a person should take to stop the hiccups.

WHAT DO YOU THINK?

- What is Benjy's main problem in the story?

- Do you think Benjy will be relieved when the show is over? Explain your answer.

- What would you suggest that Benjy do to make the show run more smoothly?

By the Dawn's Early Light

THE STORY OF THE STAR-SPANGLED BANNER

Notable Trade Book in Social Studies

BY STEVEN KROLL
ILLUSTRATED BY DAN ANDREASEN

The War of 1812

Between 1793 and 1814, France, led by the power-hungry Napoleon, waged war against many European countries.

As England began needing more sailors for the Royal Navy, there were fewer and fewer British commercial ships. Soon the United States had pretty much taken over trade between the French and Spanish colonies and Europe.

England and France tried to impose restrictions on American shipping, and the Royal Navy began boarding American ships and seizing both British deserters and American sailors for their service. Finally, on June 18, 1812, a poorly prepared United States declared war on Great Britain.

For almost two years there were battles on land and sea. Then, in March 1814, Napoleon was defeated in Europe, and Britain turned full attention to America.

On August 18th of that year, British forces reached the mouth of the Patuxent River. Between the 19th and the 25th, British troops defeated the inexperienced American militia at Bladensburg, Maryland, burned a defenseless Washington, and returned to their ships.

AUGUST 31, 1814

Francis Scott Key was a well-known Washington lawyer. He lived just outside the city center in Georgetown where he was also a lieutenant in the Georgetown Light Artillery. Since the burning of Washington on August 24th, he had been on duty every day.

On August 31st, he had only just come home, when there was a sharp knock at his door.

He flung it open, and there was Richard West, his brother-in-law.

"The British have arrested Dr. Beanes!" said Richard. "He's a prisoner on one of their ships."

Francis was outraged. Dr. William Beanes was a close friend from Upper Marlborough, Maryland. "But why?" he almost shouted.

"Dr. Beanes was looking after wounded British soldiers. After the army left, three stragglers began making trouble. The doctor had them thrown in jail. The British got angry—"

"Something must be done!" said Francis.

"A few of us hoped you might use your influence with President Madison."

Francis got released from military duty. Early the next morning, after a hug from his wife, Polly, and their six children, he mounted his horse and rode into Washington.

The smell of burning was everywhere. The Capitol was gone, along with the Executive Mansion. Temporary presidential quarters had been set up at the French Minister's house, and when Francis walked inside, everyone looked worried.

He was shown into a front room with a guard at the door. The president sat alone. He was pale and hollow-eyed and looked very small.

Francis made his request. Mr. Madison turned and smiled sadly. "I give you permission to visit the British fleet as an official American envoy under a flag of truce. John Mason, Commissary General of Prisoners, will allow Colonel John S. Skinner, his agent in charge of prisoner exchange, to go with you."

"Thank you, sir," said Francis.

He returned home and asked Polly to take the children to Terra Rubra, their estate in western Maryland. The following day, he set off through stifling heat for Baltimore.

General Samuel Smith was busy preparing his men for the defense of Baltimore and Fort McHenry when Francis arrived. Colonel Skinner was there and listened carefully to President Madison's instructions. He mentioned that he knew Dr. Beanes personally and had in his possession letters from wounded British officers describing the doctor's kindness to them after the Battle of Bladensburg. He arranged to hire a small boat so he and Francis could sail down Chesapeake Bay to meet the British.

By the time Francis and Colonel Skinner were ready to leave, the heat was breaking and a storm was coming up. When it began to pour, they took shelter at a local inn. The rain continued, and it wasn't until September 5th that they were able to sail their small cartel boat with its white flag of truce down the Patapsco River toward Chesapeake Bay.

They searched for the British fleet until nightfall, but they had no luck until late in the afternoon of September 7th. The tall ships were lying off the mouth of the Potomac. Colonel Skinner sighted Vice Admiral Sir Alexander Cochrane's eighty-gun flagship, H.M.S. *Tonnant*. As they drew closer, Francis could see the line of gun ports, black checkerboard squares against a yellow background.

They reached the *Tonnant*. Francis and the colonel climbed aboard and were taken to Admiral Cochrane's cabin.

The admiral was friendly but formal. "No," he said when Francis finished his plea. "As a noncombatant, Dr. Beanes had no right to arrest those men."

Francis explained that the doctor might not have realized what he was doing, that he could not have violated his neutrality because by then the British were no longer occupying the territory.

The admiral gestured to a midshipman. "Call in General Ross and Admiral Cockburn."

They arrived almost at once. Major General Sir Robert Ross was tall and imposing, Rear Admiral Sir George Cockburn, red-faced and grim.

Once more Francis presented his arguments and his official letters. This time he stressed the letters of praise for Dr. Beanes from the wounded British officers.

"A pack of nonsense," said Admiral Cockburn. "We must take Beanes to Halifax and see that he's punished there."

"I do not agree," said General Ross. "I am moved by these letters from wounded officers, and as co-commander of our expeditionary forces, I will release the prisoner. However, all three of these men will remain with us until after we have completed our attack on Baltimore."

Francis and the colonel shared a look of alarm. Then they were hurried out to a small hold in the ship's prow. Dr. Beanes was there and greeted them warmly. When his two friends told him what was happening, he was horrified.

"And we must sit and watch while our country is attacked?" he exclaimed.

"I'm afraid so," Colonel Skinner replied.

The three Americans were put up on the frigate *Surprise,* and for three days the British fleet crept up Chesapeake Bay.

Meanwhile, Baltimore was getting ready. Though inexperienced, the militia was on call. The city was ringed by trenches and ramparts built by citizens. At star-shaped Fort McHenry, out on Whetstone Point overlooking the Patapsco River, a thousand troops were under the command of Major George Armistead. They had thrown up barriers outside the moat, placed sandbags around the powder magazine, and sunk many small ships and barges in the north channel of the river to slow enemy progress. They had also stationed a half-dozen small gunboats between the sunken hulls and the city.

There was a bold, new flag flying over the fort. Forty-two by thirty feet, fifteen stars and fifteen stripes, it was the work of Mary Pickersgill and her daughter, Caroline.

On Saturday, September 10th, the British fleet anchored off North Point at the mouth of the Patapsco River. Francis, Colonel Skinner, and Dr. Beanes were hustled from the *Surprise* back to their own small boat. Admiral Cochrane had decided to take personal command of the bombardment. He wanted the smaller, faster frigate as his flagship.

Sunday morning, Baltimore's church bells called the militia to arms. Monday, boats filled with British soldiers in scarlet uniforms began leaving for shore. Francis watched grimly. Things did not look good for the Americans.

With the troops underway on land, the fleet began moving upriver. As the ships came within view of Fort McHenry, the Stars and Stripes were waving overhead.

Later that afternoon, word came from shore. The Americans had retreated to positions outside the city. General Ross had been killed.

A silence seemed to fall over the fleet, but preparations continued. Francis, Dr. Beanes, and Colonel Skinner spent a restless night as sixteen smaller British ships moved into the shallower water closer to the fort.

At dawn the bombardment began. The noise was so great and the smell of burning powder so strong that the three hostages were forced to take refuge in their cabin. When the response from the fort seemed to die away for a moment, it became clear that the Americans' thirty-six-pound shells were not reaching the ships. But then the heavy shelling and rocketing began again and went on hour after hour.

At dusk Francis crawled out onto the deck. "Can you see the flag?" Dr. Beanes called after him.

Francis squinted through the smoke and the din and the glow of the setting sun. "The flag is flying," he replied.

Soon after, it began to rain. Thunder and lightning joined the booming of the guns. Very late that night, Francis struggled out on deck again. Though he could not know it, at that moment the British were trying to land a thousand men at Ferry Branch. An American sentry discovered them and Fort McHenry began to fire. As the barges fled, every available American gun pursued them.

The rainy night sky was suddenly lit up, and in that moment Francis could see the flag again. It was soaked now and drooping from its staff, but it was there, still there.

By dawn the rain had stopped and the fight was over. Peering through the clouds, Francis, Dr. Beanes, and Colonel Skinner strained to see what flag was flying over the fort. Had the British triumphed in the night? But no, there it was, unfurling in the breeze, the Stars and Stripes!

All his life, Francis had written poetry. He reached into his pocket and found an old letter. With the tune to the song "To Anacreon in Heaven" in mind, he scribbled *O say can you see* and then *by the dawn's early light*.

He wrote a few more lines, crossed out a few, but there wasn't much time. Already redcoats were leaving for the ships. The fleet was abandoning the assault!

The sails of the little cartel boat were returned to the members of its American crew. By afternoon, Francis, Dr. Beanes, and Colonel Skinner were back in Baltimore.

Cheering crowds were everywhere. The three men went straight to the Indian Queen Hotel on Baltimore Street, rested and had supper, but later that night, Francis finished the four stanzas of his poem.

The next day he went to visit his brother-in-law, Judge Joseph Nicholson, who had been at Fort McHenry. Judge Nicholson loved the new poem. "Let's get it printed," he insisted.

The judge rushed over to the *Baltimore American,* but the printers weren't back from defending the fort. A young apprentice, Samuel Sands, agreed to set the verses in type and run off the handbills. Because Francis hadn't thought of a title, Judge Nicholson came up with "The Defense of Fort McHenry," but it wasn't long before everyone was singing what had come to be known as "The Star-Spangled Banner."

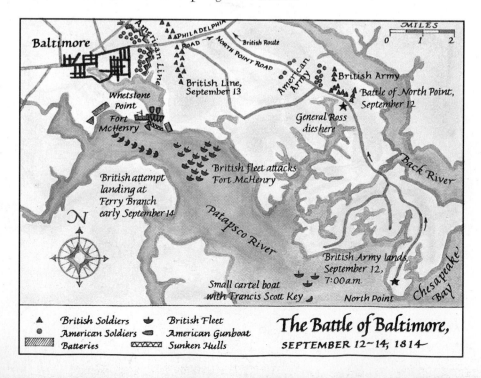

The Battle of Baltimore,
SEPTEMBER 12–14, 1814

THE STAR-SPANGLED BANNER

O say can you see by the dawn's early light
What so proudly we hail'd at the twilight's last gleaming,
Whose broad stripes and bright stars through the perilous fight
O'er the ramparts we watch'd were so gallantly streaming?
And the rockets' red glare, the bombs bursting in air,
Gave proof through the night that our flag was still there.
O say does that star-spangled banner yet wave
O'er the land of the free and the home of the brave?

On the shore dimly seen through the mists of the deep,
Where the foe's haughty host in dread silence reposes,
What is that which the breeze, o'er the towering steep,
As it fitfully blows, half conceals, half discloses?
Now it catches the gleam of the morning's first beam,
In full glory reflected now shines in the stream.
'Tis the star-spangled banner, oh, long may it wave
O'er the land of the free and the home of the brave!

And where is that band who so vauntingly swore
That the havoc of war and the battle's confusion
A home and a country should leave us no more?
Their blood has wash'd out their foul footstep's pollution.
No refuge could save the hireling and slave
From the terror of flight or the gloom of the grave,
And the star-spangled banner in triumph doth wave
O'er the land of the free and the home of the brave.

O thus be it ever when freemen shall stand
Between their lov'd home and the war's desolation!
Blest with vict'ry and peace may the heav'n-rescued land
Praise the power that hath made and preserv'd us a nation!
Then conquer we must, when our cause it is just,
And this be our motto, "In God is our Trust,"
And the star-spangled banner in triumph shall wave
O'er the land of the free and the home of the brave.

O say can you see ~~through~~ by the dawn's early light
What so proudly we hail'd at the twilight's last gleaming,
Whose broad stripes & bright stars through the perilous fight
O'er the ramparts we watch'd, were so gallantly streaming?
And the rocket's red glare, the bomb bursting in air,
Gave proof through the night that our flag was still there,
O say does that star spangled banner yet wave
O'er the land of the free & the home of the brave?

On the shore dimly seen through the mists of the deep,
Where the foe's haughty host in dread silence reposes,
What is that which the breeze, o'er the towering steep,
As it fitfully blows, half conceals, half discloses?
Now it catches the gleam of the morning's first beam,
In full glory reflected now shines in the stream,
'Tis the star-spangled banner — O long may it wave
O'er the land of the free & the home of the brave!

And where is that band who so vauntingly swore,
That the havoc of war & the battle's confusion
A home & a Country should leave us no more?
— ~~Their blood~~
Their blood has wash'd out their foul footstep's pollution.
No refuge could save the hireling & slave
From the terror of flight or the gloom of the grave,
And the star-spangled banner in triumph doth wave
O'er the land of the free & the home of the brave.

O thus be it ever when freemen shall stand
Between their lov'd home & the war's desolation!
Blest with vict'ry & peace may the heav'n rescued land
Praise the power that hath made & preserv'd us a nation!
Then conquer we must, when our cause it is just,
And this be our motto — "In God is our trust,"
And the star-spangled banner in triumph shall wave
O'er the land of the free & the home of the brave. —

This is a photograph of the original manuscript of the poem that
Francis Scott Key wrote in his room at the Indian Queen Hotel
on Baltimore Street the evening after he had witnessed the
Battle of Baltimore.

AUTHOR'S NOTE

For those concerned with additional detail, it was the fort's storm flag, measuring twenty-five by seventeen feet, that was flying overhead during the battle. The larger flag, the fort's garrison flag, was raised in celebration as Francis Scott Key sailed back to Baltimore. Both flags had been made by Mary Pickersgill.

After writing his poem, Key returned to Terra Rubra and then to Georgetown and his successful law practice. When his friend Andrew Jackson became president in 1829, he was appointed United States District Attorney for the District of Columbia. Always opposed to slavery, he was a founder of the American Colonization Society, which began a settlement of freed slaves on the west coast of Africa called Liberia. He and Polly had eleven children altogether and eventually retired to Terra Rubra.

With the collapse of the assault on Baltimore, the British fleet sailed to Jamaica. A peace treaty was signed at Ghent (in what is now Belgium) on December 24, 1814, but word of that did not reach America for some time and the final battle of the war was actually fought and won by Andrew Jackson at New Orleans on January 8, 1815.

Over the years, "The Star-Spangled Banner" became more and more popular. In the 1890s, it became the official song of the Army and the Navy. In 1916, President Woodrow Wilson ordered that it be played on official occasions, but not until 1931 did the Congress, by decree, make the song the national anthem of the United States of America.

STEVEN KROLL

Editor Ilene Cooper talks to
Steven Kroll about writing.

How much did you know about Francis Scott Key and "The Star-Spangled Banner" before you wrote the book?

I knew that Key had been out in Baltimore harbor on a British ship, watching the battle. I had no idea what he was doing there. It was always puzzling to me, but I never bothered to find out the reason until it came time to write the book. It turned out to be a fascinating story.

One thing that I found amazing was that Key and the others were set free after the battle was over.

Wars were fought differently back in those days. There was a certain amount of gentlemanly behavior. Key and the others were accidental prisoners—they happened to be in the wrong place at the wrong time. With no way of returning them, the British made them stay.

For a book like this, how much time is spent doing research, and how much time is spent writing?

It's about 75 percent research and 25 percent writing.

Do you remember the first important thing you wrote?

Yes. It was my sixth-grade autobiography. I got some good comments from my teacher, and that got me interested in writing. Then, one night during a walk in the rain, I saw that the wet sidewalks looked as if they were made of glass. I rushed home, and without taking off my wet raincoat, I pulled out my typewriter and wrote a story called "A World Made of Glass." It was terrible! But right then I realized how much I loved writing stories. It was an extraordinary moment for me.

RESPONSE CORNER

Patriotic Poet

Francis Scott Key was an interesting man. Write a poem about his life using details from the story. You may wish to set your poem to music, as he was famous for doing. Share your poem with your classmates.

SING A SONG

Moving Music

Find the words to "The Star-Spangled Banner" near the end of the selection. Choose two groups of singers. Everyone should sing the first verse. Then have the two groups take turns singing the other stanzas. Make it a goal to memorize the national anthem.

Flag Facts

The American flag has a rich history. Find out more about how the flag developed into the red, white, and blue banner to which we pledge allegiance today. How many different national flags has the United States had? What different nicknames have been given to our flag? Use your findings to create a class booklet titled "Stars and Stripes Forever."

What Do You Think?

- Why was Francis Scott Key inspired to write his poem?

- What did you find out about the national anthem of the United States that you did not know before?

- If you had met Francis Scott Key after the battle of Fort McHenry, what would you have asked him?

Art & Literature

You have read about some people who use creative ways to express what they feel. How does the painting **Woman at the Piano** *fit in with these selections? How might a story or a painting help you find a way to express your own feelings?*

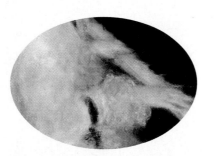

Woman at the Piano
by Pierre-Auguste Renoir

The paintings of Pierre-Auguste Renoir show his interest in how light affects color. Although the woman in this painting is sitting in a dark room, she is bathed in light. The light shines on her face and hands. It also highlights her white dress. Notice how the black line on the dress flows gracefully from her shoulder to the floor.

Oil on canvas, 1875, 93.2×74.2 cm,
Mr. and Mrs. Martin A. Ryerson Collection

Yang the Youngest

Lensey Namioka
Yang the Youngest
and
His Terrible Ear

Illustrated by Kees de Kiefte

Horn Book
Magazine
Fanfare

Terrible Ear and His and

WRITTEN BY LENSEY NAMIOKA

ILLUSTRATED BY KEES DE KIEFTE

All of the Yangs are talented musicians. All of them, that is, except their youngest member, Yingtao, who is tone-deaf. Yingtao's talents seem more suited to the baseball diamond than the concert hall.

When Yingtao's father insists that he play his screeching violin at the family's first open house, Yingtao is petrified. But he and his friend Matthew hatch a clever plan to save the day, and the Yang family's musical reputation.

SATURDAY CAME. I STILL HADN'T HEARD FROM MATTHEW.

I wanted to go over to his house to talk with him, but Father was keeping an eye on me, making sure I was staying home to practice.

Then I thought of calling Matthew up, but every time I went into the kitchen to call, someone was there. Second Sister was cutting up tea bags, or Mother was preparing the refreshments for the recital.

As the hour for the recital approached, I spent my time looking out the window, hoping for a sign from him. There was nothing.

The recital was being held in our living room, and it was to begin at two in the afternoon. Since Father had only six students, we could easily squeeze everybody in. The audience were mostly relatives—close relatives—of the young players, and we expected about twenty-five people.

We had actually never seen fortune cookies until we came to America.

Mother was going to serve orange soda to the young people and tea to the adults. She also planned to serve fortune cookies. We had actually never seen fortune cookies until we came to America. After Father got his first paycheck, he treated the family to a dinner in Chinatown. Although Mother was a good cook, we were glad to have a change. The food was Cantonese, which was a little different from the Shanghai food we had at home, but it was good and not totally strange.

The one strange item came at the end. When the waiter presented the bill, he also handed us a small plate with six funny-looking cookies. They were shaped like a small, round cake, folded in half, with the corners bent back.

"What are these?" asked Father.

"They are fortune cookies," said the waiter. "Each cookie has a piece of paper with your fortune on it." He showed us how to break the crisp cookie open and get at the tiny slip of paper with a message.

We excitedly broke open our cookies and read the messages. Mine said, "Listen carefully, and your inner voice will tell you what to do." Even my fortune cookie was telling me to listen carefully.

Everyone liked the fortune cookies very much. From that time on, Mother bought them for special celebrations. For the recital, she bought the largest package in the store.

"When the recital is finished, we'll really have something to celebrate," she said. She was smiling bravely as she spoke, but her voice trembled a little.

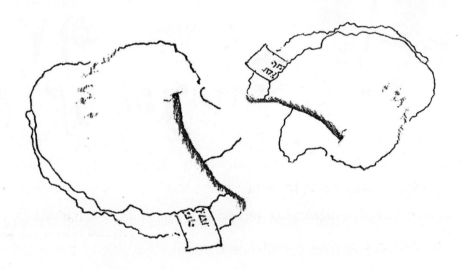

The only problem was how to get everyone seated. We finally borrowed enough chairs from our neighbors for the grown-ups. The kids in the audience would just have to sit on the floor.

Eldest Brother set up the screen in the living room. While he wasn't looking, I moved the screen a little so that it stood right in front of the door to the kitchen. This way Matthew could move to his place behind the screen without being seen.

If he came.

I could hardly swallow my lunch, I was so anxious about Matthew. Of course, the rest of the family thought I was just suffering from stage fright.

"You'll be all right if you just concentrate, Yingtao," Father said heartily.

"Don't finish your rice if you don't feel like it," said Mother. In our family—in any Chinese family—not finishing your bowl of rice is a terrible thing. So Mother was really trying to be kind.

Maybe maybe if I got

"Once you get the first few measures right, the rest will come easily," said Eldest Brother. "I know you can do it."

Even Second Sister had a kind word to say. "You have a good sense of rhythm, Fourth Brother. We all have confidence in you."

Could they be right? Maybe if I concentrated, maybe if I got the first few measures right . . . Maybe there was just a chance that I might not disgrace the Yang family after all.

For once, Third Sister was the only one who didn't say anything to cheer me up. Probably because she knew how hopeless it was.

After lunch Mother looked at the living room one last time and nodded. Then her eyes went to Second Sister's pictures of the Chinese scenes. "You've done a good job," she said softly.

374

We were still putting out the refreshments when the first of Father's students arrived with their parents. They were not only on time; they were early. I guess the parents were curious about how a Chinese family lived.

The kids probably just wanted to get it over with. Most of them didn't look happy about playing in front of people. I knew how they felt.

But stage fright was the least of my worries today. I hung around the backdoor, waiting and hoping for Matthew to arrive. When it was nearly two o'clock and most of the guests had arrived, there was still no sign of him. Slowly, reluctantly, I went to my room and got my violin out. Even the instrument seemed unwilling to leave its case.

if I concentrated...
the first few measures right...

"He's here!" It was Third Sister's voice. "He sneaked in through the backdoor without anyone seeing him!"

I spun around, and there, standing behind her, was Matthew.

For a moment we just stood there looking at each other. Neither of us could speak. I was too relieved to say anything, and Matthew too happy.

Then he grinned and made a thumbs-up sign. "I told my folks that I was coming down with something. I said it was better if I didn't go, in case the other kids caught it."

Then he grin

"Come on, we have to hurry down," whispered Third Sister. She was right. The others would be suspicious if we didn't show up soon.

I copied Matthew's thumbs-up sign, and hurried after Third Sister. According to our plan, Matthew was to wait in my room until it was time for the quartet, and then he would come downstairs, go through the kitchen, and get to his place behind the screen.

The program began right on time. Father had arranged the recital in order of age. His youngest student would play first, and then the next youngest, and so on. The last number was our quartet.

First on the program was Peter Schultz, who was five years old and the only boy among Father's students. Maybe he was too young to worry about being called a nerd, a wimp, or a sissy.

I was the same age as Peter when I got my first violin. But unlike me, Peter was not tone-deaf. His problem was that he couldn't count time. He didn't care if he played his notes too soon or too late, as long as he played them all. Mother accompanied Peter on the piano, and she had to scramble to stay with him.

At the end of the piece Peter bowed and beamed until his face almost split in two. We all clapped hard.

The rest of Father's students were girls. Four of them studied the violin and one of them the viola.

ned and made a thumbs-up sign.

The string players in our school orchestra, the violinists, violists, and cellists, were almost all girls. But for some reason it was all right for boys to play wind instruments, like the trumpet and the clarinet. It couldn't have been easy for Matthew to keep on playing the violin, when the other boys teased him about it.

The girl who played next in the recital was terribly nervous. She was biting her lip as she played, and I found myself biting my lip, too. Once she had to stop in the middle of the piece because she had lost her place.

She looked ready to cry, but Father went over and talked softly to her for a minute. She started the piece over again, and this time she finished it. We clapped extra hard.

One of the older girls played a piece with a lot of fast notes. Some of the little kids in the audience said, "Ooh!"

At the end of the piece the girl bowed and quickly ran back to her parents. They hugged her, and I could hear them telling her how proud they were of her playing.

My parents had never told me they were proud of my playing. They never would, either.

I began to look over the other parents in the audience. Suddenly I recognized a couple sitting in the back row. It was Matthew's parents. When Mr. Conner caught my eye, he gave me a big wink. Eric wasn't with them, so he had managed to find an excuse to stay away.

The next three pieces seemed to pass very quickly. Much sooner than I expected, it was time for our quartet.

I jumped up and rushed over to help set up the music stands. As I was putting out the sheet music for the

Where is the glue?

quartet, I noticed that the edge of one of Second Sister's paintings had come loose. There was a big gap, and I could see through it. If I could see through it, so could the audience.

"What's the matter?" Eldest Brother asked me. "Why are you taking so long?"

"The painting is coming loose here," I said. "I'll try to glue it back."

"Never mind!" hissed Second Sister. She seemed in a hurry to get the quartet over with. "Come on, let's get started."

"I won't be a minute," I muttered, and rushed into the kitchen.

Matthew was standing beside the refrigerator. "What's happened?"

"Haven't got time to explain," I gasped. "The glue! Where is the glue?"

Third Sister had used a tube of glue to put up the paintings, and I didn't know where she had put it. Then I saw my bowl of leftover rice on the counter.

I grabbed a bit of it and kneaded it together with my fingers until it became a sticky paste. Then I rushed back to the screen and quickly dabbed at the loose edge of the painting with my homemade paste. Third Sister soon saw what I was doing and helped me smooth the paper down.

"I didn't know that painting was so important to you," growled Second Sister. But she looked pleased.

The audience was getting restless, especially the children. We finally settled down in our seats. One of the mothers gave a "shush," and the children quieted. I heard a faint rustling behind the screen.

I glanced at Third Sister to see if she had also heard the rustle. She smiled at me, and her dimples flashed.

When I see her smile like that, I know she's thinking of some mischief. Now she was probably smiling because we were playing a trick on the audience.

Eldest Brother lifted his bow and began to play. Second Sister followed with her entrance, then Third Sister. As she played the deep notes of her cello, it was nearly time for my entrance. I lifted my bow. My fingers were sticky from the rice paste, but at least it gave me a better grip on the bow.

Eldest Brother gritted his teeth and Second Sister stiffened her shoulders as they prepared themselves for the sour notes they expected me to produce.

Then I drew my bow across the strings—or I pretended to. By now, I was really good at keeping my bow just a tiny bit above the strings. I was an expert at bow sync.

A ripple of notes came out as I moved my bow back and forth. Eldest Brother and Second Sister were so surprised that they both stopped playing for a moment. Only Third Sister's cello kept on going smoothly.

But Eldest Brother and Second Sister recovered quickly. They had both played in a lot of recitals back in China. Unexpected things often happen during a performance. They found their places again, and the quartet went ahead. To my great relief, Matthew was keeping up perfectly with the others.

It didn't take long for Eldest Brother to figure out what was going on. From his seat, he could tell the second violin part wasn't coming from me. And soon he knew it was coming from behind the screen.

I saw Second Sister look at me. She had also figured out what was happening. She probably recognized Matthew's way of playing. But there was nothing she could do except continue to play, and play beautifully.

Everything was fine, until I took hold of the corner of the music to turn it over. The rice paste made my fingers stick to the paper. I broke out in a sweat as I tried to shake the paper loose.

Meanwhile the second violin part continued to issue smoothly from behind the screen. Did the audience

notice that while I was struggling with the sheet music, my violin was playing by itself?

Maybe not. A lot of notes were flying around, and the audience couldn't always tell exactly which notes were coming from which player. Only the composer, Haydn, would know exactly, and he had been dead for almost two hundred years.

By the time I finally got my fingers free, my eyes were almost blinded by salty sweat. I wiped my brow and went back to swishing my bow back and forth.

I gave the audience a quick peek and saw that they all looked quite content. Mother smiled, and Father looked pleasantly surprised. They were proud of me.

My mouth filled with a bitter taste. My parents were proud of me for something I didn't do.

Suddenly I wished I had never thought of the trick. Third Sister was right. It would have been better for me to play the second violin part, even if I sounded terrible. At least that would have been honest.

But it was too late to change. Besides, Matthew was in this, too. The quartet kept on playing, and I went on moving my bow back and forth—silently.

The music became faster and louder as we got near the end. Eldest Brother had a short solo part with a dazzling swirl of notes that climbed higher and higher. After that, all four of us—all five of us?—played together, and we finished with a big, crashing chord.

The audience burst out clapping, even the little kids. I stole a look at Matthew's parents. They were clapping as hard as everybody else.

It was time for the four of us to stand up and take a bow. Third Sister seemed to be having some trouble. We were crowded together, and she had to get her

I had never thought of the trick.

cello out of the way before she could bow properly.

Third Sister stepped back a little to give herself more room. She moved her cello to her left, and bumped hard against the screen.

Crash! In full view of the audience stood Matthew, with his violin still in his hands.

There was dead silence. I could see the audience trying to understand what was going on. Father and Mother were the first to suspect the truth. Their eyes went from me to Matthew and then back to me again. I swallowed hard, wanting to melt into a puddle and sink into the ground with shame.

Why was Matthew still standing there? He had promised to steal away as soon as the quartet was over! But I couldn't really blame him for staying. I think he wanted to hear the clapping. After all, he had earned it.

Father broke the silence. "So that's why the quartet sounded so different!" Shock was being replaced by anger on his face.

Mr. and Mrs. Conner just stood stunned, with their mouths open. Finally Mrs. Conner found her voice. "Matthew? What are you doing there? I thought you were sick!"

Matthew grinned sheepishly but didn't say anything.

Third Sister cleared her throat. "I'm glad you all liked the quartet," she said and smiled at the audience.

That was when I realized she had knocked over the screen on purpose. She must have planned on doing it all along.

"Matthew isn't one of my father's regular students," she continued, "but we wanted to show you what a talented musician he is. So we played this little trick on you. We hope you enjoyed it."

She looked at me shyly, silently apologizing. I quickly smiled, letting her know that I wasn't angry at her.

There was a murmuring as the audience finally understood what had happened, that Matthew had been playing behind the screen. The kids loved the whole thing. They started cheering and clapping. After a while their parents joined in.

My parents were the only ones not cheering.

Lensey Namioka

Editor Ilene Cooper talks to Lensey Namioka.

Ilene Cooper: Was your family musical like the Yangs?

Lensey Namioka: I'd say so. My father has composed music, and my sister is a professor of musicology, so they had very good "ears." But not me! Once my sister hid my violin exercise book. She confessed years later that she just couldn't take listening to me practice anymore! Still, my family was very supportive of other things I did. I wanted to show in my book that just because you're not good at one thing, it doesn't mean you can't be good at something else.

Cooper: What else in the story comes from your own life?

Namioka: I was born in Beijing, China, and came here with my family when I was nine years old. I didn't know English when I came here, and I had to learn it at school.

Cooper: Was that difficult?

Namioka: It wasn't as bad as it sounds. Kids learn fast, and I had good friends like Matthew.

Cooper: What was the biggest surprise to you?

Namioka: Everything! The food, the stores, the automobiles. I was shocked at how noisy the kids were in school. In Chinese schools, discipline is very important.

Cooper: Yingtao preferred playing baseball to practicing the violin. What did you prefer doing to practicing?

Namioka: Actually, I *did* like playing the piano. It was really only the violin that I disliked. I hated tuning it up! I preferred reading. I was a real bookworm. After I found the public library, it became my home away from home.

SPEAK UP

by Janet S. Wong

You're Korean, aren't you?

        Yes.

Why don't you speak Korean?

        Just don't, I guess.

Say something Korean.

        I don't speak it.
        I can't.

C'mon. Say something.

        Halmoni. Grandmother.
        Haraboji. Grandfather.
        Imo. Aunt.

Say some other stuff.
Sounds funny.
Sounds strange.

        Hey, let's listen to you
        for a change.

Listen to me?

        Say some foreign words.

But I'm American,
can't you see?

        Your family came from
        somewhere else.
        Sometime.

But I was born here.

        So was I.

Strike Up the Band!

Can you use your voice to make the sound of a musical instrument such as a trombone? Or a violin? Or a bass drum? Form a band with a group of other "musical" classmates and hold a recital.

Listen careful

Response

RESEARCH PROVERBS

Useful Proverbs

The Yang family enjoyed the messages inside the fortune cookies. Many of these "fortunes" are really **proverbs**, or wise sayings. Research proverbs, and list some you like. Share your list with a group.

Choose Your Strings

Yingtao and Matthew played the violin, but Third Sister preferred the cello. Write a paragraph describing the musical instrument you would most like to play and why.

Corner

What Do You Think?

- How does Yingtao try to solve his problem in the story?
- Do you think Yingtao's solution to his problem was wise? How would your solution have been the same or different?
- Who would you say is the stronger character – Yingtao or the second voice in "Speak Up"? Why?

A Very Young Musician

by Jill Krementz

I LOVE TO PLAY THE TRUMPET. I LOVE MUSIC.

I don't know if I want to be a professional trumpet player when I grow up. All I know for sure is that I'd like to be a good musician. My name is Josh Broder and I'm ten years old.

I live in Portland, Maine, with my parents and my older brother, Yank. He's eighteen, and started out playing piano until he switched to the saxophone. He's studying composition and jazz performance at The New England Conservatory of Music. He's already decided to be a professional musician.

PHOTOGRAPH © 1991 BY JILL KREMENTZ

The first wind instrument I ever played was the shofar, which is a hollowed-out ram's horn. I heard my brother play it, so I just picked it up one day and gave it a try. I was only eight years old, but horn playing seemed to come naturally to me. My mom and dad encouraged me to try playing the trumpet. It was hard at first, but I stuck with it and pretty soon I was enjoying it. My brother was a big influence, too. He taught me a lot, and we started jamming together—me on the trumpet and Yank on the saxophone. That was the most fun of all.

I still play the shofar. My dad is president of the Jewish Home for the Aged, so I go there and play on the High Holidays.

PHOTOGRAPH © 1991 BY JILL KREMENTZ

I go to the Waynflete School and I'm in the fifth grade. My teacher's name is Mrs. Lightbody and my best friend is Matt Marston. My favorite subjects are art and science. My best sport is gymnastics. When I go back and forth to school, I usually carry my trumpet along with my school books.

Quite a few of my friends play musical instruments; and this year I was invited to join the jazz band, which is made up of all eighth graders. There are sixteen people in our ensemble. The instructor, Ray Morrow, starts each class by passing the trash can around so we can throw out our gum. Then he says, "No food, no candy, and no talking." He's a tenor saxophonist, and he taught my brother how to play when Yank was in high school. The jazz band rehearses a couple of times a week. Being a part of this older group has really built my confidence—and they've taught me a lot.

Mark Fenderson is my trumpet teacher and I have a lesson once a week at the music studio. I take an hour of private instruction and a half hour of music theory, which is done on a computer. In my practice sessions we work on the fundamentals of trumpet playing and musicianship. Mark teaches me things that are specific to my trumpet playing; but he goes beyond that and covers general musical concepts such as rhythm, intonation, and style.

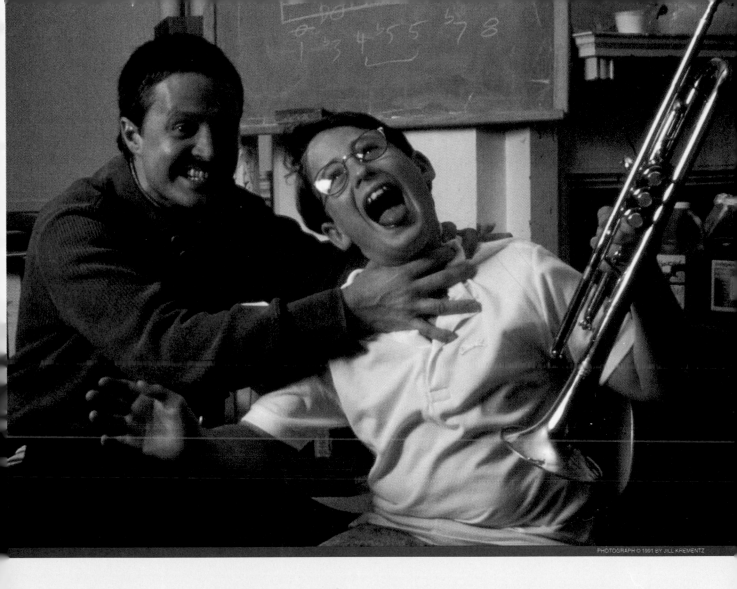

Mark has a three-level reminder system to help me remember what he's told me. The first step is a gentle tap on the head with a music book. If the book doesn't work, he says he'll move to heavier objects—a tennis racket or a two-by-four. The third and by far the most effective reminder is to strangle me.

Mark makes me laugh and that's important. The main thing is to focus on what I'm doing without a lot of tension. A good musician should enjoy what he or she is doing. It's all process, not product. When you sit down to play, you're not supposed to worry about how it's going to sound to other people. You just concentrate on playing your best; and if you make a mistake, you keep on going.

I try to practice every night for forty minutes. If I'm working on something new, I'll study my score ahead of time. It's crucial to be able to read new music accurately.

Early in the morning, before school and on weekends, I practice with the Deering High School Marching Band. It was a big honor to be asked to join the band and to play with people who are older and have more experience than I do.

This year I marched with the band in the Veterans Day parade. It's hard to march and play at the same time. The music clips onto a lyre attached to the slide of my horn. It jiggles up and down as I high-step, so it's hard to read. And the mouthpiece is another problem! When I'm marching, my trumpet is moving, so it's hard to keep the mouthpiece on my lips. Besides that, it was freezing!

For the past two summers I've gone to a sleep-away camp called Interlochen. "Interlochen" means "between the lakes," and it's in the woods of Michigan. There are over thirteen hundred campers from all around the world who come here to study art, music, drama, and dance—and to have fun.

The camp lasts for eight weeks, and we all sleep on bunks in wooden cabins. The campers are separated by age into divisions—Junior, Intermediate, and High School. This year I was elected to represent my group—Junior Boys—in the Senate, which is our camp government. It's like a student council. I couldn't wait to go to camp again this summer because I knew I was going to have a great time and make some new friends.

Each morning, after breakfast and roll call, I check the blackboard to see if there are any special events I should know about.

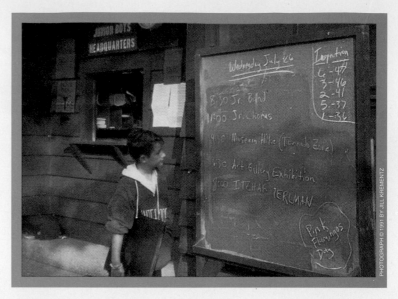

Then it's off to band practice, which is always my first class of the day. Our conductor's name is Mrs. Pickney.

It's the conductor's job to make the group perform together at the correct tempo and with the proper expression. Some conductors use their hands and others use a baton. Mrs. Pickney uses both.

A band is made up of brass, woodwind, and percussion instruments. When there are string instruments, it's an orchestra.

You learn a lot about the other instruments when you play in a band. The woodwind section includes clarinets, bass clarinets, oboes, saxophones, flutes, piccolos, English horns, bassoons, and double bassoons. They're called "woodwinds" because many of these instruments used to be made of wood. Now some of them are made of metal, but they still have mouthpieces with wooden reeds, which you blow into to make the sound.

The saxophone is made of brass, and it combines a lot of the features of the clarinet and the oboe. Technically, it's a woodwind because its mouthpiece has a wooden reed; but since it was never made out of wood, it's sort of in a class by itself. It was invented in 1840 by a Belgian instrument maker named Adolphe Sax.

The only woodwind that doesn't use a reed is the flute. It's one of the oldest instruments—in ancient times, it was made out of clay. Flutes and recorders are part of the same family; but flutes have mouthpieces on the side, and recorders are played from the end.

The percussion instruments include the various kinds of drums—like the snare drum, the timpani, and the big bass drum—and lots of other things like triangles, castanets, cymbals, and gongs. A cymbal on a stand is called a hi-hat. In most compositions the percussion instruments aren't played much of the time, but it still takes plenty of skill to do it right. Everyone knows if you make a mistake!

The timpani are called kettledrums because that's what they are—big "kettles" of copper or brass with a skin stretched over the open top, or "head." The player uses padded drumsticks and can make a lot of different sounds, from just a whisper to a big roar that sounds like thunder.

The brass section sits in the back of the band because it's the loudest. It includes the trumpet, trombone, French horn, and tuba. This year there were three trumpet players in the band—Dorie, Louis, and me.

The French horn originated in France as a hunting horn and is very difficult to play. French horn players always seem to put one of their hands inside the instrument bell, and this is called "stopping." The effect is a more muffled tone that sounds smoother and more velvety.

When we're learning a new piece, Mrs. Pickney rehearses each section separately until we get it right. Then when we all play together, it's like a miracle—all these different people playing different instruments to make music. We probably play our best when we give concerts. There's a lot of pressure when you're playing for an audience and you can't hear what the band sounds like. But when you hear the applause at the end, it's one of the greatest feelings I know.

At Interlochen, the students who are studying dance put on ballet recitals and the drama students put on plays. The artists exhibit their crafts and paintings, and sometimes they even exhibit themselves. We all have a chance to see these performances. We also have the opportunity to show off what we've learned. For me, that's one of the things that makes camp so much fun.

All summer long we have famous performers who hold master classes for the students and who perform in the evenings. This year Itzhak Perlman and Billy Taylor—two of my favorites—were guest artists. Itzhak Perlman played a violin concerto with the camp's World Youth Symphony Orchestra. Billy Taylor played piano with his trio.

▲ *Josh with Billy Taylor*
◀ *Itzhak Perlman performs*

When I got home from camp, my mom and dad took me to a Wynton Marsalis concert on Long Island to celebrate my eleventh birthday. He's one of my favorite musicians so this was a special treat. The concert was at a club called Wings. Since I usually set up the sound system for my brother's perfor-mances, I knew Wynton

would probably be there an hour or two before the concert for a sound check. So I went early, hoping to meet him. Was I ever lucky! He did arrive early, and since I was the only one there, besides the waiters, I sat and watched while he and the rest of his ensemble rehearsed.

Wynton Marsalis is not only a great trumpet player, he's also a great musician. He can play anything from classical concertos to modern jazz. He asked me if I had brought along my horn. I had, and he asked me to play for him. I was scared to death, but I played my long tones and some slur exercises.

Then he played his trumpet. He put my hand on his windpipe so he could demonstrate deep breathing—using a lot of air when you're playing—which is essential to trumpet playing. He told me how important it is to practice, to relax when I play, and to be humble. He said I should work on my scales; make every exercise musical; practice every day; and when I'm practicing to concentrate on every detail—to always know the reason why I'm practicing something. If I do all these things, he said, I'll be really good.

Wynton started playing when he was six and practicing seriously when he was twelve. His brother, Branford, is a great musician, too. Besides playing tenor saxophone, Branford has acted in quite a few movies. They both learned a lot from their father, who is head of the jazz department at the University of New Orleans.

At the end of the lesson, Wynton told me that I should always help other musicians and practice every day—he said that it shows in your tone.

While we waited for his concert to begin, I told my mom and dad that I would remember this birthday until I was a hundred years old.

The concert was wonderful! Wynton and the ensemble played "The New Orleans Function," which is a favorite of mine. It's one of the pieces from his album called "Majesty of the Blues." Between each set, he talked to the audience about the growth and history of jazz.

It's hard to believe that he's only twenty-seven years old. He's won eight Grammies, and he's the only musician who has ever won a Grammy for both jazz and classical music in the same year.

During the concert, I tried to imagine what it would be like if that was me up there. Wynton made it look so easy, but I know that hours and hours of practice go into every piece. I could tell that he loves music and loves to play for people.

Meeting Wynton Marsalis and getting to play for him was one of the most exciting things that ever happened to me. I still haven't decided if I want to be a full-time trumpet player when I grow up. I know I have a lot to learn. For now, I just want to be a better musician. But if I do stay with serious playing, I hope I'll always be as nice to young musicians as Wynton was to me.

Meet Jill Krementz

PHOTOGRAPH © 1991 BY JILL KREMENTZ

JILL KREMENTZ works as a journalist, photographer, and portraitist. Her pictures can be seen regularly in *The New York Times, Los Angeles Times, New York* magazine, *Time, Newsweek,* and many other major periodicals. She has written and photographed more than two dozen books for young readers and adults, including *A Very Young Skier, A Very Young Dancer, A Very Young Rider, A Very Young Gymnast, A Very Young Circus Flyer, A Very Young Skater, The Fun of Cooking, A Visit to Washington, D.C.,* and the "How It Feels" series dealing with the death of a parent, adoption, divorce, and chronic illness.

Ms. Krementz received the 1984 *Washington Post*/Children's Book Guild Nonfiction Award for "creatively produced books, works that make a difference." She lives in New York City with her husband and young daughter.

RESPONSE CORNER

ORCHESTRA ART

Work with one of four groups to research a family of instruments — brass, percussion, strings, or woodwinds. Make a poster listing all the instruments in that family, and include illustrations of as many of the instruments as possible. Display your poster along with those of the other three groups to create an entire orchestra.

WRITE A PARAGRAPH

PROCESS OR PRODUCT

Josh is taught that a good musician thinks of his or her work as a process, not a product. What do you think this statement means? Do you agree with what Josh is being taught? Write your opinion in a paragraph.

DISCUSS A TOPIC

FACT & FICTION

If this story had been written as fiction, would you have liked it? Discuss your answer with a partner. Tell how the story and the information given might have been different.

WHAT DO YOU THINK?

✳ What is Josh doing to become a better trumpet player?

✳ What did you learn about becoming a musician that you didn't know before?

✳ Suppose that a friend decided to learn a musical instrument. What information about Josh's experiences would you share with your friend?

Beethoven Lives Upstairs

Barbara Nichol

Illustrated by
Scott Cameron

On Thursday, March 29, 1827, the people of Vienna flooded into the streets. They came to pay their respects to Ludwig van Beethoven, the great composer, who had died three days earlier.

At three o'clock in the afternoon nine priests blessed the coffin, and the funeral procession left Mr. Beethoven's house for the church. So dense were the crowds that the one-block journey took an hour and a half.

I wasn't in Vienna on that famous day. I was a student of music in Salzburg at the time. But if you had looked carefully, you might have spotted in the crowd a little boy with a serious face. He is Christoph, my nephew, and there was a time when he came to know Mr. Beethoven quite well.

It was not a happy time in Christoph's life. He was only ten years old, and his father had recently died.

The first of Christoph's letters arrived at my door in the autumn of 1822. I was surprised that he had written. I had not seen my nephew for some years. . . .

7 September 1822

Dear Uncle,

I hope you will remember me. It is Christoph, your nephew, who writes. As to the reasons, I will not keep you in suspense. I write, Uncle, because something terrible has happened. A madman has moved into our house.

Do you remember that when Father died, Mother decided to rent out his office upstairs? Well, she has done it, and Ludwig van Beethoven has moved in.

Every morning at dawn Mr. Beethoven begins to make his dreadful noise upstairs. Loud poundings and howlings come through the floor. They are like the sounds of an injured beast. All morning Mr. Beethoven carries on this way. After lunch he storms into the street. He comes home, sometimes long after the house is quiet for the night, tracking mud and stamping his way up the stairs above our heads.

Mother says I mustn't blame him. He's deaf and can't hear the noise he makes. But he wakes up the twins, and they start their crying. They cry all day.

Uncle, I must make this one request. I beg you to tell my mother to send Mr. Beethoven away.

Your nephew, Christoph

My dear Christoph,   10 October 1822

I arrived home last night to find your letter on the table in the hall. Do I remember you? Of course I do!

I should tell you that I have received a letter from your mother as well. As you know, she is concerned about you and wants you to be happy. She assures me that Mr. Beethoven is peculiar perhaps, but certainly not mad.

Christoph, Mr. Beethoven will settle in soon, I'm sure. I know that life will be more peaceful before long.

Your uncle, Karl

Having answered my nephew's letter, I left Salzburg for some weeks on matters related to my studies. In truth, I expected no further messages. The three letters that follow arrived in my absence.

22 October 1822

Dear Uncle,

I hope you will forgive my troubling you, but I am sure that you will want to hear this news. Our family is now the laughing-stock of Vienna.

I opened the door this morning to find a crowd in front of our house. They were looking up at Mr. Beethoven's window and laughing, so I looked up too. There was Mr. Beethoven, staring at a sheet of music. And Uncle, he had no clothes on at all! It was a dreadful sight!

You should see him setting out for the afternoon. He hums to himself. He growls out tunes. He waves his arms. His pockets bulge with papers and pencils. On the street the children run and call him names.

Mr. Beethoven is so famous that sometimes people stop outside our house, hoping they will see him. But if anyone asks, I say he has moved away.

Your nephew, Christoph

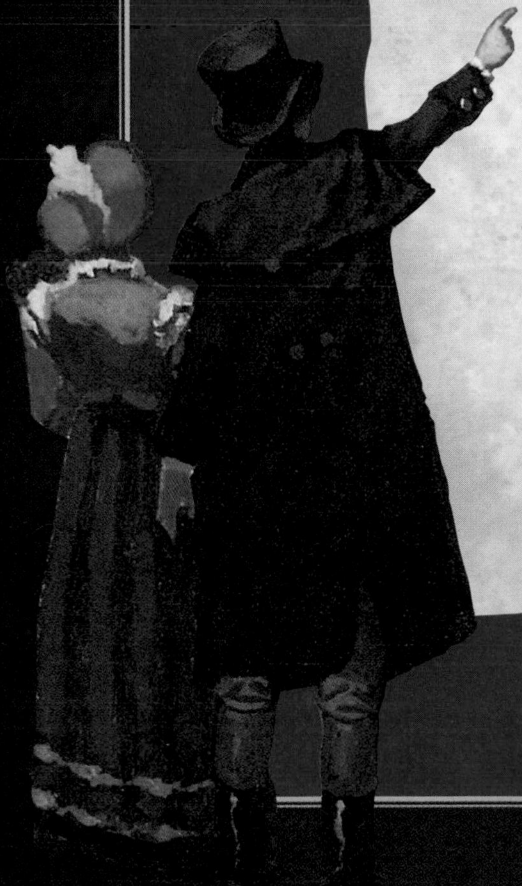

29 October 1822

Dear Uncle,

I have now seen with my own eyes that Mr. Beethoven is mad. I will tell you the story in the hope that you will do something at last.

Last night, when I was getting ready for bed, I happened to look up. There were beads of water collecting on the ceiling above my head.

As usual, Mother was busy with the twins, so I climbed the stairs and crept along the hall to Mr. Beethoven's room. I looked in. He was standing there with no shirt on. He had a jug of water in his hands. He was pouring the water over his head, right there in the middle of the room, and all this time stamping his feet like he was marching or listening to a song.

You should see my father's study! Do you remember how tidy he was? Well, now there are papers lying everywhere— on the floor, on the chairs, on the bed that isn't made. There are dirty dishes stacked up and clothing crumpled on the floor. And another thing, he has been writing on the wall with a pencil!

I said nothing to Mr. Beethoven, of course. Luckily, he did not see me, and I ran back down the stairs.

Uncle, if you are thinking of coming to our aid, there could be no better time than now.

Christoph

5 November 1822

Dear Uncle,

Another week has passed, but life is no calmer here.

I've been thinking. If Mr. Beethoven were to leave, surely we could find someone nice to live upstairs. The rooms are large, and Father's patients always talked about the view of the river. Father used to carry me down to the riverbank on his shoulders, even down the steep part right behind the house.

I think that of all the places in the house, I like the outside best. I can be alone there and get away from all the noise inside. But on this day even the stray dog outside was making his pitiful voice heard.

Yours truly, Christoph

22 November 1822

My dear Christoph,

Today I have returned home from a visit away to find three of your letters waiting. Christoph, I will admit that Mr. Beethoven does not seem to be an easy guest.

Perhaps I can help, though, by saying that as strange as Mr. Beethoven seems, there are reasons for the way he acts.

They say he is working on a symphony. And so, all day long, he is hearing his music in his head. He doesn't think, perhaps, how very strange he sometimes seems to us.

Tomorrow I am leaving Salzburg again and traveling with friends to Bonn, the city where Mr. Beethoven was born. I know I will find something to tell you about and I will be sure to write on my return.

Uncle Karl

10 December 1822

Dear Uncle,

It has now been a full three months since Mr. Beethoven moved in, but our household has not yet become like any sort of ordinary place.

Mr. Beethoven has a friend named Mr. Schindler who visits almost every day. He always says, "Poor Mr. Beethoven. He is a lonely man."

You know that Mr. Beethoven is deaf. When he has visitors, they write what they want to say in a book. He reads their message and answers them out loud. He has a low and fuzzy voice.

Mr. Beethoven's eyes are weak as well. When he works too long by candlelight, his eyes begin to ache. He sometimes sits alone, with a cloth wrapped around his head to keep out the light. He sits, not seeing and not hearing, in his chair.

Uncle, there is no hour of the day when I forget that Mr. Beethoven is in the house.

Your nephew, Christoph

I returned to Salzburg in late January of 1823.

22 January 1823

Dear Christoph,

I have this very day returned from the place where Mr. Beethoven was born. It seems his family is well remembered there.

They say Mr. Beethoven's grandfather was a musician, in charge of all the music at the palace. And Mr. Beethoven's father was a musician, too. But Christoph, this father was an unhappy man who took to drink. Mr. Beethoven was not a happy child.

People who lived near their house remember hearing music coming from the attic late at night. Sometimes Mr. Beethoven's father would come home long after dark and get the young boy out of bed. He would make him practice his piano until dawn.

The little Beethoven would play all night, tired and cold, his face awash with tears. Finally, as the sun came up, he would go to bed to the sound of morning bells.

I will send this letter right away, in the hope that you will answer soon.

Affectionately, Uncle

4 February 1823

Dear Uncle,

This afternoon a messenger arrived, bearing a note for Mr. Beethoven.

The messenger said to me, "This is from Prince Karl Lichnowsky. But the prince says that if Mr. Beethoven's door is closed, he is not to be disturbed."

Mr. Beethoven must be a terrible man if even a prince is afraid of him.

Your nephew, Christoph

Dear Christoph,   15 February 1823

I've been thinking of your story about the prince. Christoph, I don't think the prince is afraid of Mr. Beethoven. I believe he is showing him respect. In Vienna, music is so loved that even a prince will tread carefully around a composer.

Alas, Mr. Beethoven has not returned their kindness. He has not been gentle with the fine people of Vienna, and they have done everything they can to please him. Mr. Beethoven has always had rough manners. He turns down their invitations, dresses carelessly to visit, and arrives late for their dinners.

Sometimes he is very angry if he is asked to play his music. There is one famous story of a grand lady who got down on her knees one evening to beg Mr. Beethoven to play. He refused. And there is another tale about a prince who teased Mr. Beethoven for not playing at dinner. Mr. Beethoven flew into a rage. "There are many princes," he said, "but there is only one Beethoven."

My belief, Christoph, is that a prince has more to fear from Mr. Beethoven than has a little boy.

Affectionately, Uncle

Dear Uncle,   26 February 1823

No news today but this—do you remember I once told you about a stray dog who was whining on the street? He is a small and spotted dog, and I have found a way to make him stop his crying.

Today he seemed quite pleased to share my sugar cake from lunch.

Christoph

Dear Christoph,   2 March 1823

I write again so soon because I have been making inquiries on your behalf.

I spoke today with a man who once worked for Mr. Beethoven, copying out music for the players. He told me that Mr. Beethoven never stays in one home very long. He moves often—as often as three times a year.

Sometimes Mr. Beethoven wants a sunnier home, sometimes shadier. Sometimes he says he cannot live on the ground floor; then he cannot live on the top. And I hear he has been asked to leave from time to time as well.

He has a restless nature, so perhaps before too long you will have your wish and quieter people will be living upstairs.

But in the meantime, tell me . . . is it true, as I have also heard, that Mr. Beethoven has three pianos in his room?

Your uncle

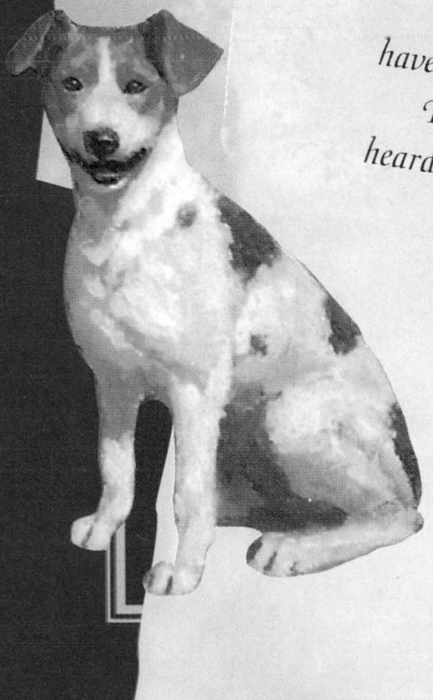

10 March 1823

Dear Uncle,

No, it is not true that Mr. Beethoven has three pianos. He has four! And you should see them! To begin with, some of his pianos have no legs. He takes the legs off to move them and so that he can play them when he is sitting on the floor. That way he can feel his playing through the floorboards, which he must do because, of course, he cannot hear.

But it's surprising that his pianos can be played at all. Many of the strings are broken and curled up. They look like birds' nests made of wire. And the pianos are stained inside from the times he's knocked the inkwell with his sleeve.

And Mr. Beethoven has all sorts of bells on his desk, and four ear trumpets to help him hear, and something called a metronome as well. It's a little box with a stick on it. The stick goes back and forth and back and forth and tells musicians how fast they should play. Mr. Beethoven has a name for me. He calls me "the little gate-keeper" because I am always sitting outside on the step.

Yours truly, Christoph
Gatekeeper

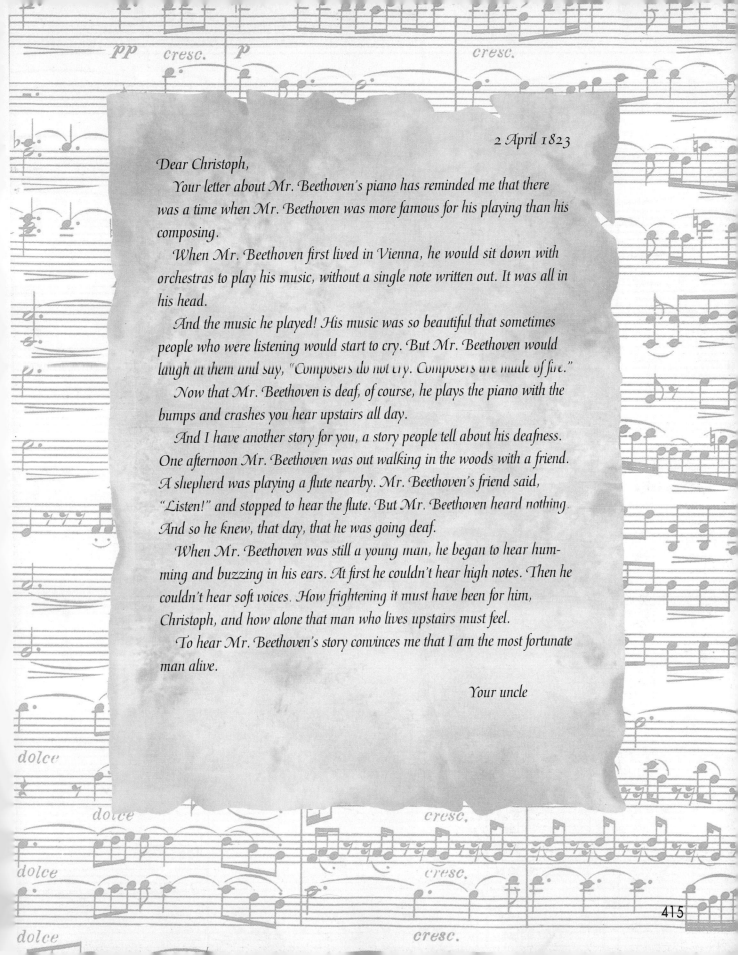

2 April 1823

Dear Christoph,

Your letter about Mr. Beethoven's piano has reminded me that there was a time when Mr. Beethoven was more famous for his playing than his composing.

When Mr. Beethoven first lived in Vienna, he would sit down with orchestras to play his music, without a single note written out. It was all in his head.

And the music he played! His music was so beautiful that sometimes people who were listening would start to cry. But Mr. Beethoven would laugh at them and say, "Composers do not cry. Composers are made of fire."

Now that Mr. Beethoven is deaf, of course, he plays the piano with the bumps and crashes you hear upstairs all day.

And I have another story for you, a story people tell about his deafness. One afternoon Mr. Beethoven was out walking in the woods with a friend. A shepherd was playing a flute nearby. Mr. Beethoven's friend said, "Listen!" and stopped to hear the flute. But Mr. Beethoven heard nothing. And so he knew, that day, that he was going deaf.

When Mr. Beethoven was still a young man, he began to hear humming and buzzing in his ears. At first he couldn't hear high notes. Then he couldn't hear soft voices. How frightening it must have been for him, Christoph, and how alone that man who lives upstairs must feel.

To hear Mr. Beethoven's story convinces me that I am the most fortunate man alive.

Your uncle

415

21 April 1823

Dear Uncle,

Do you remember my telling you that Mr. Beethoven leaves each afternoon for a walk? Did you wonder where he goes? Well, now I know, and I will tell you the story.

Mother sometimes says that instead of just staying on the front steps it would be nice if I'd spend some time inside. I used to believe she meant it until this morning.

I thought of something to play with the twins. I rolled up a bit of cardboard like an ear trumpet and put one end in little Teresa's ear. I said, "GOOD MORNING, BABY!" very loudly, and she started to scream. Mother said it hurt her. So I went outside again and sat in my usual place on the step.

Then Mr. Schindler came downstairs. He said to me, "The master needs new pencils," and off I went to the shop.

When I came back, Mr. Schindler was gone. No one was upstairs but Mr. Beethoven, and he was writing at his desk. I stamped my feet on the floor to get his attention and when he didn't notice I stamped harder until at last I was stamping as hard as I could. Then suddenly he turned around and saw me. When he laughs, he sounds like a lion.

So today I went along with him on his walk. At times Mr. Beethoven forgot that I was with him. He would hum and sometimes wave his arms. He took out his papers and made some little notes.

We walked outside Vienna into the tall woods and then past the woods and into the fields. Uncle, if you were to come to visit me, I would show you where we walked today.

Christoph

30 June 1823

Dear Uncle,

Spring has come and gone, and now it is summer. The house is quiet because tonight Mr. Beethoven has gone to Baden, where he will spend the hottest months. He will finish his symphony and then he will come back.

Tonight as I write you it is evening, but I cannot sleep with the sun still shining through the shutters. From my room I can hear Mother playing piano as she used to when I was small.

I have been sitting here thinking about something Mr. Schindler said. He said, "Mr. Beethoven works so hard because he believes that music can change the world."

In July of 1823 the following note arrived, unfinished and unsigned. Christoph was preoccupied, I suspect, by the pleasures of summertime and was too busy for letter writing. The note was sent to me by his mother, included in a letter of her own.

In the autumn of 1823 Mr. Beethoven returned to Vienna from his summer lodgings.

Dear Uncle,

29 October 1823

Mr. Beethoven has come home, and so our house is in an uproar again. Someone has given him another piano, and there was a lot of trouble getting it up the stairs.

And then last night he had a party. A lot of people went in and out very late, and the more cheerful they became upstairs, the noisier it was for us.

Finally, it was impossible to sleep. I could hear two ladies singing. I had seen them earlier, laughing on the stairs. They are called sopranos because they are singers who can sing very high.

Mr. Beethoven has a housekeeper. She says that when the sopranos come up the stairs, Mr. Beethoven rushes like a schoolboy to change his coat. And he won't let her make the coffee for them. It must be perfect, with exactly sixty beans for every cup. He counts them himself.

Uncle, I have asked Mother if you can come to visit. She said she would be delighted if you would. She thinks you would enjoy the goings-on.

Christoph

4 January 1824

Dear Christoph,

How glad I was to receive your letter. I hope you will forgive my very late reply. Did you know that your mother has written to me as well? She tells me there's a steady stream of great musicians up and down your stairs.

Since Mr. Beethoven is writing his Ninth Symphony in your very house, perhaps you will be interested in the things I have heard. According to the stories, Mr. Beethoven has felt that he is not appreciated in Vienna. He almost agreed to perform his new symphony in Berlin! I'm happy to say, though, that so many people begged Mr. Beethoven to change his mind that, luckily, he did.

And there is other news: they say the orchestra members are complaining about their parts. The bass players say their instruments aren't nimble enough for Mr. Beethoven's quick notes. The sopranos say their notes are just too high. All over Vienna the musicians are struggling with their tasks. His symphony will put to music the poem "Ode to Joy."

I hear as well that because Mr. Beethoven is deaf, he will lead the orchestra with another conductor—one who can hear—conducting alongside him.

Amid these great events, little gatekeeper, how is life at home? Do your twin sisters still torment you with their terrible shouts? Perhaps before too long I shall hear them for myself.

Uncle Karl

27 March 1824

Dear Uncle,

I know this will come as a surprise, but this time I write you with good news.

I was standing on the upstairs landing today when my favorite soprano came by to get tickets for the concert. At least she is now my favorite.

She had something to ask of Mr. Beethoven and she wrote her request in his book. Then she wrote another request, handed him the book, and winked at me.

He read her words and said, "Certainly. The boy and his mother will have tickets as well."

And so Mother and I will be going to the Ninth Symphony. I wrote "thank you" as neatly as I could in his book.

As for the twins, Uncle, of course they still torment me. It is what they were put on earth to do.

Now I have a new name for my sisters. I call them "the sopranos." It makes my mother laugh.

Yours truly, Christoph

20 April 1824

Dear Uncle,

I know now that all of us have been quite happy of late. And the way I know it is that in the past few days our happiness has vanished once again. With the symphony just two weeks away, Mr. Beethoven's moods are fierce.

Caroline, his housekeeper, is going to leave to marry the baker next door. She told Mr. Beethoven today, and he became very angry. He picked up an egg and threw it at her.

Then Mr. Schindler came rushing down the stairs like a scalded cat. He had told Mr. Beethoven that his new coat won't be ready for the concert in time. He tried to talk to Mr. Beethoven about another coat but, as Mr. Schindler said, "The master is in no mood for details."

And I have not helped matters. Today, when I was in his room, I disturbed some of his papers as I was passing by his desk. They fluttered to the floor. I am afraid these papers had been ordered in some very special way because Mr. Beethoven said, "Now I must do work again that I have already done."

Uncle, just when life was getting better, I have ruined things again.

Your nephew

28 April 1824

My dearest Christoph,

How shall I console you? Perhaps by telling you that Mr. Beethoven is famous for his temper and that his moods are not your fault.

Imagine how frustrating his life must be. Imagine how lonely to hear no voices. Imagine hearing no birds sing, no wind in the trees, no pealing of bells. Imagine: he hears no music played, not even his own!

So Mr. Beethoven has a great temper. How could he not? But if you listen to his music, you will hear that his heart is great as well, too great to be angry for long at an innocent boy.

You write me that, for the moment, your happiness has vanished. I can give you my promise, Christoph, that unhappiness has a way of vanishing as well.

Your uncle and friend, Karl

Dear Uncle,

Mr. Beethoven has forgotten the incident with the papers. He squeezed my shoulder in a friendly way when he passed me in the hall this afternoon.

Now the house is quiet, and I am alone. The concert is tomorrow night, and so, of course, I cannot sleep. I think of Mr. Beethoven alone upstairs. I have not heard him stir for quite some time. I wonder what he's thinking about. I wonder if he's awake tonight like me.

Perhaps he is hearing something beautiful in his head.

7 May 1824

Dear Uncle,

Tonight I have been to the Ninth Symphony. It is very late. I have already tried to sleep, but it seems I cannot do so before I describe this night to you.

The concert looked as I expected. There was Mr. Beethoven on the stage, waving his arms as I have seen him do so many times upstairs. And there were the singers. I had seen them often too, tramping up and down our halls. And there were the musicians scowling at their charts. These sights were so familiar.

It was the music, Uncle, that took me by surprise.

And when the music ended, the audience was on its feet. Everyone was standing and cheering and clapping and waving scarves and crying and trying to make Mr. Beethoven hear them.

But he couldn't hear us and he didn't know that we were cheering until one of the sopranos took his sleeve and turned him to face the crowd. Four times the audience finished their clapping and then began to clap and cheer again. Up on the stage Mr. Beethoven bowed and bowed.

As the carriage took us home, I could hear the music in my head. But my thoughts kept turning back to Mr. Beethoven himself.

He has so many troubles, how can he have a heart so full of joy?

I cannot describe the music, Uncle. I can only tell you what the music made me think.

Uncle, how difficult Mr. Beethoven's life must be. To feel so much inside, even so much joy, must be almost more than he can bear.

Christoph

In June of 1824 I finally paid a visit to Vienna, to the home of my sister, her twin girls, and Christoph. It was Christoph, of course, who took the most delight in explaining the many eccentricities of the genius up the stairs. This letter, the final portion of which is now missing, is the last in which my nephew mentions Mr. Beethoven. It arrived at my home in Salzburg almost a year after my visit to Vienna.

31 March 1825

Dear Uncle,

As you know, Mr. Beethoven moved away soon after your visit. But I have seen him again and thought you might like to hear about it.

It was on the street. I saw him rushing by, humming to himself as always. I ran up and caught him by the sleeve. He looked confused at first, but then he recognized me. He said, "It's the little gatekeeper," and took my hands in his.

I took his book and asked if he was well. He had hoped his health would be better living away from the river. He told me his health has not improved. I wrote in his book that when I grow up I'm going to be a doctor like my father and then I will make him better.

He asked about Mother and the twins, and he was glad to hear that Mother is teaching piano again. And then I told him that we miss him. He squeezed my hands and looked down at the ground.

And as for other news, the twins have finally stopped their screaming. I know, however, that our good luck will not hold. I have seen them exchanging looks in their carriage and can see that they are hatching some new plan.

But Uncle! Best of all! Mother has agreed to let me keep the spotted dog.

I have named him Metronome, because of his wagging tail.

Response Corner

RESEARCH THE EAR

How We Hear

Why was Ludwig van Beethoven losing his hearing? Research how the ear works. Draw a scientific diagram of the human ear, labeling all the important parts.

WRITE A LETTER

A Message from the Master

Suppose that Beethoven has written Christoph a letter after leaving Vienna. Write that letter as if you were Beethoven, using the proper form. Tell Christoph how you felt about living upstairs from him. Share your letter with a partner.

Music Around the World

Beethoven's music was popular all over Europe and is now a treasured part of European culture. Work with a partner. Select another part of the world, and prepare an oral report on its musical heritage.

What Do You Think?

- In what way does Christoph's opinion of Beethoven change?

- If you had had Beethoven upstairs from you, what would have been the hardest things to live with? What would have been the best?

- If you could have met Beethoven, what questions would you have written in his book?

431

There are many talented characters in this theme. Who do you think is the most talented? Why?

The characters in this theme use their creativity in many different ways—including broadcasting, music, and writing. Explain the way (or ways) you use your own creativity.

ACTIVITY CORNER

Prepare a short talk for the radio program *Kidsview.* Read aloud a one-minute review of any selection in the theme.

THEME

PLANET OF LIFE

How do we fit into the natural world?

Knowing the answer to that question

can give us a deeper appreciation of

life on Earth. Read about some people

who respect the natural world and who

try to live in harmony with it.

THEME PLANET

CONTENTS

434

OF LIFE

BOOKSHELF

Sugaring Time
by Kathryn Lasky

There is a pause between the winter-time and the springtime, when the sweet syrup runs inside the maple trees.
Signatures Library

To Space & Back
by Sally Ride with Susan Okie

Blast off with Sally Ride and the space shuttle crew on this true American adventure.
Signatures Library

Good-Bye My Wishing Star
by Vicki Grove

When her parents can no longer afford to keep their farm, Jens finds that keeping a journal makes saying good-bye a bit easier.

Notable Trade Book in Social Studies

Sequoias
by Michael George

Learn about the physical characteristics, growth patterns, and longevity of the majestic sequoia tree. Gorgeous photographs of the giant trees fill the book.

Earth, Sky, and Beyond: A Journey Through Space
by Jean-Pierre Verdet

This examination of the planets, stars, and sun begins with our own Earth. The book also includes brilliant drawings of artificial satellites and spacecraft.

THE AMERICAN

A PHOTO ESSAY BY GEORGE ANCONA

TEXT BY JOAN ANDERSON

The American Family Farm
A Photo Essay by GEORGE ANCONA   Text by JOAN ANDERSON

ALA Notable Book
SLJ Best Books

WILL
Cab

FAMILY FARM

Willie Adams's house and farm in Greensboro, Georgia, are tucked away behind the towering pines that line the east Georgia highway.

"At the fork in the road, bear left," Willie says, "and go down the hill and over a bridge. You'll see our sign. The house is at the end of the road."

Willie lives with his wife, Linda, daughter, Shonda, son, Cedric, and his mother, Rosie.

"I spent my childhood following my grandfather as he steered the horse-drawn plow and worked these ninety-two acres," Willie says. "In those days, the fields around here were full of cotton, peanuts, and corn."

Despite hard times, Willie's grandfather did whatever was necessary to hold onto the land.

"Then, when I was just fifteen, he took ill and could no longer work," Willie remembers, "and things had to change if the farm was to survive."

"That's how I eventually got into chicken farming," he says. "There was no way I could manage growing crops and go to school at the same time. Besides, with synthetic fiber becoming more and more popular, cotton was on its way out. My mother and I were forced to change our way of farming altogether."

They phased out crops and began raising beef cattle, improving their pastureland to allow them to feed the new herd. Twelve years ago, Willie added two poultry houses to his farm. "In this business you always have to look ahead to what will sell. Poultry farming doesn't depend on weather, because the chickens are kept in specially built houses. As long as they are fed properly, you're pretty much guaranteed a healthy chicken at the end of eight weeks."

"We live a simple life—real quiet and peaceful," says Rosie, sitting on the porch with her grandchildren on her lap. "There's always a breeze on this front porch, because the house sits on a little knoll and catches the air.

"It sure is a perfect place to raise children. Lets 'em see down-to-earth living. That way they learn how things are. Living on a farm allows you to go down to grass roots and know that something can always be created from the soil."

Every day, Cedric sets off for the fields with his red wagon.

"He collects whatever is growing out there," his grandmother says. "Willie did the same thing when he was little, and look what happened to him!"

Everyone has a place here. Linda Adams tends to the poultry houses when her husband is off in the fields. In the afternoon she says good-bye to the children and goes to work in a nearby sock factory.

"Most of the women out here work away from the farm at least part time," she says. "It adds a steady income for us, along with what we get from the chickens. If farming is in your blood and you want to stay on the land, you do what needs to be done to make that possible."

Twice daily, Willie drives five miles in his pickup truck to a tract of U.S. Forest pastureland where his seventy Beefmaster cattle graze. "I rent the

land for a small fee," he says. "It's one way the government is trying to help the small farmer.

"Here in Georgia the cattle can stay out all year long," Willie says as he unloads buckets of feed. "They're good animals. I wouldn't feel like a farmer if I didn't have a herd of cows."

"A few years back something very exciting happened to me," says Willie. "I began meeting other black farmers who seemed to love agriculture as much as I did. At the time, we were all struggling, working independently of each other. Most of our wives had jobs, and none of us could afford hired hands. Gradually it occurred to me that perhaps we could help each other, that surely there would be strength in our combined ideas. And so I formed a cooperative in which the members would experience a sense of kinship, share knowledge and labor from time to time, and offer each other moral support—just like it would be if we were brothers working the same farm. The co-op is like an extended family farm."

Today ten members, all of whom share common roots, belong to the cooperative. They are Willie and Linda Adams, I. V. and Annie Henry, Leroy Cooper, Melvin Cunningham, Roger Lemar, Frank Smith, Robert Williams, and Mrs. E. M. Neal.

Descended from Africans brought as slaves to this country over one hundred years ago to till the white man's land, these fifth-generation farmers truly know the cycles of agriculture.

Willie is in constant contact with the co-op members, discussing individual needs and problems and trying to make arrangements for one farmer to help another.

"We share large machinery, trailers, and trucks for hauling live-stock," he explains. "We save a lot of money by not owning identical equipment." The members are always on the lookout for used equipment that can be bought inexpensively and restored for communal use.

"Some of us are better mechanics than others," Willie says. Today he is calling Melvin Cunningham to repair his tractor, and in return for his time Melvin will use the tractor to work his land. Similarly, Willie recently borrowed a truck from one of the co-op members to pick up seeds a feed store was giving away. He managed to get enough to be able to share them all around.

This being June in Georgia, it is time for the first cutting of hay.

Willie is off to I. V. Henry's place, hoping that I. V., who owns the only baler in the co-op, will have time to harvest one of Willie's fields.

Willie finds his friend ready to hook the baler to his tractor, and he goes to help. I. V. then takes off across the broad field, where freshly cut yellow hay waits to be gathered up into massive round bales. "Round bales can sit out in the fields longer," I. V. says, "because the hay is gathered in such a way that it is better protected from the elements. Good thing, too, because none of us has enough loft space to store the square bales, which need more protection.

"This baler is an amazing machine," he adds, pleased to have found it secondhand. "It gathers the hay in a round formation and ties it together with twine in the process. Machines like this one make farming a whole lot easier than it was in the old days."

I. V. Henry has been a farmer since he was ten years old. His parents separated at that time, and he had no choice but to take up the chores of his father. "I learned early on that if you could raise it you didn't have to buy it," he says. "Since the only income most black folks had back then came

from picking cotton, we learned real quick to use our extra land to raise anything and everything we wanted to eat.

"Even today, things aren't that easy," I. V. continues, running his hands through a barrel of grain. "We never know whether a bank will give us a loan or turn us down. And on top of that, there are lots of folks out there who are anxious to buy us out. With the co-op we can figure out our options better."

Because I. V. is Willie's closest co-op neighbor, the two men frequently help each other with heavy chores. In a few weeks, I. V.'s chickens will have matured, and Willie will help him herd them into boxes on turn-over day.

"Chicken farming is a one-man job until the day we ship them out," I. V. says. "Then we need all the help we can get. After the birds are gone, the entire house must be cleaned within twenty-four hours to prepare for the new shipment of baby chicks."

Weary after a long day, I. V. pauses to reflect a moment. "You know, Booker T. Washington once said: 'No race can prosper till it learns that there is as much dignity in tilling a field as in writing a poem,' and I think he was right."

"We're out to beat the statistics that say black farmers are losing their land at a rate of 9,000 acres a week," says Willie. He and his cooperative have found a way to perpetuate a lifestyle, preserve the land of their forefathers for future generations, and prosper in the process.

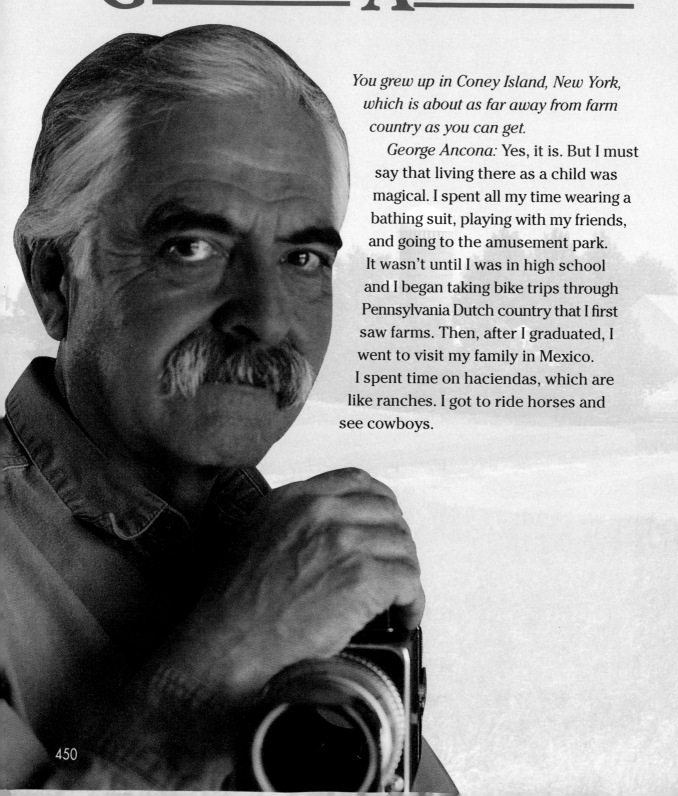

AN INTERVIEW WITH THE PHOTOGRAPHER:
GEORGE ANCONA

You grew up in Coney Island, New York, which is about as far away from farm country as you can get.

George Ancona: Yes, it is. But I must say that living there as a child was magical. I spent all my time wearing a bathing suit, playing with my friends, and going to the amusement park. It wasn't until I was in high school and I began taking bike trips through Pennsylvania Dutch country that I first saw farms. Then, after I graduated, I went to visit my family in Mexico. I spent time on haciendas, which are like ranches. I got to ride horses and see cowboys.

Was your visit to Mexico your first exposure to your Latin heritage?

   Ancona: Oh, no. My home life was full of my heritage. We spoke Spanish at home—at least I *thought* I spoke Spanish, until I went to Mexico. My cousins teased me about my accent. They called me a *gringo*. Still, the closeness of the family, the food, the music—that felt very much the same to me.

Do you still go back to Mexico?

   Ancona: Oh, yes. I'm working on a book about the Maya, so I've been spending a good deal of time in the Yucatan. My relatives are from there.

There is a strong family feeling in The American Family Farm. *Is that what attracted you to this subject?*

   Ancona: Sure. In farm families there is a sense that "we are all in this together." But I was also interested in the strong sense of place: This is the land, it's been here for generations, and the people are tied to it. They'll never leave.

How did you find the families that appear in the book?

   Ancona: Joan Anderson, the author, did the initial research. Then she and I talked to various families, and we got to know each other. We were particularly interested in the Adams family because we wanted to know about an African American farm family in the South.

When you begin work on a photo essay, do you plan out what you want to shoot, or do you just begin taking pictures?

   Ancona: I begin by shooting a lot. That gets people used to me, because sometimes they're nervous around a camera, or they're too eager to pose. After a while, though, the camera becomes ordinary, and I just become the crazy guy snapping away.

RESPONSE CORNER

DRAW A MAP

America's Breadbasket

Use resources to find information about farming in present-day America. Work with a partner to create a map showing where certain crops are grown. Make a map key to explain any symbols you use on your map. Compare your map with those of your classmates.

WRITE A PARAGRAPH

Co-op Pros and Cons

Think about the cooperative to which Willie Adams and the other farmers belong. List some of the good and bad things about working in a co-op. Then use your list to help you write an opinion paragraph. Tell whether you think cooperatives make good business sense.

The Changing Farm

Farming was much more difficult before the invention of modern farm machines. Find out about one of the machines that has made farming easier. Create a poster that shows it and tells about it. Display your poster in the classroom.

What Do You Think?

- What important ideas did you learn about farming?

- What do you think about farming as a way of life?

- Do you think the American family farm can survive? Explain your response.

words and pictures by
Raymond Bial

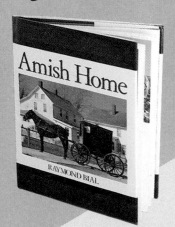

Amish Home

Author's Note The Amish do not allow themselves to be photographed because of the biblical passage cautioning against the making of "graven images" and because of *Gelassenheit,* a German word that roughly means "humility." They believe that it is prideful to draw attention to themselves. As one Amish lady told me, "You may not take any pictures of me, but you may photograph anything I own, because worldly goods do not matter to me." Another young man, as he shoed a workhorse, shyly grinned and remarked, "Sure, you can take all the photographs you want, just so I don't get in any of them!"

Out of respect for these gentle and industrious people, there are no portraits in this book. Yet one can also know people by their crafts, and there are many photographs of buggies, quilts, clothing, and other possessions in *Amish Home.* Although the Amish do not place any value on these "worldly goods," they are hardworking, productive people, and the objects around them very much reflect the spirit of their lives.

When visiting an Amish settlement, you may at first think that you are traveling down any country road. The sun gleams on the ribbon of asphalt. Queen Anne's lace and black-eyed Susans crowd the shoulder, and the fields unfold green in every direction. However, as you drive along, you quickly discover that you have entered another world.

You may first notice a horse and buggy clip-clopping along the road. Among the Amish, the horse and buggy serve not only as a practical means of transportation, but as symbols of their way of life, because these deeply religious people do not believe in owning and driving automobiles.

Many people consider the Amish to be old-fashioned because they have rejected much of modern technology, including radios and televisions. Actually, the Amish do not oppose progress so much as they conscientiously adhere to their own beliefs. These beliefs are rooted in their religion, which emphasizes the importance of family and community, and their agrarian way of life. Far from being "the plain people," as they are often called, the Amish live in accordance with a complex and dynamic system of values.

 For the sake of their community the Amish have given up many individual freedoms, and they do not value material wealth. But unlike the Puritans and other ascetic religious groups, they do not believe in depriving themselves. They enjoy good food and many social activities. They are genuinely pleasant and respectful to friend and stranger alike. They love their children and have added many touches of humor, originality, and beauty to their lives.

Believing that they must live apart, the Amish consider themselves to be "in the world, but not of it." Whether parked in the yard, sheltered in a barn, or moving slowly down a country road, their buggies demonstrate that they have prevailed over worldly progress and that they are unlike others, to whom they refer collectively as the "English." Among themselves, the Amish speak a dialect similar to Low German and conduct religious services in a language similar to High German. With others, they speak English.

Because they cannot easily travel more than a few miles in their buggies, the Amish remain near home and visit relatives and friends within their closely knit rural community. The Amish cherish their families and their neighbors, and visiting is an integral part of their lives.

457

Amish buggies are made in a simple, box-like design that represents the lack of pretension in the lives of the Amish. Bases and frames of the buggies are now constructed of fiberglass, which is more durable than wood. Buggies may sport other modern features such as vinyl tops, ball-bearing wheels, hydraulic brakes, and battery-powered windshield wipers. They are also outfitted with fluorescent triangles and reflector lights for safety. Some Amish install carpet and upholstery in one of several colors, which might be considered "fancy." However, these innovations are permitted as long as the basic design of the buggies remains unchanged.

Buggy styles and colors vary from one region to another, yet these are simply variations on the theme of "plain living." Costing as much as $3,000, the buggies are made in special shops. It may take a full ten days to build one, but the buggy can last for a lifetime.

During their teenage years, many Amish boys go through a wild period called *rumpaspringa*, which means "jumping around" or "running around." They may soup up their buggies with plastic reflectors, stereos, carpeting, dashboards, and speedometers. Parents and church leaders tolerate this flouting of rules so their children can get a taste of the outside world and then decide for themselves whether or not they wish to be baptized as adults into the Amish faith. With a good horse, buggies usually travel 12 mph. With an older horse they may average 10 mph, but if you ever clock one going 15 mph, one Amishman quipped, "you can be sure it's a teenage driver!"

Horses also symbolize Amish culture and values. The animals are seemingly everywhere—grazing in pastures of sweet grass, congregating in barnyards, and taking advantage of shade trees along fencerows. If they are sleek animals, they are likely Standardbreds used to pull buggies. These horses are often retired harness racers, and the Amish appreciate their grace and spirit. Most Amish keep one or two driving horses.

Large, muscular draft horses with clumpy hooves are used for fieldwork. Amish farmers often have six to eight of these horses, because they may use tractors only in their farmyards as power sources for jobs such as grinding feed and transporting ear corn into cribs.

The Amish do not use tractors for fieldwork because of high equipment and fuel costs. They are quick to point out that horses replace themselves, while other farmers must purchase an expensive new tractor every few years. In addition, the manure of horses and other livestock is useful as fertilizer, though chemical fertilizers are sometimes used as well. The Amish know that high production costs would require them to expand the size of their farms, and the only way to do so would be at the expense of their neighbors. Smaller farms enable the Amish to live closer to one another in their rural communities.

During the spring, Amishmen competently guide the powerful horses over the bare fields as they plow, harrow, and plant their crops. Horses are also used to cultivate and harvest crops, as well as to bale hay and straw. The Amish care deeply about their land and follow sound farming practices such as crop rotation. They are particularly adept at transforming land of poor fertility into productive farms. Acre for acre, they are among the best farmers on earth.

In Amish country you may next notice what is *not* there. No utility lines are strung to the houses, because the Amish cannot have electricity in their homes. The Amish do not object to electricity itself, which may be used in wood-working and related businesses. They simply do not want television and radio to threaten family life. As one Amishman noted about his English neighbors, "The center of attention in their home is the tube. They're home together, but they're not sharing anything."

The Amish spend their leisure time reading books and magazines. They do not believe in formal education beyond eighth grade, because they prefer to concentrate on practical skills that will be of greatest value to them as farmers, housewives, and craftsmen. Yet the Amish are hardly opposed to learning and they are generally

 better informed about world events than many of their English neighbors.

The Amish also do not permit telephones in their homes, although they may use their English neighbors' phones, pay telephones, or special phones placed in small wooden buildings along country roads. They are not opposed to the telephone itself, but to its convenience. If they had the devices in their homes, they fear that people would not go to the trouble of hitching a horse to a buggy and driving down the road to visit a friend or relative.

Seeking religious freedom, the first Amish settled in Pennsylvania in the early 1700's. Although they do not actively seek new members, their population has grown because they have large families, averaging seven or eight children. There are now more than 100,000 Amish living in twenty-five states, primarily in Pennsylvania, Ohio, Indiana, Illinois, and Iowa. No Amish remain in Europe, although they originated there.

The Amish did not appear overly different from their English neighbors until the early twentieth century. As the rest of the country bought Model T automobiles, they continued to drive their horses and buggies. Believing that "the old is the best," the Amish also did not change their dress, at least not outwardly, while the rest of the world embraced the latest styles.

PATCHWORK QUILTING:
An American Art

from *Cricket*

by **Anita Howard Wade**

illustrated by **Joyce Audy Zarins**

Fabric for clothing and bedding was scarce out West. Frontier women saved every scrap and devised creative ways to sew them together by hand. Someday those pieces would reappear as a colorful patchwork quilt.

As soon as her daughter was old enough to thread a needle and stitch a seam, the woman taught her to sew. By candlelight each evening, the girl worked on quilt tops for her hope chest. It was important for a young woman to bring a collection of quilts, clothing, and embroidered linens to her new home when she married. Since there were few stores out on the prairie, and money was scarce, she had to make the bedding her future family would need. Factory-made comforters were not even available until about 1890.

Sorting through her scrap bag, the girl chose pieces of fabric and trimmed them neatly into squares, triangles, and strips. She laid the shapes on the table and shifted them around to form a

LOG CABIN · WINDMILL · EVENING STAR · BEAR TRACKS

colorful pattern. When she was satisfied with the design, she stitched the pieces together into a block. She sewed five to nine blocks together in a row, then joined several rows to complete the quilt top.

Inspired by the shapes and activities around them, early American quilters developed hundreds of wonderful patterns and gave them interesting names like *log cabin, windmill, evening star,* and *bear tracks.* If there weren't enough scraps to form well-ordered blocks, a frugal pioneer woman made a *crazy quilt* by sewing odd-shaped scraps in a random pattern onto a base, such as an old woolen blanket. She decorated the quilt with intricate embroidery along the seams, snips of ribbon and lace, and delicate embroidered flowers, animals, and people.

Later, when the young woman announced her engagement, widely scattered neighbors gathered eagerly for an important social event—the quilting bee! The well-prepared country bride brought several tops she had pieced by hand, and her friends proudly displayed the *friendship quilt* top they'd brought as a wedding gift. Each contributor had made a block and embroidered it with her own initials. Together, the women began "quilting."

As the women skillfully worked their fine, even stitches in and out across the quilt, they exchanged gossip, recipes, quilting patterns, and fabric scraps. Boys and girls too young to sew were paid pennies for keeping the needles threaded. By the end of the day, the quilts were finished. The men and older boys, who had been helping the bride's father with farm chores, returned, and everyone enjoyed a potluck supper, games, and dancing.

The young couple could use their new quilts in many practical ways. Quilts could be hung from ceiling beams to divide cabins into rooms, tacked up in doorways and windows to keep out winter drafts, and spread out on the grass for picnics. Quilts could cover rough wood or dirt floors as mats for babies, and they could warm travelers on chilly winter rides in sleighs or wagons. Piled on the floor or on beds, quilts often served both as mattresses and as blankets. They were sold at bazaars to raise money for churches and schools. If a crop failed, a farmer might use a handsome homemade quilt to pay a debt.

Pioneer women used their imaginations and the materials they had at hand to make warm and beautiful bedding for their families. At the same time, they created their own unique form of art: the American patchwork quilt.

465

MAKE A CHART

Have Horse, Will Travel

Compare and contrast using a horse and buggy with using an automobile. Talk about the good and bad points of each with a small group of classmates. Make a comparison chart for the two types of transportation.

RESPONSE

WRITE A PARAGRAPH

A New Way of Life

The Amish have a simple way of life. Think about how you and your classmates could live more simply. Write a how-to paragraph for a bulletin board titled "Steps to a Simple Life."

What Do You Think?

- What do you think the author wanted you to learn about the Amish by looking at an Amish home?

- What did you find most interesting or surprising about the Amish?

- What is the difference between the lifestyle described in "Amish Home" and the lifestyle described in "Patchwork Quilting: An American Art"?

CORNER

Art of the Amish

The art of the Amish quilt is shown all through the selection. Design your own colorful quilt in the Amish style, and display it for your classmates.

ART & LITERATURE

You have read about farmers who respect nature and work to preserve it. How are the people in the painting *Still Life and Blossoming Almond Trees* taking care of the Earth? What do you think these people would have in common with the farmers in the selections you have read?

Still Life and Blossoming Almond Trees
by Diego Rivera

Diego Rivera was a Mexican artist who created murals, or large paintings on walls. His murals tell about the changes that took place in Mexico during his lifetime. Many of Rivera's murals are frescoes, which means that they are painted on moist plaster using water-based paints. Some frescoes last a long time. In fact, before Rivera started painting murals, he studied frescoes in Europe that were painted hundreds of years ago.

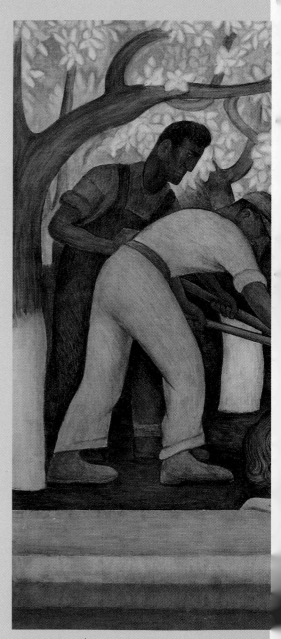

Fresco, 1931, $62\frac{1}{4}$" x 105" University Art Museum, University of California, Berkeley, CA

The People Who Hugged the Trees

AN ENVIRONMENTAL FOLK TALE

adapted by Deborah Lee Rose
from a story of Rajasthan, India
with pictures by Birgitta Säflund

*I*n long-ago India, when warrior princes ruled the land, there lived a girl who loved the trees. Her name was Amrita.

Amrita lived in a poor village of mud houses, on the edge of the great desert. Just outside the village grew a forest.

Every day Amrita ran to the forest, her long braid dancing behind her. When she found her favourite tree, she threw her arms around it. "Tree," she cried, "you are so tall and your leaves are so green! How could we live without you?" For Amrita knew that the trees shaded her from the hot desert sun. The trees guarded her from the howling desert sandstorms. And where the trees grew, there was precious water to drink. Before she left the forest, Amrita kissed her special tree. Then she whispered, "Tree, if *you* are ever in trouble, I will protect you."

The tree whispered back with a rustle of its leaves.

One day just before the monsoon rains, a giant sandstorm whirled in from the desert. In minutes the sky turned dark as night. Lightning cracked the sky and wind whipped the trees as Amrita dashed for her house. From inside, she could hear the sand battering against the shutters. After the storm ended, there was sand everywhere—in Amrita's clothes, in her hair and even in her food.

But she was safe and so was her village, because the trees had stood guard against the worst of the storm.

As Amrita grew, so did her love for the trees. Soon she had her own children, and she took them to the forest with her.

"These are your brothers and sisters," she told them. "They shade us from the hot desert sun. They guard us from the terrible desert sandstorms. They show us where to find water to drink," she explained. Then Amrita taught her children to hug the trees as she did.

Each day when she left the forest, Amrita fetched water from the village well. She carried the water in a large clay pot, balanced on top of her head.

One morning by the well, Amrita spotted a troop of men armed with heavy axes. They were headed toward the forest. "Cut down every tree you can find," she heard the chief axeman say.

"The Maharajah needs plenty of wood to build his new fortress."

The Maharajah was a powerful prince who ruled over many villages. His word was law. Amrita was afraid. "The tree-cutters will destroy our forest," she thought. "Then we will have no shade from the sun or protection from the sandstorms. We will have no way to find water in the desert!" Amrita ran to the forest and hid. From her hiding place, she could hear the *whack* of the axes cutting into her beloved trees.

Suddenly Amrita saw the chief axeman swing his blade toward her special tree.

"Do not cut down these trees!" she cried and jumped in front of her tree. "Stand back!" thundered the axeman. "Please, leave my tree," Amrita begged. "Chop me instead." She hugged the tree with all her strength. The axeman shoved her away and swung his blade. He could see only the tree he had been ordered to cut. Again and again the axeman chopped until Amrita's tree crashed to the ground. Amrita knelt down, her eyes filled with tears. Her arms tenderly grasped the tree's dying branches.

When news of Amrita's tree reached the village, men, women and children came running to the forest. One after another they jumped in front of the trees and hugged them. Wherever the tree-cutters tried to chop, the villagers stood in their way.

"The Maharajah will hear of this!" threatened the chief axeman.

But the people would not give in.

The Maharajah was furious when the axemen returned emptyhanded. "Where is the wood I sent you to chop?" he stormed. "Your Highness, we tried to cut down the trees for your fortress," answered the chief axeman. "But wherever we went, the villagers hugged the trees to stop us."

The Maharajah sliced the air with his battle sword. "These tree-huggers will pay for disobeying me!" He mounted his fastest horse and rode out for the forest. Behind him came many soldiers, riding long-legged camels and elephants with jeweled tusks.

The Maharajah found the
people gathered by the village well.
"Who has dared to defy my order?"
he demanded. Amrita hesitated a moment,
then she stepped forward.

"Oh Great Prince, we could not let the axemen destroy our forest,"
she said. "These trees shade us from the baking desert sun. They protect
us from the sandstorms that would kill our crops and bury our village.
They show us where to find precious water to drink."

"Without these trees I cannot build a strong fortress!" the Maharajah insisted.

"Without these trees we cannot survive," Amrita replied.

The Maharajah glared at her.

"Cut them down!" he shouted.

The villagers raced to the forest as the soldiers flashed their swords. Step by step the soldiers drew closer, as the sand swirled around their feet and the leaves shivered on the trees. Just when the soldiers reached the trees the wind roared in from the desert, driving the sand so hard they could barely see.

The soldiers ran from the storm, shielding themselves behind the trees. Amrita clutched her special tree and the villagers hid their faces as thunder shook the forest. The storm was worse than any the people had ever known. Finally, when the wind was silent, they came slowly out of the forest.

Amrita brushed the sand from her clothes and looked around. Broken tree limbs were scattered everywhere. Grain from the crops in the field littered the ground.

Around the village well drifts of sand were piled high, and Amrita saw that only the trees had stopped the desert from destroying the well and the rest of the village.

Just beyond the well the Maharajah stood and stared at the forest. He thought for a long time, then he spoke to the villagers.

"You have shown great courage and wisdom to protect your trees. From this day on your trees will not be cut," the Maharajah declared.

"Your forest will always remain a green place in the desert."

The people rejoiced when they heard the Maharajah's words. They sang and danced long into the night and lit up the sky with fireworks.

In the forest, the children strung flowers and bright colored paper through the branches of the trees. And where Amrita's tree had fallen, they marked a special place so they would never forget the tree's great sacrifice.

Many years have passed since that day, but some people say Amrita still comes to the forest to hug the trees.

"Trees," she whispers, "you are so tall and your leaves are so green! How could we live without you?"

For Amrita knows that the trees shade the people from the hot desert sun.

The trees guard the people from the howling desert sandstorms.

And where the trees grow there is water, and it is a good place for the people to live.

In the original legend, Amrita Devi and several hundred villagers gave up their lives while protecting their forest nearly three centuries ago. The Indian government has commemorated their sacrifice by naming the Rajasthani village of Khejare as India's first National Environment Memorial.

Today, the people of India still struggle to protect their environment. One of the most dedicated groups is the Chipko ("Hug the Tree") Movement, whose members support nonviolent resistance to the cutting of trees.

In 1987, the Chipko Movement received the distinguished Right Livelihood Award (the "alternative Nobel") for "dedication to the conservation, restoration, and ecologically responsible use of India's natural resources."

Three Wishes

by Karla Kuskin

Three wishes
Three.
The first
A tree:
Dark bark
Green leaves
Under a bit of blue
A canopy
To glimpse sky through
To watch sun sift through
To catch light rain
Upon the leaves
And let it fall again.
A place to put my eye
Beyond the window frame.

Wish two:
A chair
Not hard or high
One that fits comfortably
Set by the window tree
An island in the room
For me
My own
Place to sit and be
Alone.

My tree
There.
Here my chair,
Me,
Rain, sky, sun.
All my wishes
All the things I need
But one
Wish three:
A book to read.

illustrated by Hui Han Liu

RESPONSE

Newsmakers

Work with a small group to present the story as a television news broadcast. Write an introduction to the news story that will grab your audience's attention. Give the facts of the situation. Follow the story with more information on what is being done to save the trees. Present your broadcast to the rest of the class.

Join the Cause?

Create a "Save the Trees" poster based on details from the story. Include information about the *who, what, where, when, why,* and *how* of joining your tree-saving group. Display your poster in the classroom.

CORNER

Tree Tales

The people in the folktale hugged the trees to save them from being chopped down. Read an American folktale about Johnny Appleseed or Paul Bunyan. Discuss with a small group how the folktales are alike and how they are different. Tell which one you liked better and why.

What Do You Think?

. How do Amrita and her village solve their problem?

. Do you think that Amrita is right to try to stop the Maharajah's axe-man? Why or why not?

. Karla Kuskin writes about a tree in her poem "Three Wishes." How are her feelings about trees similar to Amrita's?

FOLKTALES

FROM AROUND THE WORLD

from

Still More Stories to Solve

as told by

George Shannon

Illustrated by

Peter Sis

THE LINE

Birbal was jester, counselor, and fool to the great Moghul emperor, Akbar. The villagers loved to talk of Birbal's wisdom and cleverness, and the emperor loved to try to outsmart him.

One day Akbar, the emperor, drew a line across the floor.

"Birbal," he ordered, "you must make this line shorter. But you cannot erase any bit of it!"

Everyone present thought the emperor had finally found a way to outsmart Birbal. It was clearly an impossible task. Yet within moments the emperor and everyone present had to agree that Birbal had made the line shorter without erasing any part of it. How could this be?

(The solution appears on page 490.)

TWO HORSES

There was once a king who had two sons. When he grew old and close to death, he sent for his sons.

"I want you to ride your horses to Jerusalem. The one whose horse arrives last will inherit everything I own."

The two princes mounted their horses. But, since each knew his horse had to arrive last if he was to win, both sons rode as slowly as they possibly could. One was forever trying to lag behind the other. When they finally reached the outskirts of Jerusalem, both sons stopped. Neither dared go a step closer for fear of getting there first and thus letting the other one arrive last and inherit the kingdom.

They sat for a day. Then two. They sat for a week and began to feel as if they'd spend the rest of their lives sitting at the edge of Jerusalem with nothing to their names. Then, suddenly, both sons had the same idea. They each jumped on a horse and rode to Jerusalem as fast as they could go. What made them change their minds and find a way to end the competition?

(The solution appears on page 491.)

NEVER SET FOOT

Long ago in Ethiopia there lived a man named Abunawas who was famous for his cleverness. One day the emperor made him a guard, and trouble was frequent from that point on. No matter what the emperor told him to do, Abunawas was able to find a way out of doing it.

When he wanted to go dancing, for example, after being ordered to watch the palace gate, Abunawas simply took the gate with him where he went to dance.

One day the emperor got so angry he told Abunawas he never wanted to see his face again. But this only created new problems. After that, when the emperor passed by, it meant Abunawas could turn around and bow with his seat to the emperor instead of the respectful way with his face.

The emperor finally got so angry he ordered Abunawas to leave the country.

"You can go anywhere," said the emperor. "But if you ever set foot on Ethiopian soil again, I'll have your life!"

The other people of the palace had enjoyed Abunawas's cleverness and were sad to see him go. But they weren't sad for long. A few days later Abunawas was smiling and walking outside the palace.

The emperor was furious and called for the guards to hang him at once. But after Abunawas had spoken, there was nothing the emperor could do but let him stay in Ethiopia and go wherever he wanted. How could this be?

(The solution appears on page 491.)

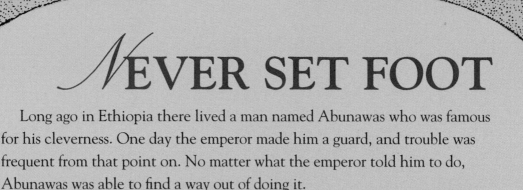

489

SOLUTIONS
HOW IT WAS DONE

THE LINE

Birbal simply drew a longer line next to the first one— which made the first line shorter than the second.

TWO HORSES

Each jumped on his brother's horse to finish the race. If one could ride the other's horse to the city first, it meant his own horse would arrive last and he would inherit the kingdom.

NEVER SET FOOT

The emperor said, "If you ever set foot on Ethiopian soil again, I'll have your life." When Abunawas left the country, he filled his shoes with Egyptian soil. After that he walked on Egyptian soil even in Ethiopia.

THE THIRD PLANET

PLANET

○ ○ ○

EXPLORING

THE EARTH

FROM

SPACE

SALLY RIDE & TAM O'SHAUGHNESSY

493

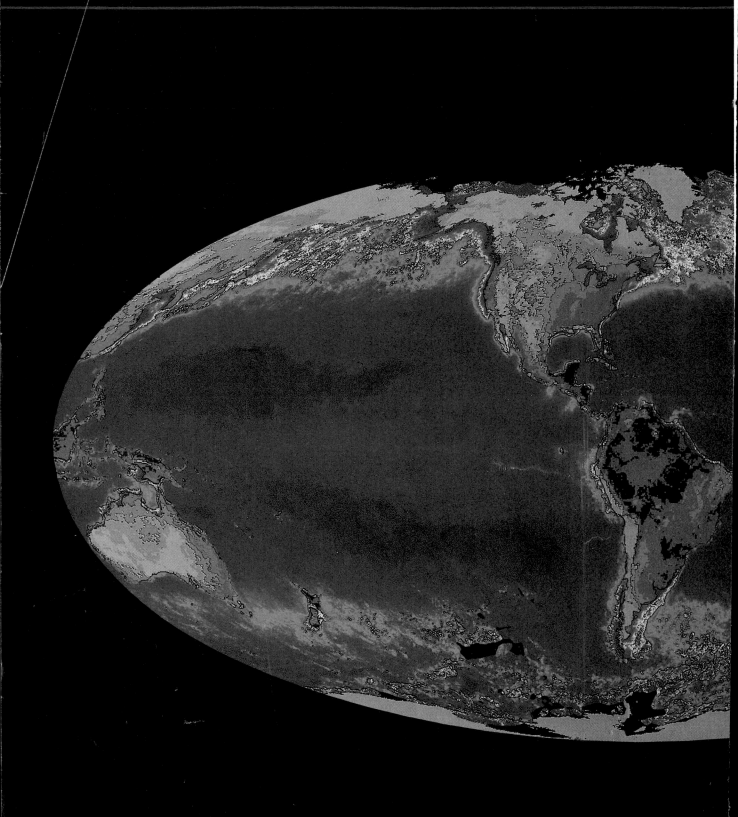

THE LIVING THINGS OF THE EARTH

inhabit a thin realm of water, air, and land called
the *biosphere.* The biosphere extends several
miles up into the atmosphere and
several feet down into the soil. It
includes rivers and lakes and
reaches deep into the oceans.
This image, put
together from satellite
data, is the first global
map of plant life in the
biosphere. It shows the
location of phytoplank-
ton in the water and
plants on land. Because
there are other living
creatures wherever there
are plants, the map shows the
distribution of life on Earth.

On land, some areas are rich in plant life
(green), while others are too hot or cold or dry
for plants to flourish (yellow). In the ocean, the richest
areas of phytoplankton are along the coasts (yellow,
orange, and red), where rivers and deep ocean currents
bring nutrients to the waters. The deserts, the north and
south poles, and vast areas of ocean are almost barren,
while forests and coastal waters are teeming with life.

Deserts like the Sahara in Africa, the Gobi in Asia, and the Great Sandy Desert in Australia are dry, desolate places where water is extremely rare and precious. It seldom rains, but when it does, small lakes and ponds suddenly appear. Millions of seeds, waiting in the dry ground, soak up tiny drops of water and sprout to life. Desert animals drink and bathe in the water, which will soon disappear. Because the rain never lasts long, the only plants and animals that live in the desert are those that are able to conserve water. But some years there is so little rain that even the plants and animals of the desert go thirsty.

1984

Satellite data show that during years of drought the Sahara Desert spreads south into the grasslands of the Sahel (1984, above). The computer picture from 1988 shows that when the rains return, a wave of vegetation reappears across the grasslands.

Not many people live in the desert. Those who do live near water. Almost all of the 60 million people in Egypt live along the Nile River. They depend on the Nile for many things, including irrigation of the land along its banks. The agricultural land hugging the Nile *(below)* looks like a green ribbon winding through the dry Sahara Desert.

Lake Nasser is a human-made lake farther up the river. It was created when the Aswan Dam was built across the Nile. The smaller picture was taken after several years of drought, when the water in the lake was very low. The white outline around the edges of the lake and the gray lake bed in the lower left are under water when the lake is full. Satellite instruments measure the size of this lake and others in deserts, to help people manage their water.

NILE RIVER

ASWAN DAM

1988

A satellite is lifted from the payload bay of the Space Shuttle.

In some places near the equator, rain falls year-round. The warm temperatures and wet weather result in lush tropical rain forests in Central and South America, Africa, and Asia. The rain forests are alive with thousands of kinds of plants and animals. Colorful birds whistle and squawk, strange insects click and buzz, and bright-eyed monkeys scream as they swing through the jungle. Giant trees, wrapped in thick vines, shade the ferns and mosses that cover the wet forest floor.

There are more species of animals and plants in the rain forests than anywhere else on Earth—so many that most have not even been named. People living in the forests and, more recently, scientists have learned that many of the exotic plants are valuable. Some of them are sources of food, and others are sources of important medicines.

In some parts of the world, the rain forests are in danger. Large sections of the Amazon rain forest in Brazil are being cut down and burned so that the land can be used for farming and cattle ranching. Until recently, the government of Brazil encouraged this because it gave people their own land and a way to make a living. But tropical soils are not good for growing crops or grazing cattle. After only a few years, the nutrients in the soil are completely used up; farmers and ranchers must move on, and clear new sections of the forest.

As the trees disappear, so do countless rare plants and animals that make their homes in the rain forest. The people of Brazil have begun to realize that a healthy rain forest is valuable and should be protected. Because satellite pictures show rain forest destruction very clearly, they are being used to monitor this huge jungle. Even a rain forest the size of the Amazon can be photographed in only a few hours by satellite.

▼ This image of the border between Mexico and Guatemala shows thriving, uncut rain forest on the Guatemalan side (right). On the Mexican side (left) the land has been cleared to grow corn and graze cattle.

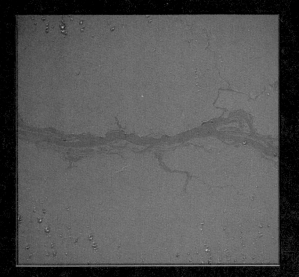

▲ *Above: Dense, undisturbed rain forest surrounding the Rio Negro river in the Amazon region (left) and smoke rising from fires as the forest is cleared (right).*

▽ *Below: This picture of part of Brazil shows roads cutting into the rain forest and patches of forest cleared away near these roads.*

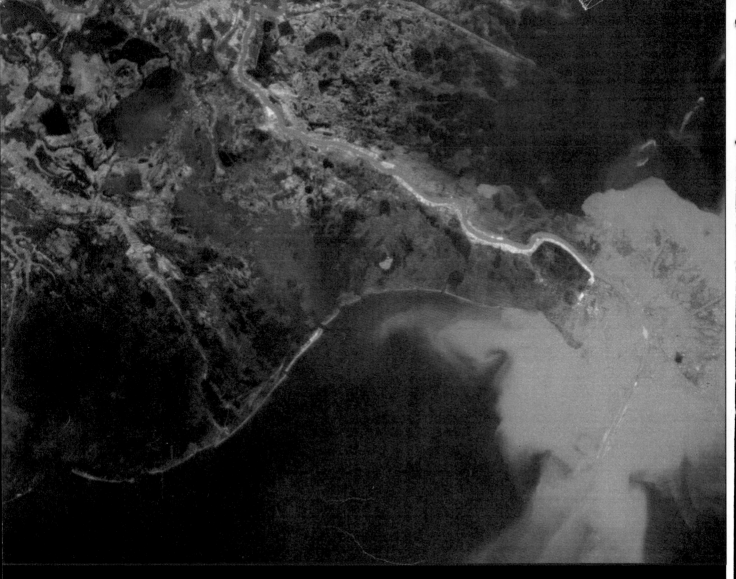

▲ *A false-color satellite image of the Mississippi River delta.*

Some of the richest ecosystems on the planet are found where large rivers empty into the ocean. These areas, where fresh water mixes with salt water, are called river *deltas.* From space, the Mississippi River delta looks like a giant bird's foot. The mighty river collects soil and nutrients as they drain off the land, and carries them to the sea. When the Mississippi River meets the Gulf of Mexico, it drops its load and new land is created. The mud flats, small islands, and salt marshes are packed with life. Flocks of birds feast on small worms; rows of turtles bask in the sun; frogs hide in the tall marsh grasses.

The Mississippi delta depends on the steady supply of soil and nutrients washed down by the river. Satellite instruments watch the muddy river dump its load and keep track of the shaping and reshaping of the delta.

The Ganges River, which empties into the Indian Ocean on the border between India and Bangladesh, forms the largest delta in the world. It is a constantly changing maze of mud flats and marshes. Like the Mississippi delta, it relies on the soil and nutrients carried down by the river. Mangrove trees, which can survive in the shallow, salty water, are the heart of this ecosystem. Their tangled roots anchor the mud flats, creating a vast stretch of mangrove marshes.

The dark area in the picture below is a wildlife preserve in the Ganges delta called the Sundarbans. It is the largest mangrove forest in the world. Here, Bengal tigers roam the dense forest, and crocodiles keep watch in the swamps.

The land around the Sundarbans is home to one of the largest human populations on Earth. Once this part of the delta was also covered in thick mangrove forests. But now most of the trees have been cut down. The marshes have been drained to grow food for the huge population. Without the protection of the mangrove trees, the delta is being worn away by heavy rains and stormy seas.

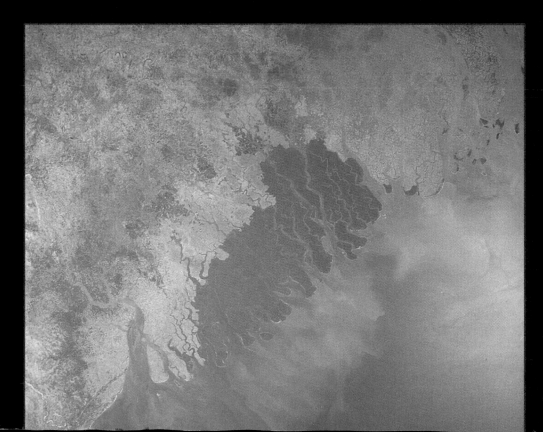

When the number of human beings on the planet was small, their effect on the planet was small. But over the past 100 years, the number of people on Earth has exploded. Now our presence is felt around the world—and our impact can be seen even from space.

Huge cities spread out over miles of land. Los Angeles *(right)* and its surrounding communities are home to more than 10 million people.

With more and more people on the planet, more and more land must be used to grow food. In the Imperial Valley near Los Angeles, dry desert has been turned into fertile fields. The lake in this picture holds salt water, not fresh water, and cannot be used for irrigation. Fresh water has to be pumped miles and miles across the desert to water the plants and make them bloom.

IMPERIAL VALLEY

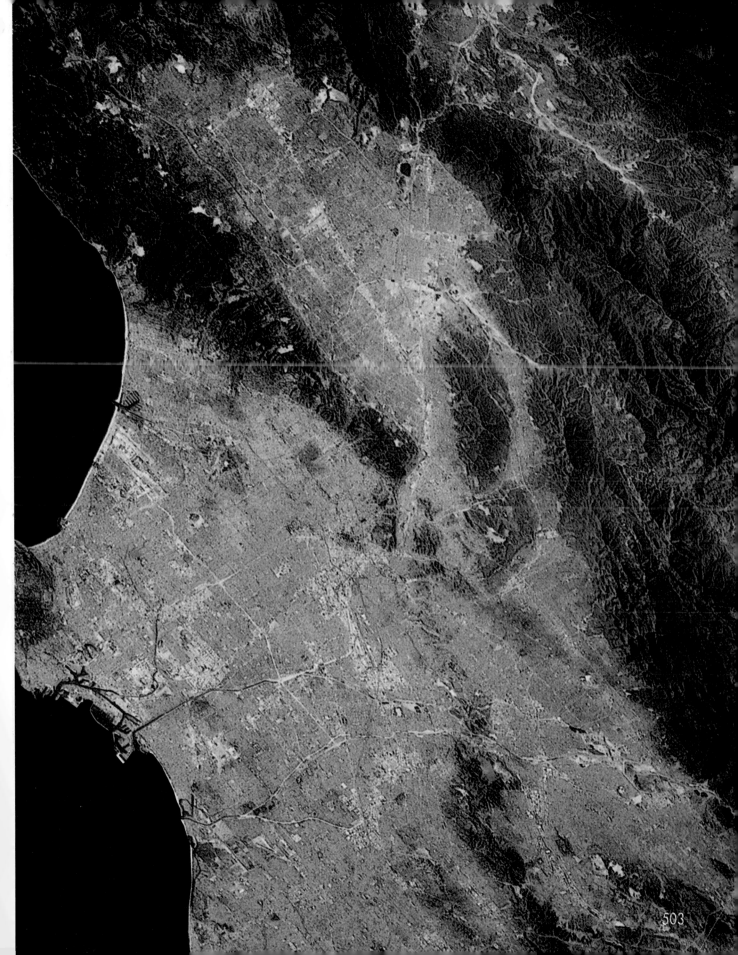

503

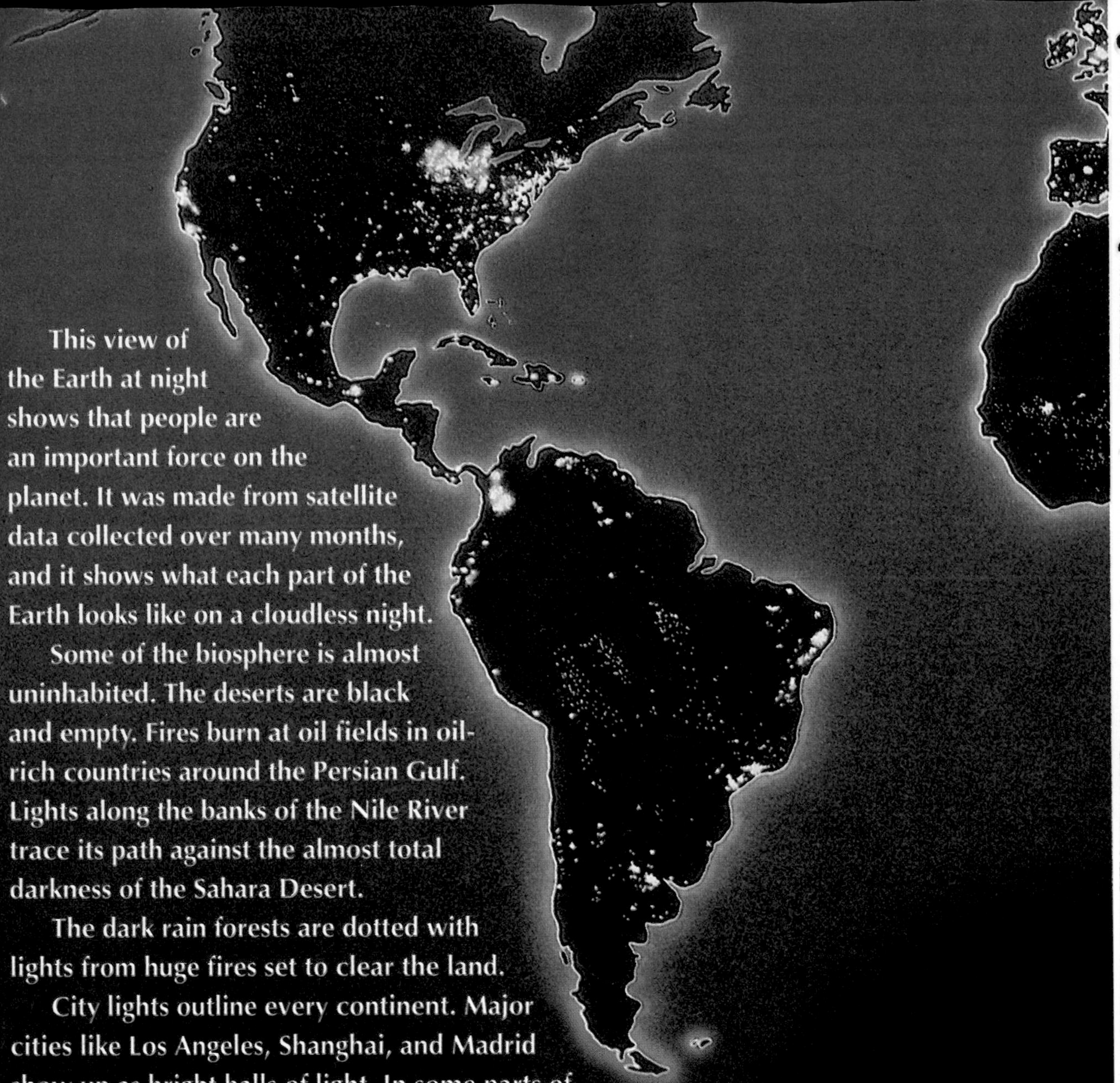

This view of
the Earth at night
shows that people are
an important force on the
planet. It was made from satellite
data collected over many months,
and it shows what each part of the
Earth looks like on a cloudless night.

Some of the biosphere is almost
uninhabited. The deserts are black
and empty. Fires burn at oil fields in oil-
rich countries around the Persian Gulf.
Lights along the banks of the Nile River
trace its path against the almost total
darkness of the Sahara Desert.

The dark rain forests are dotted with
lights from huge fires set to clear the land.

City lights outline every continent. Major
cities like Los Angeles, Shanghai, and Madrid
show up as bright balls of light. In some parts of
the world—the eastern United States, Europe, and Japan—
the lights of the cities blend together until it's difficult to tell where one stops
and another starts.

Our planet is different from any other. As we explore the Earth, we are
learning about its oceans, atmosphere, land, and life. We are finally
beginning to understand our home planet and how we are affecting it.

504

SALLY RIDE

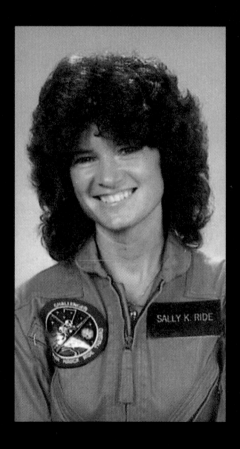

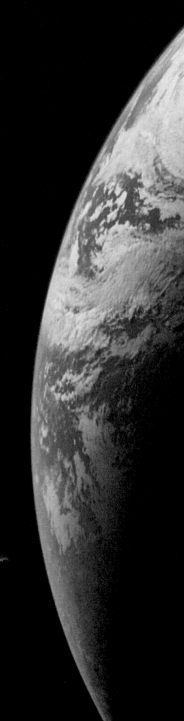

As a Child, Sally Ride

loved to play tennis. She also loved to learn about the stars and the planets. She became so good at tennis that Billie Jean King, the number-one tennis player in the world, once told her that she could be a professional. But Sally chose to pursue her other great interest instead.

Sally enrolled in Stanford University to study physics. Then, in 1978, she saw a want ad from the National Aeronautics and Space Administration. NASA was looking for new astronauts. Sally, along with 8,079 other hopefuls, applied for the job.

After the first rounds of testing, that large number was down to 208, including Sally. Even tougher physical and mental tests followed. Sally, who was both an athlete and a scientist, passed them all and was chosen to be an astronaut. The rest is history.

In June of 1983, Dr. Sally Ride (by now she had her doctoral degree from Stanford) became the first American woman in space when she flew as a mission specialist aboard the space shuttle *Challenger*. She writes about this mission and about her life as an astronaut in her book *To Space & Back*.

Sally Ride left NASA in 1987. Today she teaches physics at the University of California, but she continues to share her experiences as an astronaut and a scientist through her writing and public speaking.

Night

Stars over snow,
    And in the west a planet
Swinging below a star —
    Look for a lovely thing and you will find it,
It is not far —
    It never will be far.

— SARA TEASDALE

illustrated by Tony Novak

Summer

Shadows linger, even in the dim halls.
How cool at the north window: a scent of lotus.
The rain stops; green vegetables like a screen;
And three, five cicadas sing to disturb the evening sun.

— TRAN THANH-TONG
(WITH BURTON RAFFEL)

April Rain Song

Let the rain kiss you.
Let the rain beat upon your head with silver liquid drops.
Let the rain sing you a lullaby.

The rain makes still pools on the sidewalk.
The rain makes running pools in the gutter.
The rain plays a little sleep-song on our roof at night—
And I love the rain.

— LANGSTON HUGHES

RESPONSE CORNER

WRITE A PARAGRAPH

OBSERVING EARTH

Using what you learned from the selection, tell why you think it is important to explore the Earth from space. Write your thoughts in a paragraph. Add your paragraph to a class book titled "The Long View of Our Planet."

CREATE A TIME LINE

CLIMATE TIME LINE

Create a climate time line for your region. Check resources in your classroom or school library. Make a chart of the average temperatures for each month along with kinds and amounts of precipitation.

JEWELS OF THE NILE

Make a fact sheet about the Nile River in Egypt. Include information on its length, width in different places, source, and effects on the people. Compare your fact sheet with that of a partner, and add new ideas.

WHAT DO YOU THINK?

· What are some ways in which people are making an impact on the Earth?

· What did you learn that you didn't know before?

· How does Sally Ride's view of the weather compare with the views of the three poets?

511

THEME WRAP-UP

The characters in this theme come from many cultures, backgrounds, and time periods. What attitude do they all have in common?

What are the pros and cons of living a life with low technology and living a life with high technology? Explain your answers.

ACTIVITY CORNER

Think globally, and act locally. Work with a small group to develop and carry out one activity in your school that would help, in some small way, to save the planet.

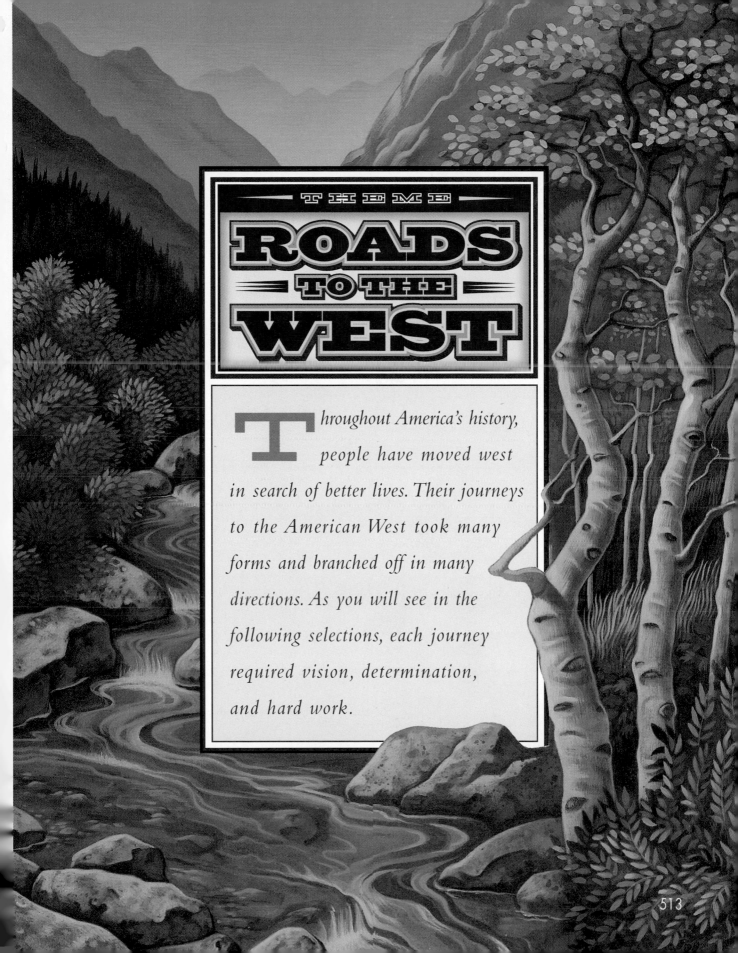

THEME

ROADS TO THE WEST

Throughout America's history, people have moved west in search of better lives. Their journeys to the American West took many forms and branched off in many directions. As you will see in the following selections, each journey required vision, determination, and hard work.

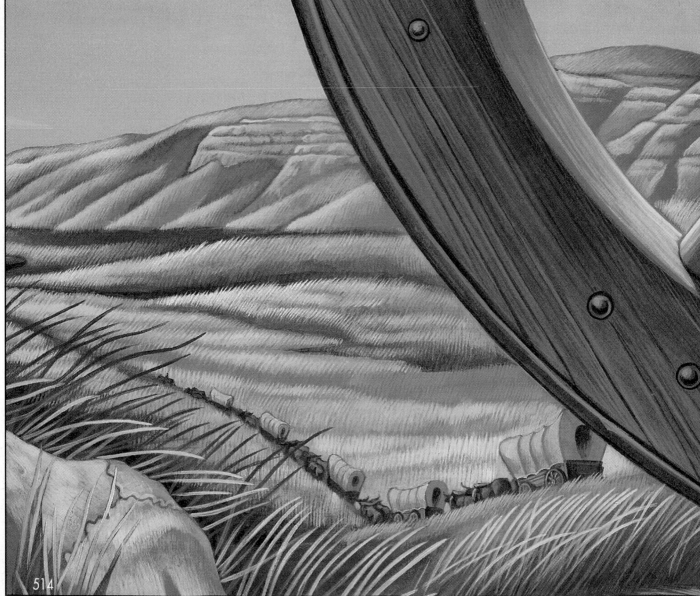

THEME
ROADS TO THE WEST

CONTENTS

BOOKSHELF

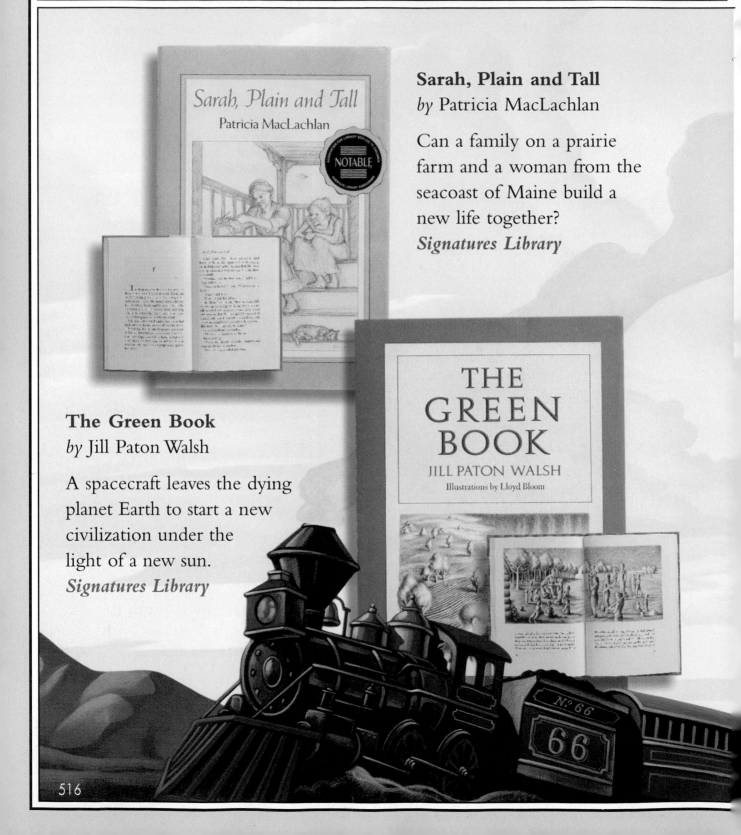

Sarah, Plain and Tall
by Patricia MacLachlan

Can a family on a prairie farm and a woman from the seacoast of Maine build a new life together?
Signatures Library

The Green Book
by Jill Paton Walsh

A spacecraft leaves the dying planet Earth to start a new civilization under the light of a new sun.
Signatures Library

Maudie in the Middle

by Phyllis Reynolds Naylor and
Laura Shield Reynolds

Young Maudie, stuck in the middle of
seven siblings, feels unimportant to her
family until a crisis shows her otherwise.

. . . If You Traveled West In a
Covered Wagon

by Ellen Levine

How did pioneer families travel west to
Oregon in covered wagons? The pioneers'
tricks of survival are explained in this
beautifully illustrated book.

Along the Santa Fe Trail

by Marion Russell, adapted by Ginger
Wadsworth

This is a true adventure story, adapted
from Marion Russell's memoirs,
about a family joining a
wagon train bound
for California.

Award-Winning
Author
and Photographer

SPANISH PIONEERS
OF THE SOUTHWEST

by Joan Anderson
photographs by George Ancona

TWENTY YEARS before the Pilgrims arrived on the east coast of North America, Don Juan de Onates led troops and settlers into the northern portion of New Spain (which is now New Mexico) to establish not only the first Spanish colony in North America but, more importantly, the first colony of Europeans in the New World. They crossed the Atlantic, landed on the east coast of Mexico (part of New Spain), and eventually traveled northward, where they were granted large parcels of land in exchange for setting up a Spanish community. In 1610, Don Pedro de Peralta founded Santa Fe and made it the capital of the new lands belonging to Spain. By the 1650s, many Spanish settlements were being established in the Southwest. The king of Spain dictated how the settlements should look and insisted that settlers build *torreones*, or round, high forts, in all of them.

This book is about one such place—El Rancho de las Golondrinas. It was owned in the 1650s by Manuel Vega y Coca and eventually fell into the hands of the Baca family. We will experience life as it was in the mid 1700s when Golondrinas was inhabited by fifty or so Baca family members. Aside from being a self-sufficient fort where the Bacas farmed and raised sheep, Golondrinas was also a hotel, or hacienda, for traders, military expeditions, and other travelers along the dangerous Camino Real.

These first colonists clung firmly to their Hispanic culture and language. Their spirit has left an indelible mark on the attitudes, values, religion, and customs of the Southwest.

The only reward in collecting wood today, Miguel thought, was that soon there would be a fiesta celebrating the coming of spring. Mamá and the other women of Golondrinas needed all the firewood that could be gathered to light the *hornos* and kitchen fireplaces. Miguel's stomach growled at the thought of food—the *dulces*, the green corn, and especially his favorite dish. He had left the hacienda at dawn with only a loaf of bread and some water. The sun was already making its westward descent toward the Sandía Mountains, which was Miguel's sign to head home.

"Come on, Gaspar," he said, nudging his faithful burro. "We've been out here long enough." Miguel tugged at his burro's reins and led Gaspar down the hillside into the valley. They trudged across the great dusty plains that served as the hacienda's backyard.

Miguel walked carefully and deliberately. He didn't want to tangle with any rattlesnakes coiled inconspicuously around desert brush, or Navajo scouts who spied on the Spanish settlers from nearby mesas.

Just last year, Miguel's brother Pedro had been taken captive in a Navajo raid. Miguel lived in fear of meeting the same fate. He shuddered every time he recalled that awful day.

All the villagers had scrambled to safety at the sound of the bell. Pedro too had run, but his pace was slowed because he carried with him a baby lamb. Miguel had watched helplessly as a Navajo scooped up his brother and rode away.

"Hurry up, Gaspar," he ordered, now more anxious than ever to get home.

It was difficult to see the hacienda from a distance, because the brown adobe fortress blended right into the landscape. Squinting hard, he finally spotted it and quickened his step, pushing Gaspar's hind end up the very last hill.

"Finally!" Miguel sighed as they approached the pine gate. "I return, Mamá," he bellowed triumphantly.

"Such a big load, Miguel!" his mother exclaimed. "And you've even cut the wood this time. *Bueno. Bueno.* Here, let me help you."

Miguel smiled at his mother's welcome. There was such relief in her eyes at his safe return. Miguel was the only Baca child old enough to help around the hacienda. His little sister, Rosa, spent her days at play, and baby Juan was just six weeks old.

Everywhere in the *placita* the people of Golondrinas were busy working. Because Nuevo Mexico was so far away from any city, they had to make everything they needed for daily life.

Doña María, the *patrón*'s wife, was brightening up a simple muslin *colcha* with embroidery, while her husband, Don Hernando, was working over the wooden loom, weaving fabric from which heavy blankets and ponchos would be fashioned. Margarita, the *patrón*'s sister, was carding freshly sheared lamb's wool, and Tía Lupita, Miguel's aunt, was hanging goat's-milk cheese from the beams in the cool storage room, where fruits and vegetables were being dried.

Just as Miguel was about to settle into a warm corner and rest his weary limbs, his father approached.

"Miguel, you've returned," he exclaimed. "I've been scanning the land all afternoon in hopes of spotting you," he said, gesturing at the wilderness beyond the gate. "You must not have met up with any grizzlies this time?" Emilio Baca joked.

"No, Papá, I didn't go up on the mesa. But if I had, I would have been ready with my knife."

"If you weren't near the mesa, wherever did you find so many juniper and piñon branches?"

"The hills west of here, Papá."

"West!" his father said. "That's getting close to Navajo country!"

"I know, Papá, but I stay alert and so far I haven't seen one Indian."

"You're becoming very brave, Miguel," his father continued, shaking his head in amazement at his young son. "The *patrón* says that he wants to give you duty in the *torreón*."

"Me?" Miguel gasped. "Stand watch like a soldier? Do you think I'm able?" he asked, straightening his spine and feeling a new rush of energy.

"Anyone who braves mesa tops and can fend off grizzly bears is man enough to guard our home. Come, enough talk," Emilio Baca said, putting his arm around his son's shoulder. "It's time for our meal. I will remind the *patrón* of his suggestion, but not until you have helped in plowing the field. The past few years your brother Pedro helped me. Now that he is gone I must look to you, Miguel."

It was warm and cozy in the Bacas' *cocina*. The chili stew smelled delectable as the family gathered and Abuelita Luisa dished it up. Everyone sat quietly, exhausted but content to be slowing down from the toils of the day.

The chill of the night descended upon them. Emilio Baca built up the fire as his wife, Isabel, unrolled the blankets and sheepskins that would become their beds. Miguel's father took his place atop the fireplace, and the others huddled close to the hearth.

Miguel felt his muscles relax as his mother began to sing softly to the baby. For the first time all day, Miguel knew he was safe. Only here in the cozy *cocina* did he feel he could let his guard down. He couldn't let Papá know that he wasn't all that brave. So on the outside, Miguel stood tall and proud, but on the inside he trembled with fear.

Dawn came early. With only a few tiny windows in the Bacas' *cocina*, it was impossible to know when the sun came up. But the *patrón* took care that the people of Golondrinas were alerted to the early hour by ringing the hacienda's huge iron bell.

Miguel stirred upon hearing the dull clang. One. Two. Three. Four. Five. On the fifth ring he bolted upright. Glancing about the room he saw that Papá's bed was vacant! Was he already at work? Miguel quickly rolled up his blanket, gulped down a cup of *atole*, and headed out the door.

Sure enough, Papá was down by the stream near the small plot of cultivated farmland. Miguel ran as fast as he could, anxious to show his father that even though he wasn't as big and strong as Pedro, he was eager to work.

"I'm here, Papá," he announced. "What shall I do?"

"Quickly, grab hold of the yoke while I secure it to their horns. These beasts want nothing of work this morning."

Miguel did as his father said, and eventually they attached the crude wooden plow and headed for the far end of the field. The earth was hard and dry. Miguel was always amazed that things grew in such unhealthy-looking soil.

"Papá," he asked, his teeth chattering in the early morning chill, "isn't it still too cold for planting?"

"It would seem so, my son," Emilio Baca answered as the plowshare dug into

the soil and began to turn the earth. "But we must hope that the days soon become warm, as it takes many months to grow our corn and beans and wheat. Besides, Padre José will come to bless our fields during the Feast of San Ysidro. If we haven't done our work there can be no blessing, *sí?*"

"I suppose not, Papá," Miguel answered, working steadily now. It felt good to be sharing chores with someone instead of being alone tending sheep and collecting wood. Time passed quickly, and by late afternoon they were putting in the seed. Miguel felt proud of their accomplishment, especially since the

"We must open up the irrigation ditch, *sí*, Miguel? Your newly planted seeds will be crying for moist soil."

"*Sí, señor,*" Miguel answered, grabbing a long stick and pushing with all his might the board that held the water back. Suddenly it gave way and the sparkling-clean water gushed forth, heading straight for the field.

"We must make good use of this water, my boy, since we have so very little, *sí*?" The *patrón* slapped Miguel on the back, pleased that another job was done.

"Come, let's head back to the hacienda," the *patrón* said to his young helper.

patrón had been watching their progress from the rooftop of the hacienda.

Just as Miguel was placing the last of the seeds in the carefully dug holes, a voice called to him. "Miguel, come give me a hand."

Miguel dropped the seed bag and ran. Whenever the *patrón* had a request, the villagers obliged. He was, after all, the owner of Golondrinas—the person to whom they all turned for food and favors. It was an honor to help him in return.

"Look how full our stream is, after the winter's snow," he said, his voice booming, as it always did, with great joy.

During the next few days, Miguel went about his regular chores hoping that soon the *patrón* would remember his promise and permit him to stand watch in the *torreón*.

Each morning he tossed fresh straw into the corral for the barn animals to eat. He fed the chickens and turkeys, milked the goats, and held the sheep steady while they were sheared.

In the afternoons, sometimes with his father, sometimes alone, he took the sheep to the nearby hills to graze. The days were long and hard, and Miguel began to wonder why there seemed to be more work this spring than in other years. Then he realized—Pedro wasn't there this year to share in all the work.

One afternoon, while he mixed the reddish-brown earth with straw and water to make adobe bricks, Miguel heard the thunder of hooves as a horse galloped toward the hacienda. Jumping to attention, he shielded his eyes from the dust and watched as a Pueblo Indian passed by.

The Pueblos were a friendly people whom the Spanish settlers had learned

to cooperate with. They brought pottery, baskets, and fruit to the hacienda to exchange for sheepskins and sugar. Miguel marveled at how the Pueblo men wore little clothing and seemed unaffected by the cold weather. He crept up to the pine gate and nestled unobtrusively in the corner, hoping to eavesdrop on Margarita's conversation. Miguel took any chance he could to understand the mysterious world of the Indians, especially now that his brother was part of that world.

"Have you visited any Navajo villages of late?" Margarita whispered to the Pueblo. Miguel moved closer as the Pueblo nodded yes. "By chance did you spot our beloved Pedro?" she pressed.

"No, no, no," he answered, a sad tone to his voice.

"Well then," she said, trying to cover up her disappointment, "let us see what you have brought today."

Miguel watched as the Indian showed Margarita brightly colored baskets and sturdy pottery jugs, but his interest in Indian things had been suddenly dampened.

"If only I were big enough to go off and find Pedro," Miguel said, sighing. "Perhaps when I learn to handle the muskets in the *torreón* I will be able to rescue him."

The very next morning the *patrón*, Don Hernando, stopped by the Baca *cocina* and assigned Miguel to the morning watch.

His head brimming with thoughts of fighting off Indians, and his heart pounding at the thought of a dramatic rescue of his brother, Miguel climbed the rickety ladder leading to the tower. Feeling like his conquistador ancestors, he stepped out into the open and gazed

over the rugged landscape. He felt nervous about the responsibility given to him. Pacing about behind the small parapet, he rehearsed in his mind just what he was supposed to do in case of attack.

The strains of the *alabados* being sung by the women in the chapel beneath him caused Miguel to relax a bit, knowing that prayers were being offered for protection from the forces of evil.

In the distance he could see the Indian servant, Polonia, with her little girl trailing behind, fetching water from the stream. For the first time Miguel wondered what had possessed the *patrón* to take Polonia captive, and why she now seemed so content with the Spanish way of life. Didn't she miss the Indian ways? Could Pedro be experiencing the same thing? Might he be taking to the Navajo way of life? There was so much Miguel didn't understand.

RESPONSE CORNER

SPANISH IN A FLASH

Work with a partner to make a deck of flashcards with the Spanish words from the selection on one side and their English meanings on the other side. Shuffle the deck and quiz each other. Continue until each of you knows all the Spanish words.

532

NECESSITIES OF LIFE

Pioneers such as Miguel and his family had to produce everything they needed to live. Work with a partner. List the items from the modern world that you would miss the most if you had to be completely self-sufficient.

TIME TRAVELER

Imagine that you are able to travel back in time to Miguel's village. Write an action adventure story about what happens. Share your story with your classmates.

WHAT DO YOU THINK?

· How do you know that Miguel and his family are brave pioneers?

· Has this selection changed your opinion about pioneer life?

· In what ways is Miguel's life similar to yours? In what ways is it different?

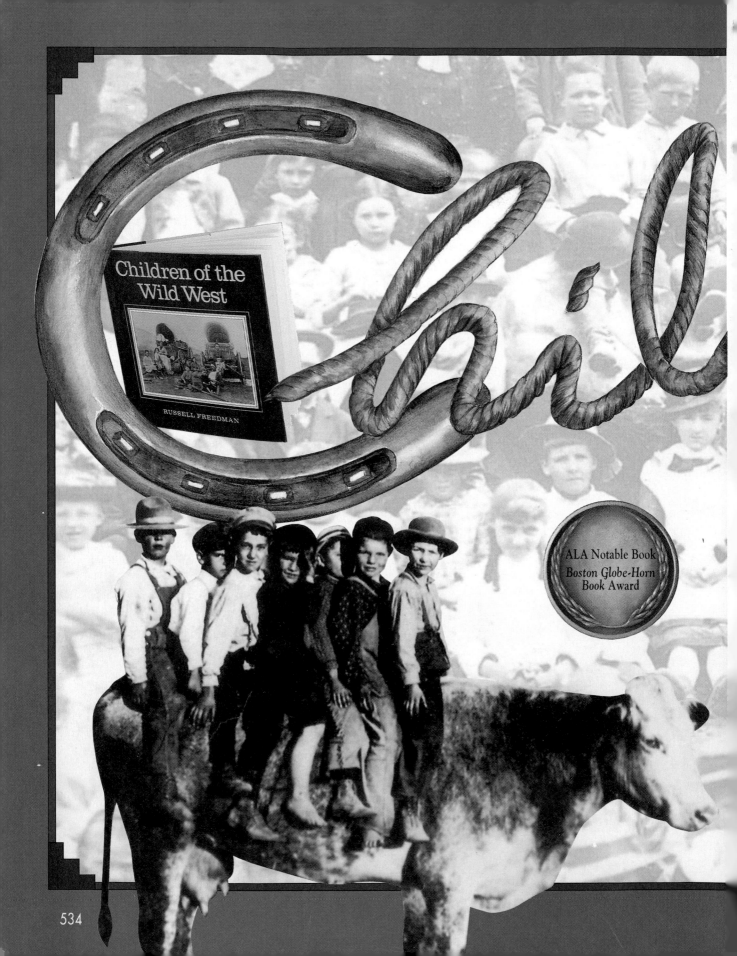

Children of the
Wild West

RUSSELL FREEDMAN

ALA Notable Book
Boston Globe-Horn
Book Award

Children

OF THE

WILD

WEST

by Russell Freedman

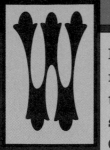

When settlers first moved into an area, there were no schools of any kind. Children were taught at home, or at the home of a neighbor. A pioneer woman would take time from her endless tasks to gather a circle of children around her and teach them reading, writing, and arithmetic. Lacking a blackboard, she used a long stick to scratch out letters and numbers on the dirt floor of the family cabin.

As soon as there were enough children in an area, families would band together to put up a proper school. Everyone contributed labor and materials for the schoolhouse, which often served as a church on Sundays.

The first schoolhouse was usually a simple cabin built of logs, sod, or adobe. Each morning students were called to class by the iron bell that hung outside the schoolhouse door. They came by foot, on horseback, and in wagons, carrying their books, their slates and tablets, and their dinner pails. Some of them had to travel several miles in each direction.

Youngsters of all ages were taught by a single teacher.

Schools, like frontier homes, sometimes had dirt floors. Since there was no running water, everyone drank from the same bucket and dipper kept in a corner of the room. The "playground" was the field outside. The "rest room" was an outhouse. Dogs of many breeds and sizes hung around the schoolhouse, whining at the door and sneaking inside to lie at their owners' feet.

Some early schools had no blackboards, no charts, maps or globes, no special equipment of any kind. Since textbooks were scarce, students brought whatever books they had at home. They arrived at school with an assortment of dictionaries, histories, encyclopedias, and storybooks. Many had copies of McGuffey's Readers, popular schoolbooks of the day that were filled with inspiring stories about hard work, honesty, and piety. Other students might have only a family Bible or an old almanac for their reading lessons.

Much of the classroom time was devoted to the three Rs, along with American history and geography. Students memorized grammar rules, recited history dates, practiced penmanship and arithmetic tables, read aloud, and competed in spelling bees. Since

ABOVE: A SOD SCHOOLHOUSE
LEFT: THE READING LESSON

the pupils might range in age from seven or eight to sixteen or older, they were not separated into grades. The teacher worked with one or two students at a time, while the others studied by themselves. Older students often tutored younger ones.

The youngsters attended classes only as their chores and the weather allowed. On an ordinary school day, many youngsters were up at 4 A.M., milking cows, chopping wood, toting water, and helping fix breakfast before leaving for school. After a full day of classes, they might do other chores by moonlight so as not to miss the next day's classes.

Since some children lived miles away from the nearest school, they might not attend classes at all until they were half grown. It was not uncommon to find youngsters twelve or fourteen years old who were just starting school for the first time. During the 1860s, fewer than half the youngsters in Oregon received any formal schooling. California did not make education compulsory until 1874, when a law was passed requiring children between the ages of eight and fourteen to attend classes during at least two-thirds of the school year.

Many frontier schools found it difficult to find and keep good teachers. The pay was low. A teacher might earn anywhere from

GETTING READY TO BOARD THE
SCHOOL BUS

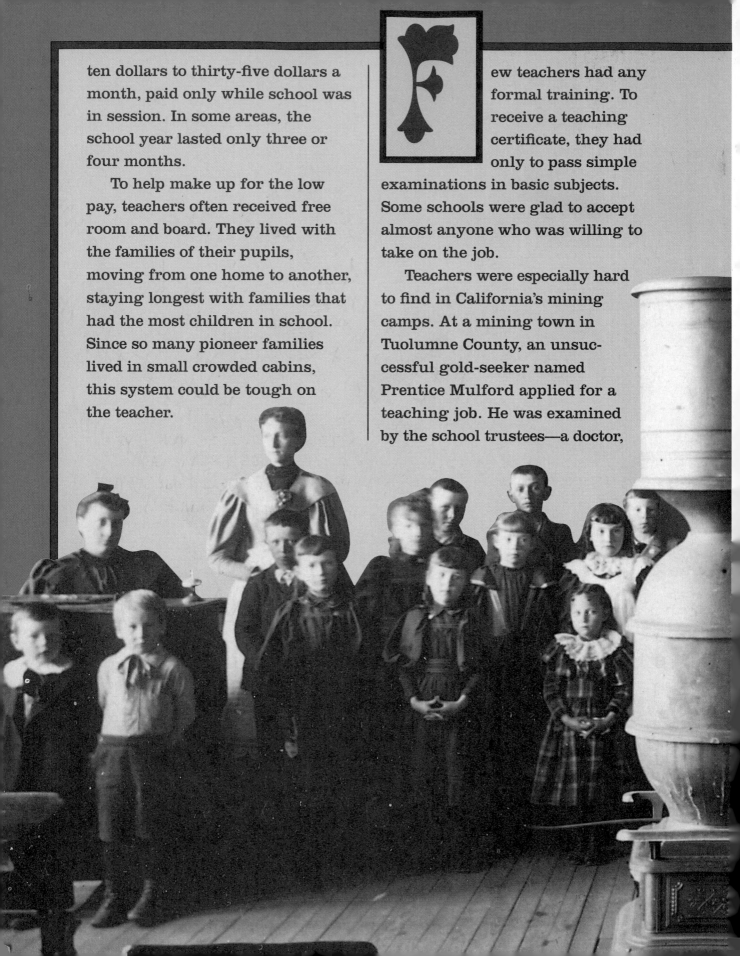

ten dollars to thirty-five dollars a month, paid only while school was in session. In some areas, the school year lasted only three or four months.

To help make up for the low pay, teachers often received free room and board. They lived with the families of their pupils, moving from one home to another, staying longest with families that had the most children in school. Since so many pioneer families lived in small crowded cabins, this system could be tough on the teacher.

Few teachers had any formal training. To receive a teaching certificate, they had only to pass simple examinations in basic subjects. Some schools were glad to accept almost anyone who was willing to take on the job.

Teachers were especially hard to find in California's mining camps. At a mining town in Tuolumne County, an unsuccessful gold-seeker named Prentice Mulford applied for a teaching job. He was examined by the school trustees—a doctor, a miner, and a saloonkeeper. "I expected a searching examination, and trembled," Mulford recalled. "It was years since I had seen a schoolbook. I knew that in geography I was rusty and in mathematics musty. Before the doctor lay one thin book. It turned out to be a spelling book."

Mulford was asked to spell *cat, hat, rat,* and *mat.* When he did this perfectly, the doctor told him, "Young man, you're hired."

Not all frontier schoolteachers

RIGHT: SCHOOL DISTRICT NO. 32

BELOW: THIS WELL-EQUIPPED CLASSROOM HAD A BIG CAST-IRON STOVE AND A REAL BLACKBOARD.

could spell as perfectly as young Mulford. In 1859, the superintendent of schools in Sacramento, California, complained that some teachers were misspelling the name of the state they were teaching in as *Callifornia* or *Calafornia.*

Some teachers were barely older than their pupils. Often they hoped to learn as much as they taught. In 1855, Charles A. Murdock organized the first public school in Arcata, California:

"There was no school in the town when we came. It troubled my mother that my brother and sister must be without lessons. Several other small children also were deprived of the opportunity. In the emergency we cleaned out a room in the store . . . and I organized a very primary school.

"I was almost fifteen, but the children were good and manageable. I did not have very many, and fortunately I was not called upon to teach very long. There came to town a clever man, Robert Desty. He wanted to teach. There was no school building, but he built one all by his own hands. He suggested that I give up my school and become a pupil of his. I was very glad to do it. He was a good and ingenious teacher. I enjoyed his lessons about six months, and then I felt I must help my father."

Eventually school boards began to adopt rules that no teacher under sixteen years of age could be hired. As late as 1880, however, the United States Census reported that California still had one boy and two girl teachers under sixteen.

LUNCHTIME: AN OLD TOBACCO TIN AND A LARD PAIL SERVE AS THE GIRLS' LUNCH BOXES.

Russell Freedman

Russell Freedman grew up in San Francisco, California, surrounded by books. Because his father worked in publishing, famous authors would often visit his home. He recalls, "I know at an early age that I wanted to be a writer, like those strange, wonderful men and women who sat at our dinner table telling stories that were always fascinating, and sometimes hard to believe."

When Freedman was older, he worked for a time as a newspaper reporter. There he learned skills that helped him become one of America's best writers of nonfiction for young people.

Freedman tries to make his readers care about a subject by telling about it as simply and clearly as possible. He also tries to spark the reader's imagination by telling a good story. He says, "Pick a subject, a good subject, and you're sure to find kids who are interested in it."

Bring 'em

Back Alive

an essay by

RUSSELL FREEDMAN

I sometimes hear that children today aren't really interested in history. It's one of their least favorite subjects. They look upon history as a kind of castor oil that one has to take—something that's good for you, maybe, but repulsive.

If that attitude exists, then it can only result from the way history is taught. I believe that history can be far more exciting than any imaginary adventure story because truth is so much stranger than fiction. Rather than castor oil, history should be thought of as a tonic. It should wake us up, because it is the story of ourselves.

The word *history*, remember, is made up mostly of the word *story*. Historians traditionally have been storytellers. Going all the way back to Homer and beyond, historians have been people who were telling, singing, reciting epic poems. They were storytellers sitting around the fire inside the cave, holding their audience spellbound on a winter's night.

When I begin a new book, I like to remember that tradition. I think of myself first of all as a storyteller, and I do my best to give dramatic shape to my subject, whatever it is. I always feel that I have a story to tell that is worth telling, and I want to tell it as clearly, as simply, and as forcefully as I can.

Nonfiction can and does make use of traditional story-telling techniques. One of the most effective techniques, for example, is to create a vivid, detailed scene that the reader can visualize—like a scene from a movie, if you will. In my book *Children of the Wild West* (Clarion, 1983), I use that device to help establish the setting and the mood, and to pull the reader into the story. After a short introduction, the book's opening chapter begins like this:

It was a typical wagon train of the 1840s. The swaying wagons, plodding animals, and walking people stretched out along the trail for almost a mile.

Near the end of the train, a boy holding a hickory stick moved slowly through the dust. He used the stick to poke and prod the cows that trudged beside him, mooing and complaining. "Get along!" he shouted. "Hey! Hey! Get along!"

Dust floated in the air. It clogged the boy's nose, parched his throat, and coated his face. His cheeks were smeared where he had brushed away the big mosquitoes that buzzed about everywhere.

Up ahead, his family's wagon bounced down the trail. He would hear the "crack" of his father's whip above the heads of the oxen that pulled the wagon. The animals coughed and snorted. The chains on their yokes rattled with every step they took.

Now, that is nonfiction. The scene is dramatized in order to make it visual, and in order to convey the texture and flavor of the event and the time. But it is entirely factual. And it introduces the story line —the narrative framework—of the book. *Children of the Wild West* is the story of children who accompanied their parents on the great westward journey, and the story of what happened to them after they arrived in the West.

Backwoods Scholars

from *A Pioneer Sampler*
by Barbara Greenwood

illustrated by Mercedes McDonald

Letters and numbers—that's what most pioneer children learned. They scratched the alphabet onto slates with slate pencils as they learned to write. Later they graduated to homemade ink, quill pens, and paper brought from home.

They learned arithmetic that would help them with everyday life. Adding and subtracting were used to determine their accounts at the general store. Multiplying and dividing helped them figure the size of a field or the number of cords in a pile of wood.

Children attended school until they were twelve or until they had learned the "rule of three," a method for finding the size of an object too large to measure easily. Early settlers needed to know how to use this rule to find heights of trees and distances across rivers.

This is how the rule of three works: Willy Robertson's father was going to cut down a tree near the cabin. To make sure it would not fall on the house and buildings, he needed to know how tall it was.

First he drove a stick into the ground. He measured the length of the stick from the ground up and the length of the stick's shadow. Next he measured the length of the tree's shadow. Now he had the three numbers he needed to find the unknown fourth.

The stick was one length long.

Its shadow was two lengths long.

The tree's shadow was thirty lengths long.

To find the height of the tree, he wrote:

	$\dfrac{\text{stick length}}{\substack{\text{stick} \\ \text{shadow length}}}$		$\dfrac{\text{tree height}}{\substack{\text{tree} \\ \text{shadow length}}}$
or	$\frac{1}{2}$	=	$\frac{x}{30}$
or	$2x$	=	30
or	x	=	15 lengths

So, using the rule of three, Mr. Robertson learned that the tree was fifteen lengths tall. Now he could measure this distance along the ground to see if the tree would fall too close to the cabin.

RESPONSE Corner

MAKE A CHART

SCHOOL SETTINGS

Make a comparison chart. On one side, list the good and bad points of going to school. On the other side, do the same for being taught at home. Which form of schooling do you think is better and why? Share your thoughts with your classmates.

DEBATE AN ISSUE

LAW AND ORDER

In 1874, the state of California said that all children ages 8 to 14 had to go to school for two-thirds of the school year. Put yourself in the place of a student in 1874. Hold a debate with classmates about the fairness of the law.

TELL A STORY

YOU WERE THERE

Russell Freedman believes that history can be shared in the form of interesting adventure stories. Research and share a true story from the Wild West. Tell the story using the words and actions of a child who lived back then.

WHAT DO YOU THINK?

- What did you learn about frontier schools that you had never thought about before?

- What surprised you about teachers in frontier schools?

- How might the essay "Bring 'em Back Alive" contribute to your enjoyment of "Children of the Wild West"?

You have read about people who began new lives by moving west. What does the painting *Among the Sierra Nevada Mountains, California* tell you about the excitement these people might have felt about their new lives? What does it show you about the hardships they may have faced while crossing a continent?

Among the Sierra Nevada Mountains, California
by Albert Bierstadt

Albert Bierstadt was born in Germany in 1830, but he grew up in Massachusetts. In 1857 he joined a team sent to map a route from St. Louis, Missouri, to the Pacific Ocean. He was amazed by the spectacular scenery of the West. Two years later he began showing his landscapes of the area. His work was well liked, and his paintings were bought by many collectors. In 1875 Congress purchased one of his landscapes, and it still hangs in the Capitol.

Oil on canvas, 1868, National Museum of American Art, Washington, DC

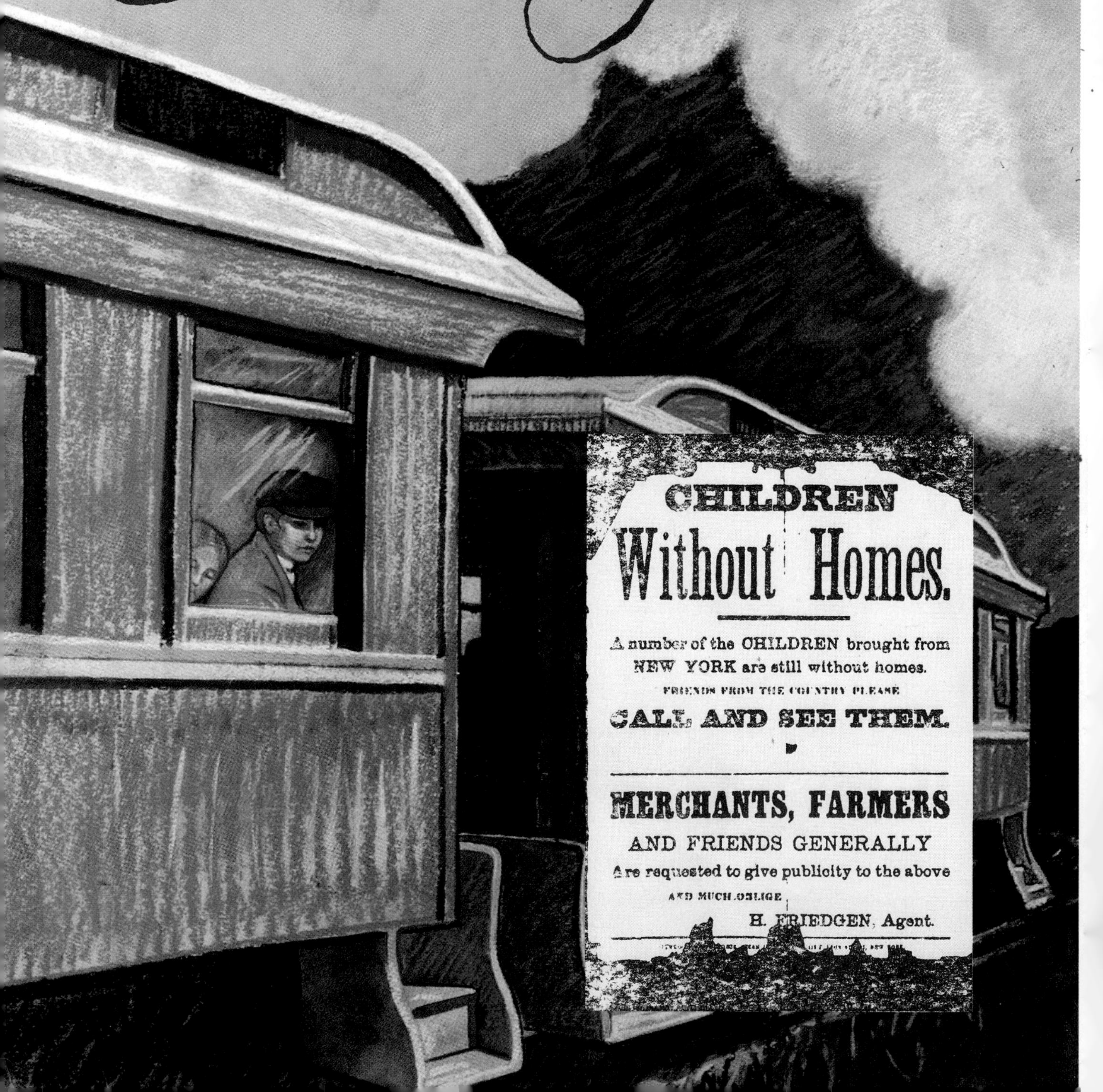

ily Apart

The Orphan Train Quartet

By Joan Lowery Nixon • illustrated by Pamela Patrick

Award-Winning
Author

When Mr. Kelly dies, Mrs. Kelly realizes she cannot properly provide for six children, ages 6 to 13. As many people in the late 1800s did, she sends her children west to Missouri on the "orphan train" in hopes that they will be placed with families who can give them better opportunities.

Frances Kelly, the eldest child, leaves New York on a train with her three brothers and two sisters. Frances has heard that families often choose boys to do farm work, and she wants to be picked with Petey, the youngest child. So Frances has convinced the guides, Andrew and Katherine, that she is Frankie Kelly, a boy.

The train started up in its usual bumping fashion. It was late and dark, with only the dim light from the swinging lantern casting wild, moving shadows across the car. As Frances stared out at the landscape, she could see clustered lights of houses that winked through the night. Then the lights became more scattered, until finally there was nothing outside the train but a black, empty world without moonlight or stars.

Frances shifted under the weight of Petey's head on her lap and leaned against the wooden frame of the window, closing her eyes. Megan sniffled beside her, and she reached over to take her hand.

"I keep thinking about what Andrew said," Megan whispered, "about how people don't take all the children in a family. We're going to be sent to different homes. It frightens me. Does it frighten you, too?"

"Yes," Frances said, keeping her voice low. "It does."

"I don't want to think about being parted from you," Megan said. "We've always been together."

Frances squeezed Megan's hand. "Maybe we won't be parted. Maybe someone will say, 'We want all those fine Kelly children!' And they'll take us to their house—a big white house with green—no, blue—shutters, and they'll have a horse for Petey to ride and—"

Megan interrupted. "None of your dreams now, Frances. Dreams are just pretending, and you know they don't come true."

"I wish this one could." Frances groaned. "Oh, if only Ma hadn't—"

But Megan interrupted, her voice breaking. "Please don't talk about Ma now. I miss her too much."

They were silent for a few minutes, and soon Megan fell asleep, her head resting heavily on Frances's shoulder. One of the smaller children in the car was crying, and Frances could hear Katherine's low, comforting murmur. Before long the only sounds in the car were the creaks and groans of the wooden seats and the clatter of iron wheels against the rails, all of which flowed into a steady rhythm. Soon Frances was sound asleep.

"WAKE UP, FRANKIE. I want to go home."

Frances awoke stiff and tired as Petey buried his face in her neck, whimpering, "I want Ma!"

"I want Ma, too! Are we ever going to see Ma again?" Peg wailed.

"There, now," Frances soothed, "of course we are." But she kept her eyes downcast, unable to meet theirs. How could she tell them this when she didn't believe it herself? Every turn of the train's wheels took them farther and farther away from Ma. Frances tried to smile, to bolster their spirits, because she was in charge. The others mustn't know that she felt like crying, too.

Frances looked up, feeling Megan's appraising eyes upon her.

Megan brushed back her long, dark hair and whispered, "What will happen to us, Frankie?"

"Why—we'll find good homes. We'll have new families and good food and warm beds," Frances parroted. She reached across Petey and gripped her sister's hand. "Oh, Megan," she whispered, "I honestly don't know what will happen."

One of the younger boys fell into the aisle and let out a yell. At the sound of it another child began to cry.

"Can't someone shut those urchins up!" Mr. Crandon bellowed as the train lurched into motion.

"They're only children," a woman snapped at him.

Mr. Crandon puffed up like a pigeon guarding the only crumb of bread. "Madam, we are entitled to as much peace and quiet as this railroad company can provide."

"I'm sorry." Andrew raised his voice over the din. "We'll feed the children at the next stop, and I can guarantee that will help the situation."

"If you can't control them—" Mr. Crandon began.

But Mike suddenly jumped into the aisle and shouted to the older children, "Hey there, chums! How about a bit of music?" He cupped his hands together and held them against his lips, creating a lively, nasal music as he hummed, and to the music he danced a few wild steps of a jig.

The children who had been crying stopped to stare, then broke into laughter as Mike leaped to click his heels together, lost his balance, and sprawled in the aisle.

Frances saw the twinkle in Mike's eyes and knew he had taken the fall on purpose.

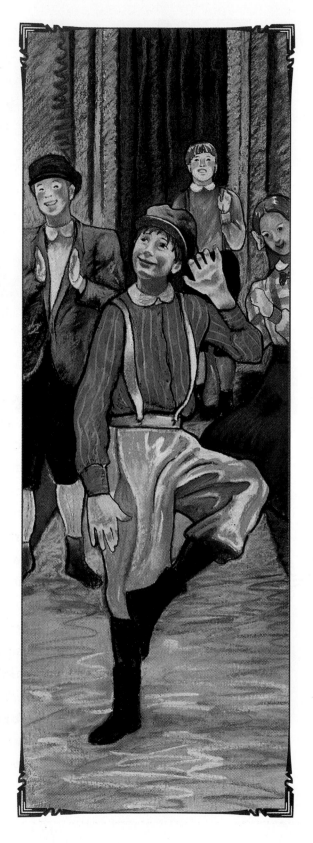

"More! More!" Petey shouted.

So Mike pranced and danced with his odd music, and when some of the older children recognized a tune, they joined in, singing the words. Frances knew "The Irish Washerwoman" and "Old Dog Tray," and when Mike began "Oh! Susanna," some of the adults on the car began to sing, too, Captain Taylor's deep baritone as loud as Andrew's.

Suddenly, with a jolt that tossed Mike sideways onto Katherine's lap, the train shook and rattled to a screeching stop.

"Good work," Katherine murmured to Mike as she helped him regain his balance.

Captain Taylor stretched forward to shake Mike's hand and said, "A wise choice of action, son."

Frances was proud of Mike. He'd been able to make them all forget their aches and fears. Ma would have been proud of Mike, too, if she could have seen him.

Her thoughts were interrupted by the frantic cry of "Fire!"

The conductor threw open the door of the passenger car. "Sparks from the train set a brushfire!" he shouted. "All able-bodied males are needed to help put it out!"

"Come on!" Mike grabbed Frances's arm and tugged her into the aisle. " 'All able-bodied males,' " he wickedly muttered under his breath. "That means you, too!"

"Don't be frightened, boys." Andrew stopped Frances with a firm grip on her shoulder and handed her a wet feed sack as she leapt from the railroad car. "It's not uncommon for sparks to set small brushfires. Just take this sack and join the others."

Deep orange and scarlet flames crawled and crackled through the burning grass, and yellow smoke rose in choking clouds.

Most of the men and boys had poured from the train, grabbed the wet sacks, and were slapping them at the smoldering grass. Frances, hands shaking with terror, copied their actions. Working hard, slamming her dripping sack on the flames, dipping it over and over into the bucket and slamming it again, she was soon absorbed in beating back the low spurts of flame.

"Look out! You're on fire!"

Frances jumped, but it was Amos Crandon Mike meant.

Mr. Crandon froze with fear as the back of his shirttail burst into flame.

"Your shirt, man! Pull it off!" Andrew shouted and began to run toward Mr. Crandon.

But Mike was faster. He dove toward the backs of Mr. Crandon's knees. Mr. Crandon bent in two and fell over Mike, sitting down hard. Mike scrambled on top of the man and pushed him on his back, rolling him over and flinging himself across him.

Mike sat up and examined the scorched shirt. "Fire's out," he announced happily.

Mr. Crandon angrily sputtered, "How dare you push me to the ground? You ought to be whipped!"

Frances wanted to defend Mike but was too furious to do anything but sputter. She was glad that Andrew seemed as surprised as Mike by Mr. Crandon's outburst. She caught her breath as Andrew spoke up: "Your shirt was on fire. Mike put it out and kept you from getting burned."

Mr. Crandon glared at Andrew. He brushed the dirt from his clothes and, muttering to himself, unaware that two large spots of very pink skin were showing through holes in his trousers, stomped to the train.

Andrew patted Mike's shoulder, and Frances said, "You did the right thing, Mike." But it wasn't at Mike that she was looking. Andrew was a fine man, a really good and kind man like Da. Oh, how Frances yearned to be called Frances Mary again!

"On board, everybody," the conductor yelled as he collected the dirty, charred feed sacks. "Fire's out. Get back on board so we can get under way."

"After this train ride is over," Mike muttered to Frances as they climbed the steps to their car, "I hope I'll never see ol' Crandon again!"

The train rattled its way west, stopping every twenty-five miles or so for water and wood. Frances gazed dreamily out over the open hills, the dim forests, the tidy squares of farmland, and the rippling, gray-gold grasslands. The train crossed trestles and bridges and passed towns that all began to look alike to Frances. Occasionally she'd wonder if this type of farm or that kind of house would be like the one where she'd live. Sometimes she'd just sit back, her arm around Petey, and let herself be rocked by the steady rhythm of the rackety wheels that clattered over and over, "New life, new life, new life."

"But I don't want a new life," Frances murmured to herself.

"Mike and I are going to be together," Danny came to tell Frances.

Terror showed in his eyes though, and Frances said what she knew he wanted to hear: "There's a very good chance you will be."

"The people who adopt the children—are most of them kind, do you think?" Megan whispered so softly that Frances could hardly hear her.

"I'm sure they are," Frances said. "Why else would they come?"

"That's a good question," Mike said, "and I haven't found an answer to it yet. Just why would anyone want us?"

Frances put on a brave face and even managed a laugh. "Because we're a fine lot, we are, and those who get us will be lucky! That's why!"

For the moment they were content, but Frances's heart ached as she realized her words meant nothing. If she was saying only what they wanted to hear, was that what Katherine and Andrew were doing, too?

Days became nights, and nights broke into early daylights with passengers so stiff they grimaced as they stretched their legs and rubbed their arms and necks. The children and the other passengers dozed, ate, and talked. Occasionally conversation in the car grew lively, especially when the topic turned to politics and the pros and cons of slavery. Frances listened and soaked up the words when someone echoed what Da had told her.

The children changed to another train in the massive Chicago railroad station. This one would take them to the Mississippi River, where they'd cross over, heading toward Hannibal, Missouri.

Missouri! Frances would be glad to see the long train ride end, but her hands grew damp and she found it hard to breathe whenever she thought about what might await her and her brothers and sisters in St. Joseph.

The car in which they rode southwest toward Hannibal looked much the same as the first one. Outside the city, even the farms and houses looked like those they had seen for so many days, and most of the passengers on their car were the same. Frances knew that everyone was as exhausted as she was, even the adults. She remembered the flounces and parasols and grand top hats the ladies and gentlemen wore when they got on the first train in Albany. Now their once-elegant suit coats and wide, bustled dresses were wilted and dusty.

When Petey put his mouth to Frances's ear and whispered loudly, "Some of the people stink," Frances could only nod in agreement.

Mike and another boy got into a shoving match in the aisle, and Frances found herself scolding Mike with an overly sharp tongue. Mike snapped back, rudely sticking out his tongue, and it was all she could do not to slap him.

Arguments exploded among all the children as quickly and often as sparks from a burning, sap-filled log. Tousled and rumpled, Peg and Danny poked at each other unmercifully, and Petey cried over every little thing. Even Megan, who was usually gentle and even-tempered, huddled into a miserable heap next to the window.

Early one evening they reached the broad Mississippi River, which they would cross by steamboat. Standing with the others who clustered at the rail of the big paddle wheeler, Frances begged, "Please, could we stay outside to watch?"

"It's cold and damp," Katherine said. She touched Frances's cheek. "You'll be soaked by the mist rising from the water."

"We don't mind," Frances said. "It's such a big river, and so many, many boats!"

Jim stepped up beside her. "Please?" he echoed. "We want to see it all!"

Katherine laughingly agreed, but while most of the children ran up and down the deck, Jim pointed out some of the types of boats to Frances.

"I'm going to work on a boat," he said. "Maybe one of those big steamboats with twin stacks." His voice filled with yearning as he added, "Maybe a captain and his wife will adopt me."

He continued to lean on the rail, eagerly studying the heavy river traffic. But Frances soon lost interest in the boats and kept an eye on the Missouri shore ahead, watching it appear from the mists as they grew nearer.

When they arrived in Hannibal, Missouri, many passengers left to journey to St. Louis, and other passengers joined them on a third train.

We're actually in Missouri, Frances thought, and she couldn't eat a bite of the food that Andrew had brought on board for their supper.

Although Danny gobbled down his meal, Mike's appetite seemed to have disappeared, too. Frances glanced at Mike just as he looked up at her, and she knew that he shared her terror of what they might have to face when they reached St. Joseph.

"Frances," he said, then quickly corrected himself. "Frankie, I'm sorry about all this. I know that being sent west has been awful hard on you, what with you and Ma so close."

Frances quickly shook her head. "We don't have to talk about it."

"But I want to, because it's my fault that all the rest of you are here, and I'm sorry I did this to you."

"Oh, Mike." Frances reached out to touch her brother's hand. "I don't blame you." She tried to make her voice light. "Look at it this way. You kept telling me I'd like living in the West. Now I'll have a chance to find out."

But Mike didn't respond to her attempt at humor. "This is our last time to be together. After we're placed, who knows when we'll see each other again?"

"We may not know when we'll be together again, but I'm sure that we will be. I'll write to you. Will you write back?"

Mike nodded. "Sure. And someday—"

But the train squealed to such a sudden stop that they were thrown off-balance.

"Outlaws!" a woman screamed as a heavily bearded man burst through the door to their car, waving a rifle at the passengers.

Shrieks and yells came from the other cars as men on horseback galloped at each side of the train. One of the men reined in his horse and poked a long gun in through one of the open windows of the children's car.

The bearded man waved a small cloth sack at the passengers. "Sit down right now! All of you! And don't do anything we don't tell you to do," he snapped.

As she dropped back onto the bench, Frances saw Captain Taylor glance at the man on horseback outside the window and back to the outlaw in the aisle. She held her breath, wondering what he would do. But he sat quietly and kept his hand away from his satchel and his gun.

"Everybody pay attention," the outlaw demanded, little drops of spittle glittering on his beard. "Put your money and valuables in this sack." When they were slow to react he yelled, "Now!" and jabbed the end of his rifle at Mr. Crandon's stomach.

"Don't do that!" Mr. Crandon squeaked. "I'll give you all my money! See! Here it is!" He fumbled for a wad of bills held with a gleaming gold money clip and dropped it into the sack.

The outlaw moved up the aisle, thrusting the open sack ahead of him, his nervous eyes darting from one passenger to another. One by one the passengers obeyed as the outlaw eyed them closely. The women even stripped off their rings and bracelets and dropped them into the sack, and some of the men gave up their pocket watches.

As the outlaw came to Katherine she said, "I have no money."

He glanced at her hand. "You have a ring. Take it off."

"Oh, please let me keep it!" Katherine said. Frances was amazed to see tears in her eyes. "It's not of much value, but it means a great deal to me."

The man quickly glanced at the man on horseback, then back at Katherine, and his voice grew even more loud and harsh. "You heard me! Drop it in the sack! Now!"

As Katherine obeyed, the outlaw outside the window called, "Get a move on! We're ready to ride!"

Cautiously, his gun held before him, the bearded outlaw began to back away from the passengers. Suddenly Mike was in the aisle, plowing into the man, and they stumbled together as the cloth bag was almost jerked from the outlaw's hand. Angrily the man regained his balance, giving Mike such a hard clout with his left hand that he knocked him sprawling. Mike bounced off the edge of the nearest seat and landed on the floor of the car, curled facedown, not moving.

Frances gasped and rushed toward Mike as the outlaw jumped from the car.

She could hear more yelling and the sound of galloping horses as he and the rest of his gang raced away from the train. The sound of gunshots exploded outside the window, and Captain Taylor shouted, "Got one of them! But just in the shoulder, blast it!"

"Mike! Wake up!" Frances begged as she threw her arms around him. Danny dove in next to her, and in the next minute Andrew and Katherine were beside her, ready to help. But Mike squirmed away from Frances, struggled to his knees,

and stood up, one fist clenched against his chest.

Frances scrambled to her feet, too, trying once more to put her arms around her brother. "Oh, Mike! Are you hurt?"

Mike pulled away to face all the other staring passengers. Frances could see him try to smile, but tears filled his eyes.

"I was a copper stealer once." Mike's voice was barely a whisper. "I promised Ma and I promised myself that I would never pick pockets again, but I couldn't let that outlaw take Mrs. Banks's ring, not when it meant so much to her."

He held out his fist and dropped the ring into Katherine's hand.

"Oh!" Katherine gasped. "Oh, Mike!" She held the ring up to stare at it as though she couldn't believe it was really there, and tears came to her eyes, too. Quickly she bent to wrap Mike in a hug.

Around them people murmured, "How did he manage that?" "What did that boy do?"

"There's more," Mike mumbled against Katherine's shoulder. When she stepped back he held out his hand, palm up, and opened his fingers. In it lay a wad of bills. As everyone stared, Mike gave the lot to Andrew. "I couldn't get it all," he apologized, "but maybe those who lost their money could divide this."

"Good, good!" Mr. Crandon stretched to see, then scowled. "What's this! What about me? He didn't retrieve my gold money clip!"

One of the women began to chirp like a frightened bird. "The bag will be almost empty! What if that outlaw notices and comes back?"

Mike shook his head. "He won't notice. I dropped my book in the bag to give it weight." He managed a shaky grin. "The tales in those novels about brave, daring outlaws are wrong. There wasn't anything grand about that man. He was dirty and fat and smelled like a New York gutter in summer."

Katherine put an arm around Mike's shoulders, hugging him again. "You risked your life!" she said. "You shouldn't have done that." As Mike ducked his head Katherine slipped the ring back onto her finger and added quickly, "But oh, Mike, my friend, I thank you with all my heart for retrieving my ring."

Captain Taylor stepped forward to shake Mike's hand. "You exhibited great courage," he said. "I'm proud of you."

Mr. Crandon's booming voice almost drowned out the captain's words. "You all heard that boy. He admitted to being a copper stealer, a common pickpocket!"

"Just a minute, Mr. Crandon!" Katherine said. "This is the boy who saved your life during the fire."

But Mr. Crandon sputtered, "Saved my life? That's debatable! All I know is that he ruined my trousers!"

"You're not being fair to Mike! He risked his life with that outlaw to try to save some of our property."

"He tried to help!" Danny echoed as he stepped in front of Mike.

Mr. Crandon wrinkled his nose as though he'd just smelled something bad. "Granted, the boy thought he was doing right," he said. "I'll give you that much. But don't you see? It simply proves my point. He's never learned the right values."

"That's not true!" Frances exclaimed, but Mr. Crandon ignored her.

"A boy like that should not be allowed in a proper home! And I'll do my best to see to it that he isn't!"

"Mr. Crandon—" Andrew began.

But a woman who had boarded the train at Hannibal raised her voice to shout over his. "I agree. Perhaps the boy could be sent back to New York."

Her companion clutched the lapels of her jacket together as though Mike had plans to steal it and stammered, "I think Mr. Crandon should take steps to see this is done. We don't need a New York pickpocket here!"

"No!" Frances could stay quiet no longer. She stepped in front of Mike and faced the surprised passengers.

"In New York," she said, "we worked very hard, but we didn't always have enough to eat. And we didn't have clean, fine clothes like those we're wearing now. And we didn't have our father. Da died last year. Mike was wrong to steal, but he thought he had to so that he could bring home a bit of meat now and then. He tried in his own way to help."

She took a long breath and hurried on before she could lose what little courage she had left. "We're people just like you, who have the same feelings you have."

The woman who earlier had spoken up for the children held out a hand, as though she were reaching for Frances, and said, "Oh, my dear child, it's plain that some of us have forgotten that you had no parents to guide you."

"We have a parent. We have a mother," Frances said, "and she and Da taught us, over and over again, the rules we should follow."

"You have a mother? But where is she?"

Frances held her chin up, willing it to stop trembling. "She sent us west," she said, trying to repeat Ma's words without thinking about them, "because she wanted us to have better lives than she could give us."

Without another word the passengers drifted back to their seats. The children, subdued and silent now, sat clustered together on the benches.

Andrew squeezed into the seat next to Frances. "Well spoken, son," he said. "I think you and Mike will do very well for yourselves in the West."

Frances glanced back at Mr. Crandon. She couldn't help being afraid, not just for Mike, but for all of them. Every minute was taking them closer to St. Joseph, to the place she had never seen that might be her home for the rest of her life. What would happen to them then?

Joan Lowery Nixon

Editor Ilene Cooper talks to Joan Lowery Nixon about her Orphan Train series:

ILENE COOPER: Where did you get your idea for *A Family Apart* and the other Orphan Train books?

JOAN LOWERY NIXON: I got it from a friend. He had read a piece in a history magazine about the Orphan Train children, and he sent it on to me. The idea excited me.

COOPER: You must have done a lot of research.

NIXON: The first thing I did was go to New York and meet with the people at the Children's Aid Society. It was the Aid Society that sent the children west. They paid for the tickets, collected clothing, advertised that they'd be coming, and paid guardians to take the children west. The Society lent me journals from the 1800s that told about the Orphan Train. The books were so old that I was almost afraid to handle them. Then I began to collect other records, such as diaries written by the Orphan Train riders themselves.

COOPER: Were most of the children true orphans, or did they, like the Kelly children, have a parent?

NIXON: Most were true orphans, but there were many immigrant children who came from one-parent homes. The parents were working long hours, and they couldn't take care of their children. The children were out on the streets and getting into trouble. Like Mrs. Kelly in the book, these parents decided their children would be better off getting out of the slums.

COOPER: You write all kinds of books—historical novels, mysteries, even picture books. How do you decide what you're going to write next?

NIXON: I look for ideas constantly. I keep a pocket file of them. I have more story ideas than I could ever possibly write. Each year I know I'm going to be writing one mystery, so everything else must fit around that.

COOPER: Are there going to be more Orphan Train books?

NIXON: Yes. There was a great response to the first four. Many readers wrote and asked me what happened next to the Kelly children. So now there are two more books. *A Dangerous Promise* is set in 1861 and is all about Mike. The next book is set in 1863 and is about Peg, who becomes a spy during the Civil War.

WESTERN

THE FORTY-NINERS
Oscar E. Berninghaus

WAGONS

 BY ROSEMARY AND STEPHEN VINCENT BENÉT

They went with axe and rifle, when the trail was still to blaze
They went with wife and children, in the prairie-schooner days
With banjo and with frying pan—Susanna, don't you cry!
For I'm off to California to get rich out there or die!

We've broken land and cleared it, but we're tired of where we are.
They say that wild Nebraska is a better place by far.
There's gold in far Wyoming, there's black earth in Ioway,
So pack up the kids and blankets, for we're moving out today.

The cowards never started and the weak died on the road,
And all across the continent the endless campfires glowed
We'd taken land and settled—but a traveler passed by—
And we're going West tomorrow—Lordy, never ask us why!

We're going West tomorrow, where the promises can't fail.
O'er the hills in legions, boys, and crowd the dusty trail!
We shall starve and freeze and suffer. We shall die, and tame the lands.
But we're going West tomorrow, with our fortune in our hands.

RESPONSE CORNER

CREATE A PAMPHLET

FIRE POWER

When the brushfire broke out and Mr. Crandon's shirt caught fire, Mike knew just what to do. How much do you know about fire safety? Research some tips and create a pamphlet with rules for what to do in case of fire. Make your pamphlet available to your family members.

WRITE TWO PARAGRAPHS

WESTWARD HO!

Many settlers traveled west by covered wagon. The Kelly children traveled west by train and steamboat. Think about two forms of travel you have tried. Write one paragraph that compares them and one paragraph that contrasts them.

CHILDREN
Without Homes.

A number of the CHILDREN brought from
NEW YORK are still without homes.
FRIENDS FROM THE COUNTRY PLEASE

CALL AND SEE THEM.

▶

MERCHANTS, FARMERS
AND FRIENDS GENERALLY
Are requested to give publicity to the above
AND MUCH OBLIGE

H. FRIEDGEN, Agent.

DISCUSS A TOPIC

LESSONS LEARNED

Frances Kelly and her brothers and sisters learned a lot in "the classroom of life." Talk with a group of classmates about the kinds of lessons people learn inside and outside of the classroom. Share at least one lesson you have learned in each setting.

WHAT DO YOU THINK?

- What kind of person is Frances? Mike? Give examples from the story that show their personality traits.

- If you could be one of the characters in the story, who would you choose to be? Explain your choice.

- How are the Kelly children like the settlers described in the poem "Western Wagons"? How are they different?

577

HECTOR

LIVES IN THE UNITED STATES NOW

THE STORY OF A MEXICAN-AMERICAN CHILD
by Joan Hewett
Photographs by Richard Hewett

*T*en-year-old Hector Almaraz is a

Mexican American. For as long as he can

remember he has lived in Los Angeles—

in this neighborhood, on this block.

Hector's parents are Leopoldo and

Rosario Almaraz. He also has three

brothers: nine-year-old Polo, and Miguel

and Ernesto, who are seven and four.

Notable Trade
Book in the Field
of Social Studies

Hector and Polo were born in Guadalajara, Mexico, and are Mexican citizens, like their parents. Their younger brothers, Miguel and Ernesto, were born in Los Angeles and are American citizens.

When Hector's parents came to California to find work, they did not understand English. But they had heard so much about Los Angeles, from sisters and brothers and their own parents, that the city seemed almost familiar.

At first they stayed with relatives. Then Leopoldo found a job, and the family moved to Eagle Rock, a residential section of the city.

They are still there. The streets and parks are safe, and an elementary school and a Catholic church are only a few blocks from their small, bungalow-style apartment.

Hector has lots of friends. Most of them live on his block. They play together after school and on Saturdays and Sundays.

Soccer is one of their favorite games. So is baseball. When it is baseball season, they dig out a bat, ball, and glove and practice batting in a backyard or alley. Other times they go to the park to play volleyball, or just to see what is going on. If no one has a flat, they ride their bikes over; otherwise they walk.

Like his friends, Hector likes to read comic books and collect baseball cards. Sometimes they gather their cards or books, meet on the front stoop, and trade. Although the children talk and joke in English, their parents come from Mexico and Central America, and Spanish is the language spoken in their homes.

When Hector and Polo are drawing or doing their homework at the kitchen table, they often tell stories to each other in English. They speak as fast as they can so their mother will not understand them. Rosario gets annoyed because she suspects they do it just to tease her.

Although Hector and Polo speak English equally well, their parents think it proper that their eldest boy be the family spokesperson. Hector enjoys the responsibility. Whenever someone who can only speak English telephones them, Hector is called to the phone. Or when Rosario has to get a prescription filled at the drugstore, Hector goes along to talk to the pharmacist.

Hector did not speak English when he started kindergarten. It was a scary time. He was away from his mother and brothers. He understood only a few English words and did not know what was going on in class. In first grade Hector had trouble learning to read. But he was determined to learn English, and by the end of the second grade he was reading and writing as well as his classmates. School started to be fun.

Now Hector is a fifth grader, one of the big kids. In United States history, his class is reading about the different immigrant groups who helped settle the West. Their teacher says, "We are a nation of immigrants. Indians, also called Native Americans, have lived here for thousands of years. Everyone else has come to the continental United States from some other place." Then she smiles and says, "Let's find out about us."

The students in Hector's class are told to ask their parents about their ancestors and then write a brief history of their families. It is an exciting project. When they finish their reports, they will glue snapshots of themselves to their papers and hang them on the wall. But first they get to read them aloud.

Philip traces his family back as far as his great-great-great-grandmother. His ancestors lived on a small Philippine island. Many of them were fishermen. Philip, his sister, and his parents are the only people in his family who have settled in the United States.

One side of Nicky's family came from Norway and Germany. His other ancestors came from Ireland and Sweden. All of them were farmers, and when they came to this country they homesteaded land, which means they farmed and built a house on uncultivated public land that then became theirs under a special homestead law.

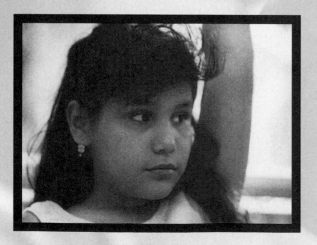

Vanessa's great-great-grandmother was a Yaqui Indian from Sonora, Mexico. Her grandfather fought in the Mexican Revolution. Another one of her ancestors was French.

Erick is descended from Ukrainian, German, and Italian immigrants. His German grandfather and Ukrainian grandmother met in a prisoner-of-war camp. When they were released, they married and came to the United States by ship.

Julie is of French, Irish, and Spanish descent. Her Great-Great-Grandma Elm was born in Texas. When Elm was a child her family moved to California. They traveled by covered wagon.

Everyone is interested in Kyria's family history. One of her African ancestors was a soldier in the American Revolution. Another fought for the Confederacy in the Civil War. Other members of her family homesteaded in Oklahoma.

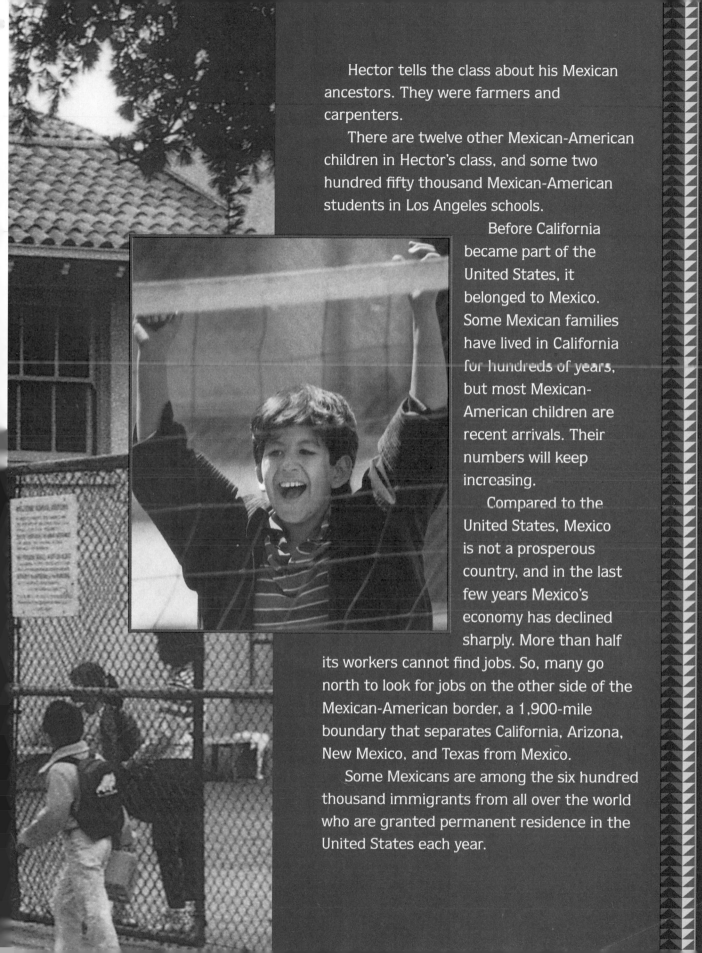

Hector tells the class about his Mexican ancestors. They were farmers and carpenters.

There are twelve other Mexican-American children in Hector's class, and some two hundred fifty thousand Mexican-American students in Los Angeles schools.

Before California became part of the United States, it belonged to Mexico. Some Mexican families have lived in California for hundreds of years, but most Mexican-American children are recent arrivals. Their numbers will keep increasing.

Compared to the United States, Mexico is not a prosperous country, and in the last few years Mexico's economy has declined sharply. More than half its workers cannot find jobs. So, many go north to look for jobs on the other side of the Mexican-American border, a 1,900-mile boundary that separates California, Arizona, New Mexico, and Texas from Mexico.

Some Mexicans are among the six hundred thousand immigrants from all over the world who are granted permanent residence in the United States each year.

DREAM
America

illustrated by Guy Porfirio

George Washington
helped get the Dream started—
praise and honor to him—
But he couldn't finish dreaming it for us.
No one can finish dreaming the Dream.

Abraham Lincoln
helped shape the Dream—
praise and honor to him—
But he couldn't finish dreaming it for us.
No one can finish dreaming the Dream.

Great men and women
can help us to dream—
praise and honor to them—
But they can't dream it all up for us.
The Dream of America must be our Dream.

— *Juan Quintana*

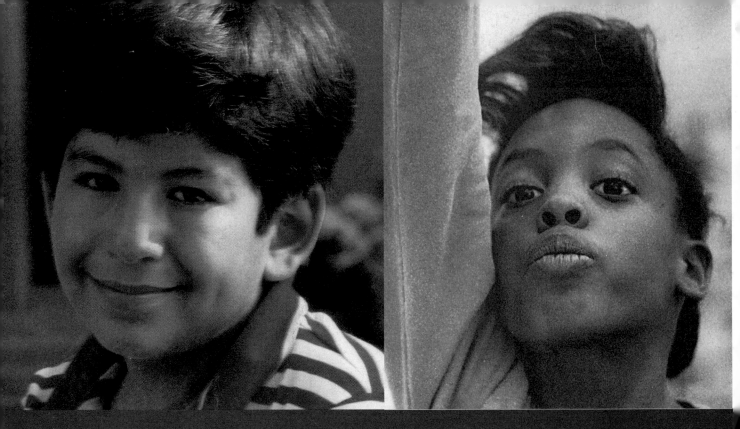

RESPONSE

ACROSS MANY BORDERS

Locate Guadalajara, Mexico, on a map of North America. Find the distance between Guadalajara and Los Angeles. Then figure out the distances immigrants from several other parts of the world would have to travel to reach other parts of America.

TIPS FROM THE TUTOR

Hector learned how to speak English in order to succeed in school. Suppose you were tutoring another person in English. What important tips would you share? Role-play the tutoring session with a partner. Then switch roles.

CORNER

WRITE A PARAGRAPH

THE AMERICAN DREAM

The United States is "a nation of immigrants." Almost all of us, or our families, have come to America in search of a dream. Find out from which country or countries your family came. Share this family history, and a glimpse of your American dream, in an information paragraph.

WHAT DO YOU THINK?

• What do you think Hector's teacher means when she says, "We are a nation of immigrants"?

• How would you feel if you, like Hector, had to move to a new country and learn a new language?

• How have the families of Hector and his classmates taken part in the American Dream described in "Dream America"?

WRAP-UP

The lives of Miguel and Hector are separated by 400 years. What can you think of that they might have in common?

Of all the children in this theme, who seems best suited to adapt to a new life in a new land? Why?

ACTIVITY CORNER

Imagine that, like the children in this theme, you became a pioneer in a strange new world. Imagine that your new world was on a new planet. Describe and name your new planet, and tell about some of its beauties and dangers.

Glossary

WHAT IS A GLOSSARY?

A glossary is like a small dictionary at the back of a book. It lists some of the words used in the book, along with their pronunciations, their meanings, and other useful information. If you come across a word you don't know as you are reading, you can look up the word in this glossary.

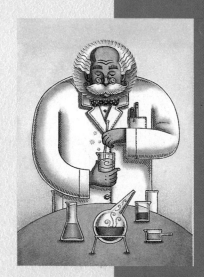

Using the

Like a dictionary, this glossary lists words in alphabetical order. To find a word, look it up by its first letter or letters.

To save time, use the **guide words** at the top of each page. These show you the first and last words on the page. Look at the guide words to see if your word falls between them alphabetically.

Here is an example of a glossary entry:

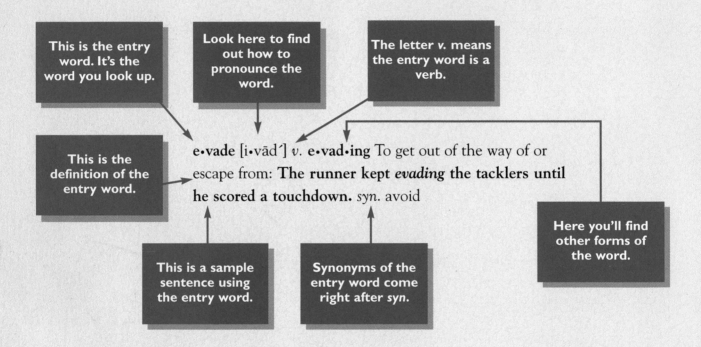

This is the entry word. It's the word you look up.

Look here to find out how to pronounce the word.

The letter *v.* means the entry word is a verb.

This is the definition of the entry word.

e•vade [i•vād´] *v.* **e•vad•ing** To get out of the way of or escape from: **The runner kept *evading* the tacklers until he scored a touchdown.** *syn.* avoid

Here you'll find other forms of the word.

This is a sample sentence using the entry word.

Synonyms of the entry word come right after *syn.*

ETYMOLOGY

Etymology is the study or history of how words are developed. Words often have interesting backgrounds that can help you remember what they mean. Look in the margins of the glossary to find the etymologies of certain words.

Here is an example of an etymology:

transmission   In Latin, *transire* means "to go across" and *mittere* means "to send." Today, transmissions can go not only across oceans but also across the galaxy.

Glossary

PRONUNCIATION

The pronunciation in brackets is a respelling that shows how the word is pronounced.

The **pronunciation key** explains what the symbols in a respelling mean. A shortened pronunciation key appears on every other page of the glossary.

- separates words into syllables
- ´ indicates heavy stress on a syllable
- ´ indicates lighter stress on a syllable

PRONUNCIATION KEY*

a	add, map	m	move, seem	u	up, done
ā	ace, rate	n	nice, tin	û(r)	burn, term
â(r)	care, air	ng	ring, song	yōo	fuse, few
ä	palm, father	o	odd, hot	v	vain, eve
b	bat, rub	ō	open, so	w	win, away
ch	check, catch	ô	order, jaw	y	yet, yearn
d	dog, rod	oi	oil, boy	z	zest, muse
e	end, pet	ou	pout, now	zh	vision, pleasure
ē	equal, tree	ŏŏ	took, full	ə	the schwa, an
f	fit, half	ōō	pool, food		unstressed vowel
g	go, log	p	pit, stop		representing the
h	hope, hate	r	run, poor		sound spelled
i	it, give	s	see, pass		a in *above*
ī	ice, write	sh	sure, rush		e in *sicken*
j	joy, ledge	t	talk, sit		i in *possible*
k	cool, take	th	thin, both		o in *melon*
l	look, rule	th	this, bathe		u in *circus*

Abbreviations: *adj.* adjective, *adv.* adverb, *conj.* conjunction, *interj.* interjection, *n.* noun, *prep.* preposition, *pron.* pronoun, *syn.* synonym, *v.* verb.

*The Pronunciation Key, adapted entries, and the Short Key that appear on the following pages are reprinted from *HBJ School Dictionary* Copyright © 1990 by Harcourt Brace & Company. Reprinted by permission of Harcourt Brace & Company.

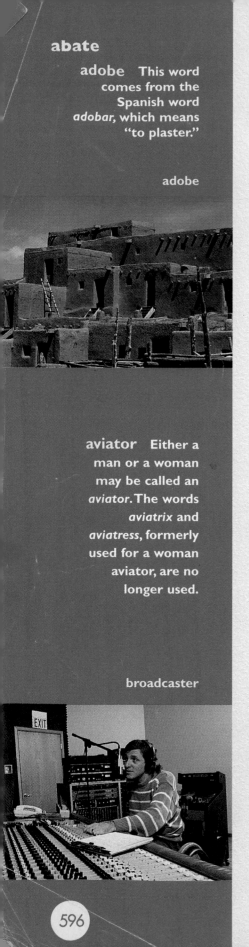

adobe This word comes from the Spanish word *adobar*, which means "to plaster."

adobe

aviator Either a man or a woman may be called an *aviator*. The words *aviatrix* and *aviatress*, formerly used for a woman aviator, are no longer used.

broadcaster

A

a·bate [ə·bāt´] *v.* **a·bat·ed** To become less: **After it rained for two days, the storm *abated*.**

a·ble-bod·ied [ā´bəl·bod´ēd] *adj.* Strong and healthy; fit.

ab·o·li·tion·ist [ab´ə·lish´ə·nist] *adj.* Wanting to end slavery in the United States: **Many *abolitionist* groups helped slaves escape to freedom.**

ac·com·plish·ment [ə·kom´plish·mənt] *n.* Something finished successfully: **Reading ten books is a great *accomplishment*.**

ad·dress [ə·dres´] *n.* A speech: **President Lincoln's most famous speech is called the Gettysburg *Address*.**

ad·journ [ə·jûrn´] *v.* **ad·journed** To end a meeting: **The student council president *adjourned* the meeting at 3:30 P.M.**

a·do·be [ə·dō´bē] *adj.* Made of sun-dried clay bricks: ***Adobe* buildings can be found in the southwestern United States.**

al·ma·nac [ôl´mə·nak] *n.* **al·ma·nacs** A book that has facts about the seasons, the heavens, and other information and features: **Some farmers look in *almanacs* to find out when to plant crops.**

an·ces·tor [an´ses·tər] *n.* **an·ces·tors** Someone in a family who lived a long time ago: **Rasheed's *ancestors* were from India.**

anx·ious·ly [angk´shəs·lē] *adv.* Nervously: **José waited *anxiously* to see the dentist.**

ap·pre·ci·ate [ə·prē´shē·āt´] *v.* **ap·pre·ci·at·ed** To value: **Your full cooperation is *appreciated*.**

as·tron·o·my [ə·stron´ə·mē] *n.* The study of stars and planets: ***Astronomy* was Maria's favorite class.**

a·vi·a·tor [ā´vē·ā´tər] *n.* A person who flies an airplane. *syn.* pilot

B

bar·i·tone [bar´ə·tōn´] *n.* A male with a medium-range singing voice: **The main singer in the opera was a *baritone*.**

black·mail [blak´māl´] *v.* To force someone to pay to keep a secret: **Someone tried to *blackmail* Simon about cheating on his test.**

bol·ster [bōl´·stər] *v.* To make stronger: **Billy ran daily to *bolster* his strength for the race.**

broad·cast·er [brôd´kas·tər] *n.* A radio or television announcer.

C

cam·pus [kam´pəs] *n.* The grounds of a school or college: **The students could not leave *campus* during the day.**

cit·i·zen [sit´ə·zən] *n.* **cit·i·zens** A person who is born in or made a member of a city or country.

com·mem·o·rate [kə·mem´ə·rāt´] *v.* **com·mem·o·rat·ed** To remember with honor: **The parade *commemorated* the end of the war.**

com·mu·nal [kom´yə·nəl or kə·myoo´nəl] *adj.* Owned and used by a group of people: **Winston works in a *communal* garden.**

com·pe·tent·ly [kom´pə·tənt·lē] *adv.* Skillfully: **Diane *competently* pulled the fish out of the water.**

com·pul·so·ry [kəm·pul´sər·ē] *adj.* Having to be done: **Training in CPR is *compulsory* for all new lifeguards.** *syn.* required

con·coc·tion [kən·kok´shən or kon·kok´shən] *n.* Something made by mixing things together: **Susan made her special *concoction*, a strawberry-chocolate shake.**

con·demned [kən·demd´] *adj.* Marked as unsafe for use: **The *condemned* building was torn down.**

con·ser·va·tion [kon´sər·vā´shən] *n.* The careful use and protection of natural resources: **When water is scarce, we must practice *conservation*.**

co·op·er·a·tive [kō·op´rə·tiv] *n.* Something owned and run by a group of people: **Benjie and Kim live in a housing *cooperative*.**

cringe [krinj] *v.* To move back in fear: **The buzzing bee made her *cringe*.**

cul·prit [kul´prit] *n.* Someone who is guilty of doing something wrong.

cul·ti·vat·ed [kul´tə·vāt´ed] *adj.* Made ready to grow plants: **Zach planted seeds in the *cultivated* garden.**

D

dem·on·stra·tion [dem´ən·strā´shən] *n.* A showing of how something works: **I saw a *demonstration* of the new computer.**

de·prive [di·prīv´] *v.* **de·priv·ing** To keep from having: **Andre is *depriving* himself of candy.**

des·o·late [des´ə·lit] *adj.* Without people; barren: **The old farm stood empty and *desolate*.**

di·a·lect [dī´ə·lekt´] *n.* The way a language is spoken in one part of a country: **The *dialect* my grandparents speak is different from mine.**

dire [dīr] *adj.* Terrible; extreme: **The flood left us in *dire* need of help.**

dire

concoction

desolate

a	add	oŏ	took
ā	ace	ōō	pool
â	care	u	up
ä	palm	û	burn
e	end	yōō	fuse
ē	equal	oi	oil
i	it	ou	pout
ī	ice	ng	ring
o	odd	th	thin
ō	open	t͟h	this
ô	order	zh	vision

ə = { a in *above*
e in *sicken*
i in *possible*
o in *melon*
u in *circus*

eccentricity

Although *eccentricities* may make you the center of attention, this word comes from the Latin words *ex* and *centros*, meaning "out from the center." The center was the normal place to be, so if people were not in the center, they were considered different and strange.

eclipse

edition

dis·mal [diz´məl] *adj.* Sad or gloomy: **Because the weather was *dismal*, we stayed home.**

dis·tri·bu·tion [dis´trə·byōō´shən] *n.* The arrangement of something in space or time: **The scientist is studying the *distribution* of plants on the hillside.**

do·na·tion [dō·nā´shən] *n.* A gift, usually to a good cause. *syn.* contribution

dread·ful [dred´fəl] *adj.* Awful: **The old piano sounded *dreadful*.** *syn.* terrible

E

ec·cen·tric·i·ty [ek´sen·tris´ə·tē] *n.* **ec·cen·tric·i·ties** A behavior that is odd: **The children thought the man's *eccentricities* were fascinating.**

e·clipse [i·klips´] *n.* **e·clips·es** A complete or partial hiding of the sun or of the moon.

e·co·sys·tem [ek´ō·sis´təm] *n.* **e·co·sys·tems** The relationship of plants, animals, and people in an area to their environment and to each other: **There are several *ecosystems* in the rain forest.**

e·di·tion [i·dish´ən] *n.* All the copies of a book printed at one time: **When the first *edition* sold out, they printed a second *edition*.**

em·pha·size [em´fə·sīz´] *v.* **em·pha·siz·es** To point out in a special way: **The teacher *emphasizes* that we should be in class on time.**

en·sem·ble [än·säm´bəl] *n.* A group that performs together: **There were four horns in the brass *ensemble*.**

en·ti·tle [in·tīt´(ə)l] *v.* **en·ti·tled** To give the right to do something: **Because she had finished her work, Cara was *entitled* to go to the gym.**

es·tab·lish [i·stab´lish] *v.* To set up: **The Pilgrims came to America to *establish* settlements.**

e·vade [i·vād´] *v.* **e·vad·ing** To get out of the way of or escape from: **The runner kept *evading* tacklers until he scored a touchdown.** *syn.* avoid

ex·clu·sive·ly [iks·klōō´siv·lē] *adv.* Only: **The picnic was *exclusively* for fifth graders.**

F

flus·ter [flus´tər] *v.* **flus·tered** To confuse or upset: **Celia was *flustered* when she was asked to sing for the class.**

for·feit [fôr´fit] *v.* **for·feit·ed** To give something up, as a penalty: **The team *forfeited* the championship because of cheating.**

for·mal [fôr´məl] *adj.* Following set rules or patterns; regular: **My grandmother had only six years of *formal* schooling.**

found [found] *v.* **found·ed** To start or set up: **The Spanish *founded* many missions in North America.**

G

grov·el [gruv´əl or grov´əl] *v.* **grov·el·ing** To crawl in fear with the face downward: **The people were *groveling* before the king because they feared his power.**

H

ham·mock [ham´ək] *n.* A long piece of strong cloth hung up by its ends to lie in.

har·vest [här´vist] *v.* To bring in a crop: **It is time to *harvest* the corn.** *syn.* pick

I

im·mi·grant [im´ə·grənt] *n.* A person who moves to another country to live.

im·pact [im´pakt] *n.* A strong effect: **The computer has a great *impact* on our lives.**

im·pose [im·pōz´] *v.* To force: **Roberto's parents wanted to *impose* a 9:00 P.M. bedtime on him.**

in·di·cate [in´də·kāt´] *v.* To show or give a sign of: **The signs above the doors *indicate* the exits.**

in·dus·tri·ous [in·dus´trē·əs] *adj.* Hardworking: **Ants are *industrious* insects.**

in·flu·ence [in´floo·əns] *n.* Power over someone's thoughts or actions without using force: **Sandra was a good *influence* on her younger sister.**

in·gen·ious [in·jēn´yəs] *adj.* Skillful and clever: **Her *ingenious* project won first prize.**

in·hab·it [in·hab´it] *v.* To live in: **Dolphins *inhabit* the oceans.**

in·quir·y [in·kwīr´ē or in´kwər·ē] *n.* **in·quir·ies** An attempt to find out information: **Aunt Shirley made *inquiries* about my mother's health.**

in·to·na·tion [in´tō·nā´shən] *n.* The ability to play or sing a note in tune: **Violet has excellent *intonation* when she sings.**

in·vis·i·ble [in·viz´ə·bəl] *adj.* Not able to be seen: **An *invisible* force field protected the spaceship.**

ir·ri·ga·tion [ir´ə·gā´shən] *n.* The bringing of water to dry land: **The farmers need *irrigation* to grow crops in the desert.**

irrigation

hammock

harvest

a	add	oŏ	took
ā	ace	ōō	pool
â	care	u	up
ä	palm	û	burn
e	end	yōō	fuse
ē	equal	oi	oil
i	it	ou	pout
ī	ice	ng	ring
o	odd	th	thin
ō	open	th	this
ô	order	zh	vision

ə = { a in *above*
e in *sicken*
i in *possible*
o in *melon*
u in *circus*

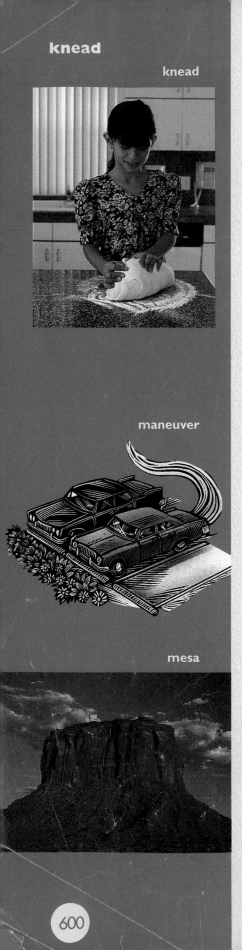

knead

maneuver

mesa

K

knead [nēd] *v.* **knead·ed** To press or squeeze together: **The baker** *kneaded* **the bread dough.**

L

land·mark [land´märk´] *n.* **land·marks** An easily recognized object, such as a tree or building.

land·scape [land´skāp´] *n.* A wide view of natural scenery: **The mountain** *landscape* **was beautiful.**

laugh·ing·stock [laf´ing·stok´] *n.* A person or thing that people make fun of: **When I struck out, I was the** *laughingstock* **of my team.**

lib·er·ty [lib´ər·tē] *n.* Freedom: **Many people come to the United States to find** *liberty.*

M

ma·neu·ver [mə·n(y)ōō´vər] *v.* **ma·neu·vered** To move with skill: **Maria** *maneuvered* **the car into the parking space.**

mar·i·ner [mar´ə·nər] *n.* **mar·i·ners** A sailor.

mem·o·ra·ble [mem´ər·ə·bəl] *adj.* Hard to forget: **Ben's birthday party at the zoo was** *memorable.*

me·sa [mā´sə] *n.* **me·sas** A steep hill with a flat top: **From the tops of the** *mesas,* **the Navajos could see for miles.**

mon·soon [mon·sōōn´] *n.* A season of strong winds and rain in Asia: **The rains of the** *monsoon* **turned the dusty road into a river of mud.**

muf·fle [muf´əl] *v.* To wrap something in order to deaden its sound: **A pillow can** *muffle* **the sound of the radio.**

mute [myōōt] *adj.* Not being able to speak: **The doll was** *mute.*

mu·ti·ny [myōō´tə·nē] *n.* Taking power from the person in charge: **The sailors planned a** *mutiny* **against the cruel captain.**

N

neu·tral·i·ty [n(y)ōō·tral´ə·tē] *n.* The condition of not taking sides: **Switzerland is known for its** *neutrality* **in European wars.**

non·cha·lant [non´shə·länt´] *adj.* Not excited or concerned: **Helen was** *nonchalant* **about running in the race.**

nu·tri·ent [n(y)ōō´trē·ənt] *n.* **nu·tri·ents** A food needed for life and growth: **The body needs** *nutrients* **from a variety of foods.**

O

or·a·tor [ôr´ə·tər] *n.* A good speech maker: **LeRoy was such a good *orator* that he won the speech contest.**

P

par·ti·tion [pär·tish´ən] *n.* A dividing wall or screen: **Our classroom has a *partition* between the study area and the art table.**

pe·cul·iar [pi·kyōōl´yər] *adj.* Strange or odd: **His old-fashioned clothes look *peculiar*.**

per·pet·u·ate [pər·pech´ōō·āt´] *v.* To make something last a long time: **They put up a statue to *perpetuate* her memory.**

pi·e·ty [pī´ə·tē] *n.* The showing of respect: **Many parents want their children to learn *piety*.**

pneu·mo·nia [n(y)ōō·mōn´yə] *n.* A lung disease: **Nadia got *pneumonia* and had to stay in the hospital.**

poul·try [pōl´trē] *n.* Chickens, ducks, or turkeys.

priv·i·lege [priv´ə·lij] *n.* **priv·i·leg·es** A special advantage: **Karen's ticket gave her extra *privileges* at the park.** *syn.* benefit

pro·fes·sion·al [prō·fesh´ən·əl] *adj.* Doing something for a living, not just for a hobby: **DeeDee wants to be a *professional* singer.**

pro·pel·ler [prə·pel´ər] *n.* Blades that spin to move a boat or an aircraft.

pros and cons [prōz and konz] *n.* The reasons for and against something: **Before I vote, I want to know the *pros and cons* of the issue.**

prose [prōz] *n.* Speech or writing that is not poetry: **The novel won an award for its beautiful *prose*.**

pros·per·ous [pros´pər·əs] *adj.* Wealthy or rich: **The family worked hard and became *prosperous*.**

pro·vi·sion [prə·vizh´ən] *n.* **pro·vi·sions** A supply of food: **We brought enough *provisions* to last five days.**

prowl [proul] *v.* **prowls** To move around quietly, searching for something: **The leopard *prowls* the land in search of food.**

Q

quar·tet [kwôr·tet´] *n.* A piece of music played or sung by four people: **The *quartet* was the second piece on the program.**

R

re·cit·al [ri·sīt´(ə)l] *n.* A concert or performance: **Jamal practiced hard for his piano *recital*.**

recital

quartet There are many words in English that come from the Latin number *quadra*, or "four," for example, *quarter* and *quart*.

propeller

provisions

a	add	o͝o	took
ā	ace	o͞o	pool
â	care	u	up
ä	palm	û	burn
e	end	yo͞o	fuse
ē	equal	oi	oil
i	it	ou	pout
ī	ice	ng	ring
o	odd	th	thin
ō	open	t͟h	this
ô	order	zh	vision

ə = { a in *above*
e in *sicken*
i in *possible*
o in *melon*
u in *circus*

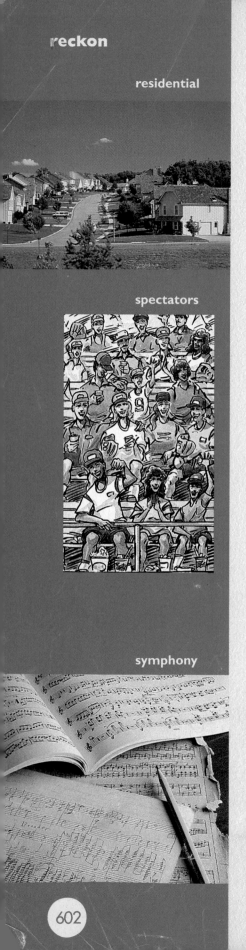

residential

spectators

symphony

reck·on [rek´ən] *v.* To guess, compute: We *reckon* the trip will take a week.

res·i·den·tial [rez´ə·den´shəl] *adj.* A place with homes, not offices or factories: The *residential* part of the city is by the lake.

res·o·lu·tion [rez´ə·lōō´shən] *n.* **res·o·lu·tions** An idea to be voted upon: The council had six *resolutions* to vote upon.

res·to·ra·tion [res´tə·rā´shən] *n.* Putting things back the way they were: The *restoration* of the old house took two years.

room and board [rōōm and bôrd] *n.* A place to sleep and food to eat: Instead of money, Sam got *room and board* for working at the factory.

S

sac·ri·fice [sak´rə·fīs´] *n.* Something that is given up as an offering: It was a *sacrifice* for Joey to give the last piece of pie to his brother.

sar·cas·ti·cal·ly [sär·kas´tik·lē] *adv.* In an unpleasant, mocking way: "I love getting flu shots," she said *sarcastically.*

scale [skāl] *n.* **scales** A pattern of tones going up and down eight notes: Flute players practice *scales* so they can play smoothly.

scour [skour] *v.* **scoured** To search every part: Dad *scoured* the house looking for his car keys.

sift [sift] *v.* To sort: The jury must *sift* through the evidence.

smug·gle [smug´əl] *v.* **smug·gling** To secretly bring something into or out of a country: The men were arrested for *smuggling* diamonds.

som·ber·ly [som´bər·lē] *adv.* In a sad way: They *somberly* waited for the bad news.

spec·ta·tor [spek´tā·tər] *n.* **spec·ta·tors** A person who watches an event: The crowd of *spectators* cheered loudly.

spokes·per·son [spōks´pûr´sən] *n.* A person who speaks for another person or group of people: The mayor is the *spokesperson* for our city.

stage fright [stāj frīt] *n.* Fear of performing in public: The actors felt *stage fright* before the play started.

stat·ic [stat´ik] *n.* Electrical noise on a television or radio.

strag·gler [strag´lər] *n.* **strag·glers** A person who falls behind the main group: The tour guide said the bus would not wait for *stragglers.*

sym·pho·ny [sim´fə·nē] *n.* A long piece of music for an orchestra.

syn·thet·ic [sin·thet´ik] *adj.* Made by people, not by nature: Nylon is a *synthetic* cloth.

tem·po [tem′pō] *n.* The speed at which a piece of music is played.

ter·ri·to·ry [ter′ə·tôr′ē] *n.* An area of land ruled by a nation: **Puerto Rico is a *territory* of the United States.**

tol·er·ate [tol′ər·āt′] *v.* To allow: **The dog will not *tolerate* people pulling its tail.**

trans·fixed [trans·fikst′] *adj.* Frozen with shock or fear: **They watched *transfixed* as the train sped toward them.**

trans·mis·sion [trans·mish′ən] *n.* A message or program sent over TV or radio: **The police received an emergency *transmission* on their radio.**

truce [trōōs] *n.* An agreement to stop fighting for a time: **A *truce* was called to get help for those who were hurt.**

tur·bu·lence [tûr′byə·ləns] *n.* Rough and violent movement of the air: **The *turbulence* caused the plane to bounce around.**

U

un·furl [un·fûrl′] *v.* **un·furled** To unroll or unfold: **The student *unfurled* the flag.**

un·rav·el [un·rav′əl] *v.* **un·rav·el·ing** To solve: **People have spent their lives *unraveling* the mystery of the pyramids.**

up·roar [up′rôr′] *n.* Noise and confusion: **There was an *uproar* when the dog chased the cat.**

V

vague [vāg] *adj.* Not clear: **Stanley gave a *vague* explanation about why he missed school.**

veg·e·ta·tion [vej′ə·tā′shən] *n.* Plant life: **The rain forest is thick with *vegetation*.**

ves·sel [ves′(ə)l] *n.* **ves·sels** A boat or ship.

ve·to [vē′tō] *v.* **ve·toed** To not allow something to be done: **The President *vetoed* the bill that Congress sent to him.**

vi·o·late [vi′ə·lāt′] *v.* **vi·o·lat·ed** To break a rule or law: **The driver got a ticket because he *violated* the speed limit.**

vis·u·al·ize [vizh′ōō·əl·īz′] *v.* To picture in the mind: **On a hot day, it helps to *visualize* a cool ocean.**

Y

yield [yēld] *v.* To produce: **I hope our tree will *yield* a lot of apples.**

transmission In Latin, *transire* means "to go across" and *mittere* means "to send." Today, *transmissions* can go not only across oceans but also across the galaxy.

vegetation

a	add	oŏ	took
ā	ace	ōō	pool
â	care	u	up
ä	palm	û	burn
e	end	yōō	fuse
ē	equal	oi	oil
i	it	ou	pout
ī	ice	ng	ring
o	odd	th	thin
ō	open	th̶	this
ô	order	zh	vision

ə = {
a in *above*
e in *sicken*
i in *possible*
o in *melon*
u in *circus*
}

INDEX OF
Titles and Authors

Page numbers in color refer to biographical information.

For permission to reprint copyrighted material, grateful acknowledgment is made to the following sources:

Harry N. Abrams, Inc., New York: "Fifth Grade" by Endo Mina from *Festival in My Heart: Poems by Japanese Children*, selected and translated from the Japanese by Bruno Navasky. Published by Harry N. Abrams, Inc., 1993.

Virginia Hamilton Adoff: "Under the Back Porch" by Virginia Hamilton. Text copyright © 1992, 1996 by Virginia Hamilton Adoff.

Anness Publishing Ltd.: Cover photograph by James Duncan from *Step-By-Step Paper Fun for Kids* by Marion Elliot. © 1994 by Anness Publishing Limited.

The Asia Society: "Summer" by Tran Thanh-tong from *A Thousand Years of Vietnamese Poetry*, edited by Nguyen Ngoc Bich. Text copyright © 1962, 1967, 1968, 1969, 1970, 1971, 1972, 1974 by Asia Society, Inc.

Atheneum Books for Young Readers, an imprint of Simon & Schuster: From *Shiloh* by Phyllis Reynolds Naylor. Text copyright © 1991 by Phyllis Reynolds Naylor. Cover illustration by Judith Gwyn Brown from *Maudie in the Middle* by Phyllis Reynolds Naylor and Lura Schield Reynolds. Illustration copyright © 1988 by Judith Gwyn Brown.

Avon Books: From *Sideways Stories from Wayside School* by Louis Sachar, cover illustration by Julie Brinckloe. Text copyright © 1978 by Louis Sachar; illustration copyright © 1985 by Avon Books.

Bantam Books, a division of Bantam Doubleday Dell Publishing Group, Inc.: From *A Family Apart* by Joan Lowery Nixon. Text copyright © 1987 by Joan Lowery Nixon and Daniel Weiss Associates, Inc.

Brandt & Brandt Literary Agents, Inc.: "Western Wagons" by Rosemary and Stephen Vincent Benét from *The Selected Works of Stephen Vincent Benét*. Text copyright 1937 by Stephen Vincent Benét; text copyright renewed © 1964 by Thomas Benét, Stephanie B. Manin and Rachel Benét Lewis. Published by Holt, Rinehart and Winston, Inc.

Carolrhoda Books, Inc., Minneapolis, MN: Cover illustration from *Song of the Chirimia* by Jane Anne Volkmer. Copyright © 1990 by Carolrhoda Books, Inc.

Children's Book Press, San Francisco, CA: "This Land Is My Land" and cover illustration from *This Land Is My Land* by George Littlechild. Copyright © 1993 by George Littlechild.

Children's Television Workshop: "Inventions" by Sara Jane Brian, illustrated by David Coulson from *3-2-1 Contact* Magazine, June 1995. Copyright 1995 by Children's Television Workshop.

Clarion Books, a Houghton Mifflin Company imprint: From *Children of the Wild West* by Russell Freedman. Copyright © 1983 by Russell Freedman. Cover photograph courtesy of Chicago Historical Society from *Lincoln: A Photobiography* by Russell Freedman.

Coward-McCann, Inc., a member of The Putnam & Grosset Group: From *Where Was Patrick Henry on the 29th of May?* by Jean Fritz, illustrated by Margot Tomes. Text copyright © 1975 by Jean Fritz; illustrations copyright © 1975 by Margot Tomes. Cover illustration by Margot Tomes from *What's the Big Idea, Ben Franklin?* by Jean Fritz. Illustration copyright © 1976 by Margot Tomes.

CRICKET Magazine: From "Patchwork Quilting" by Anita Howard Wade from *CRICKET* Magazine, September 1995. Text copyright © 1995 by Anita Howard Wade.

Crown Publishers, Inc.: From *The Third Planet* by Sally Ride and Tam O'Shaughnessy. Copyright © 1994 by Sally Ride.

Pat Cummings: Illustration by Pat Cummings from "Under the Back Porch" by Virginia Hamilton. Illustration copyright © 1992 by Pat Cummings.

Dial Books for Young Readers, a division of Penguin Books USA Inc.: "I Love the Look of Words" by Maya Angelou from *Soul Looks Back in Wonder* by Tom Feelings. Text copyright © 1993 by Maya Angelou; illustration copyright © 1993 Tom Feelings.

Doubleday, a division of Bantam Doubleday Dell Publishing Group, Inc.: "Two Horses," adapted from "The Riddle" in *Jewish Folktales* by Pinhas Sadeh. Text copyright © 1989 by Doubleday, a division of Bantam Doubleday Dell Publishing Group, Inc.

Dilys Evans Fine Illustration: Cover illustration by Lynne Dennis from *Shiloh* by Phyllis Reynolds Naylor. Illustration copyright © 1991 by Lynne Dennis.

Farrar, Straus & Giroux, Inc.: From *Whose Side Are You On?* by Emily Moore. Text copyright © 1988 by Emily Moore; cover illustration © 1988 by Eric Velasquez. Cover illustration by Peter Catalanotto from *The Green Book* by Jill Paton Walsh. Illustration copyright © 1986 by Peter Catalanotto.

Sheldon Fogelman, on behalf of Jerry Pinkney: Cover illustration by Jerry Pinkney from *Pride of Puerto Rico* by Paul Robert Walker. Copyright © 1988 by Harcourt Brace & Company.

Russell Freedman: From "Bring 'em Back Alive" by Russell Freedman in *The Story of Ourselves*, edited by Michael O. Tunnell and Richard Ammon. Text copyright © 1993 by Russell Freedman.

Greenwillow Books, a division of William Morrow & Company, Inc.: "The Line" and "Never Set Foot" from *Still More Stories to Solve: Fourteen Folktales from Around the World* by George Shannon, illustrated by Peter Sís. Text copyright © 1994 by George W. B. Shannon; illustrations copyright © 1994 by Peter Sís.

Hampton-Brown Books: "Dream America" by Juan Quintana, "What Flies Free" by Ina Cumpiano, and "The Outside/Inside Poem" by Sara Chan from *A Chorus of Cultures: Developing Literacy Through Multicultural Poetry* by Alma Flor Ada, Violet J. Harris, and Lee Bennett Hopkins. Text copyright © 1993 by Hampton-Brown Books.

Harcourt Brace & Company: From *The American Family Farm* by Joan Anderson, photographs by George Ancona. Text copyright © 1989 by Joan Anderson; photographs © 1989 by George Ancona. *Dear Benjamin Banneker* by Andrea Davis Pinkney, illustrated by Brian Pinkney. Text copyright © 1994 by Andrea Davis Pinkney; illustrations copyright © 1994 by Brian Pinkney. "Nickel-a-Pound Plane Ride" from *Local News* by Gary Soto. Text copyright © 1993 by Gary Soto.

HarperCollins Publishers: "Her Dreams" and cover illustration from *Under the Sunday Tree* by Eloise Greenfield, illustrated by Mr. Amos Ferguson. Text copyright © 1988 by Eloise Greenfield; illustrations copyright © 1988 by Amos Ferguson. From *Hector Lives in the United States Now* by Joan Hewett, photographs by Richard Hewett. Text copyright © 1990 by Joan Hewett; photographs copyright © 1990 by Richard R. Hewett. Untitled poem (Retitled: "Three Wishes") from *Near the Window Tree* by Karla Kuskin. Text copyright © 1975 by Karla Kuskin. Cover illustration by Marc Simont from *In the Year of the Boar and Jackie Robinson* by Bette Bao Lord. Illustration copyright © 1984 by Marc Simont. Cover illustration by Ruth Sanderson from *The Facts and Fictions of Minna Pratt* by Patricia MacLachlan. Illustration copyright © 1988 by Ruth Sanderson. Cover illustration by Marcia Sewall from *Sarah, Plain and Tall* by Patricia MacLachlan. Illustration copyright © 1985 by Marcia Sewall.

Holiday House, Inc.: Cover illustration by Terea Shaffer from *The Singing Man* by Angela Shelf Medearis. Illustration copyright © 1994 by Terea Shaffer.

Houghton Mifflin Company: From *Amish Home* by Raymond Bial. Copyright © 1993 by Raymond Bial.

Hyperion Books for Children: From *Morning Girl* by Michael Dorris. Text copyright © 1992 by Michael Dorris; cover illustration © 1992 by Kam Mak.

Alfred A. Knopf, Inc.: "April Rain Song" by Langston Hughes from *The Collected Poems of Langston Hughes*, edited by Arnold Rampersad. Text copyright © 1994 by the Estate of Langston Hughes.

Little, Brown and Company: From *Yang the Youngest and His Terrible Ear* by Lensey Namioka, illustrated by Kees de Kiefte. Text copyright © 1992 by Lensey Namioka; illustrations copyright © 1992 by Kees de Kiefte. Cover illustration by Kees de Kiefte from *Yang the Third and Her Impossible Family* by Lensey Namioka. Illustration copyright © 1995 by Kees de Kiefte.

Lodestar Books, an affiliate of Dutton Children's Books, a division of Penguin Books USA Inc.: From *Spanish Pioneers of the Southwest* by Joan Anderson, photographs by George Ancona. Text copyright © 1989 by Joan Anderson; photographs copyright © 1989 by George Ancona. Cover illustration by Pierre Bon from *Earth, Sky, and Beyond: A Journey Through Space* by Jean-Pierre Verdet, translated by Carol Volk. Copyright © 1993 by l'école des loisirs, Paris; English translation copyright © 1995 by Penguin Books USA Inc. Originally published in France by l'école des loisirs, 1993.

Lothrop, Lee & Shepard Books, a division of William Morrow & Company, Inc.: Cover photograph from *To Space and Back* by Sally Ride and Susan Okie. Copyright © 1986 by Sally Ride and Susan Okie. Cover illustration by Carole Byard from *Have a Happy...* by Mildred Pitts Walter. Illustration copyright © 1989 by Carole Byard.

Macmillan Publishing Company, a division of Macmillan, Inc.: Cover illustration by Eros Keith from *The House of Dies Drear* by Virginia Hamilton. Illustration copyright © 1968 by Eros Keith. Cover photograph by Christopher G. Knight from *Sugaring Time* by Kathryn Lasky. Photograph copyright © 1983 by Christopher G. Knight.

Claudia Cangilla McAdam: "Christopher Marshall: Up, Up, and Away" by Claudia Cangilla McAdam from *CRICKET* Magazine, April 1992. Text © 1992 by Claudia Cangilla McAdam.

Margaret K. McElderry Books, an imprint of Simon & Schuster: "Speak Up" from *Good Luck Gold and Other Poems* by Janet S. Wong. Text copyright © 1994 by Janet S. Wong.

McGraw-Hill Inc.: From book #60660 *The Log of Christopher Columbus* by Robert H. Fuson. Text copyright 1987 by Robert H. Fuson. Originally published by International Marine Publishing Company, Camden, ME.

Eileen McKeating: Cover illustration by Eileen McKeating from *After Fifth Grade, the World!* by Claudia Mills. Illustration copyright © 1989 by Eileen McKeating.

Joseph T. Mendola Ltd., on behalf of Steve Brennan: Cover illustration by Steve Brennan from *A Gathering of Days* by Joan W. Blos. Illustration copyright © 1990 by Steve Brennan.

Francisco Mora: Cover illustration by Francisco Mora from *Local News* by Gary Soto. Published by Harcourt Brace & Company, 1993.

Morrow Junior Books, a division of William Morrow & Company, Inc.: From *Dear Mr. Henshaw* by Beverly Cleary, cover illustration by Paul O. Zelinsky. Text and illustration copyright © 1983 by Beverly Cleary. Cover illustration by Paul O. Zelinsky from *Strider* by Beverly Cleary. Illustration copyright © 1991 by William Morrow and Company, Inc. Cover illustration by Diane deGroat from *Aldo Peanut Butter* by Johanna Hurwitz. Illustration copyright © 1990 by Diane deGroat.

National Geographic Society Book Division: From "Appalachian Highlands" and maps by William H. Bond in *National Geographic Picture Atlas of Our Fifty States*. Copyright © 1991 by National Geographic Society.

Orchard Books, New York: *Beethoven Lives Upstairs* by Barbara Nichol, illustrated by Scott Cameron. Text copyright © 1993 by Classical Productions for Children Limited; illustrations copyright © 1993 by Scott Cameron.

Philomel Books: Illustrations by Robert Sabuda from *The Log of Christopher Columbus*, compiled by Steve Lowe. Illustrations copyright © 1992 by Robert Sabuda.

Plays, Inc.: *Mary McLeod Bethune, Dream Maker* by Mary Satchell and cover from *Plays of Black Americans*, edited by Sylvia E. Kamerman. Text copyright © 1987 by Sylvia K. Burack. This play is for reading purposes only; for permission to produce, write to Plays, Inc., Publishers, 120 Boylston Street, Boston, MA 02116 USA.

Puffin Books, a division of Penguin Books USA Inc.: Cover illustration by Alan Olson from *Just My Luck* by Emily Moore. Illustration copyright © 1991 by Alan Olson.

G. P. Putnam's Sons: From *Homesick, My Own Story* by Jean Fritz, cover illustration by Margot Tomes. Text copyright © 1982 by Jean Fritz; cover illustration copyright © 1982 by Margot Tomes.

Roberts Rinehart Publishers: *The People Who Hugged the Trees* by Deborah Lee Rose, illustrated by Birgitta Säflund. Text copyright © 1990 by Deborah Lee Rose; illustrations copyright © 1990 by Birgitta Säflund.

Melodye Rosales: Cover illustration by Melodye Rosales from *Beetles, Lightly Toasted* by Phyllis Reynolds Naylor. Illustration copyright © 1987 by Melodye Rosales.

Scholastic Inc.: Cover illustration from *Good-Bye My Wishing Star* by Vicki Grove. Copyright © 1988 by Vicki Grove. From *Radio Fifth Grade* by Gordon Korman. Text and cover illustration copyright © 1989 by Gordon Korman. *By the Dawn's Early Light* by Steven Kroll, illustrated by Dan Andreasen. Text copyright © 1994 by Steven Kroll; illustrations copyright © 1994 by Dan Andreasen. Cover illustration by Elroy Freem from *...If You Traveled West in a Covered Wagon* by Ellen Levine. Illustration copyright © 1992 by Scholastic Inc.

Simon & Schuster Books for Young Readers, a division of Simon & Schuster: From *If You Were There in 1492* by Barbara Brenner. Copyright © 1991 by Barbara Brenner. From *A Very Young Musician* by Jill Krementz. Text copyright © 1991 by Jill Krementz. From *Hatchet* by Gary Paulsen. Text copyright © 1987 by Gary Paulsen. "Night" from *The Collected Poems of Sara Teasdale*. Text copyright 1930 by Sara Teasdale Filsinger, renewed 1958 by Guaranty Trust Company of New York. Cover illustration by Pat Cummings from *Mariah Keeps Cool* by Mildred Pitts Walter. Illustration copyright © 1990 by Pat Cummings.

Ticknor & Fields Books for Young Readers, a Houghton Mifflin Company imprint: "Backwoods Scholars" and cover illustration by Heather Collins from *A Pioneer Sampler* by Barbara Greenwood. Text copyright © 1994 by Barbara Greenwood; illustration copyright © 1994 by Heather Collins/Glyphics.

Time, Inc.: "Golden Gate Bridge, World's Longest Span, Opens May 28" from *Life* Magazine, May 31, 1937. Text copyright 1937 by Time Inc.

United Press International: "Boy Pilot Resumes Historic Trans-Atlantic Crossing" by Warren Perley, July 11, 1988. Text copyright © 1988 by United Press International.

Viking Penguin, a division of Penguin Books USA Inc.: Cover illustration by Ted CoConis from *The Summer of the Swans* by Betsy Byars. Copyright © 1970 by Betsy Byars.

Neil Waldman: Cover illustration by Neil Waldman from *Hatchet* by Gary Paulsen. Illustration copyright © 1987 by Bradbury Press.

Franklin Watts: Cover photograph courtesy of the American Museum of Natural History from *North American Indian Survival Skills* by Karen Liptak. Copyright © 1990 by Karen Liptak.

Albert Whitman & Company: Cover illustration by James Watling from *Along the Santa Fe Trail: Marion Russell's Own Story* by Marion Russell, adapted by Ginger Wadsworth. Illustration copyright © 1993 by James Watling.

World Book Publishing: From "Flags in American History" in *The World Book Encyclopedia*, Volume 7. © 1992 by World Book, Inc.

Joyce Audy Zarins: Illustrations by Joyce Audy Zarins from "Patchwork Quilting" by Anita Howard Wade in *CRICKET* Magazine, September 1995.